Kelsey Timmerman has been where very few donors go, and has seen the positive impact of the highly effective giving I advocate, as well as the negative impact of less desirable forms of giving. *Where Am I Giving?* offers thought-provoking and often entertaining insights into the importance of thinking carefully about where we give.

**—Peter Singer, professor of bioethics,
Princeton University, and founder of The Life You Can Save**

Charity should never be motivated by pity because that causes dependency. Charity must always be the result of compassion leading to constructive action making the recipient independent and productive member of society. *Where Am I Giving?* is a good guide to constructive giving. A must read for all charity-minded people.

**—Arun Gandhi, founder-president,
Gandhi Worldwide Education Institute, Rochester, NY**

Kelsey Timmerman has written a compassionate and compelling book about the people who run the international charities many of us donate to. To do so, he visited these organizations in person, spanning the globe, and bringing to the fore the realities that shape the daily lives of both the helpers and those being helped. Along the way, he intersperses his own advice as to what charity should—and shouldn't—mean for his readers. An inspirational book that's also a fascinating travelogue, it deserves a wide audience. We'll all be better off if our friends and neighbors read this.

**—Pauline Frommer, publisher, Frommer Guidebooks**

I loved this book. Kelsey has managed to write an exciting adventure of a how-to book on giving, volunteering, and generally making the world a better place through his own thrilling and heart-wrenching tales. Kelsey has done it all and lived it all. *Where Am I Giving?* is hugely entertaining while offering practical, real lessons and guidelines that he has lived. He has seen success and failure and shares where we can be most effective. Kelsey shows us where we can offer our time and resources, large and small, to impact the planet. He takes us along on his adventures to meet the people, learn about the causes, and show us the long-term victories and failures so we don't have to make the same mistakes. It's the most entertaining how-to book I've ever read, and few books are more timely.

**—Conor Grennan, founder of Next Generation Nepal (NGN)
and author of *Little Princes***

Traveling with Kelsey Timmerman in the pages of *Where Am I Giving?* will inspire you to do the most good you can do.

**— Will MacAskill, president of the Centre for Effective Altruism and author of *Doing Good Better: How Effective Altruism Can Help You Help Others, Do Work that Matters, and Make Smarter Choices about Giving Back***

# KELSEY TIMMERMAN

## WHERE AM I

# GIVING?

**A GLOBAL ADVENTURE EXPLORING HOW TO USE YOUR
GIFTS AND TALENTS TO MAKE A DIFFERENCE**

WILEY

For general information on our other products and services or for technical support, please contact our Customer Care Department within the United States at (800) 762-2974, outside the United States at (317) 572-3993 or fax (317) 572-4002.

Wiley publishes in a variety of print and electronic formats and by print-on-demand. Some material included with standard print versions of this book may not be included in e-books or in print-on-demand. If this book refers to media such as a CD or DVD that is not included in the version you purchased, you may download this material at booksupport.wiley.com. For more information about Wiley products, visit www.wiley.com.

*Library of Congress Cataloging-in-Publication Data:*

Names: Timmerman, Kelsey, 1979- author.
Title: Where am I giving? : a global adventure exploring how to use your
   gifts and talents to make a difference / Kelsey Timmerman.
Description: Hoboken, New Jersey : John Wiley & Sons, Inc., [2018]
Identifiers: LCCN 2018019679 (print) | LCCN 2018021118 (ebook) | ISBN
   9781119454236 (Adobe PDF) | ISBN 9781119454410 (ePub) | ISBN 9781119448129
   (hardcover)
Subjects: LCSH: Humanitarianism. | Voluntarism. | Charities. | Social action.
Classification: LCC BJ1475.3 (ebook) | LCC BJ1475.3 .T56 2018 (print) | DDC
   201/.76—dc23
LC record available at lccn.loc.gov/2018019679

Cover Design and Images: Rule 29 Creative

Printed in the United States of America

F10001993_070318

*To Annie, Harper, and Griffin,*
*who give me so much,*
*including more reasons to give*

# CONTENTS

**CHAPTER 4**

## Confessions of a Volunteer Addict (Indiana, 2010)

*Benefits of volunteering / 100-hour rule / Make where you live interesting*

**25**

**CHAPTER 5**

## What Can One Person Do? (Cambodia, 2017)

*Leaving Hollywood for a dump in Cambodia / The White Savior Industrial Complex*

**37**

**CHAPTER 6**

## Happiness Isn't Having a Lot; It's Giving a Lot (Cambodia, 2017)

*The Hero's journey / What* The Matrix *teaches us about happiness and purpose / Four pillars of meaning*

**47**

**CHAPTER 7**

## Giving Is Complicated: Ethnic Cleansing in the Most Generous Nation on Earth (Myanmar, 2017)

*Change starts with students / Problem with empathy / World Giving Index / Problem with orphanages*

**63**

**CHAPTER 8**

## Seeing Differently to Make a Difference (Myanmar, 2017)

*A not-so-noble Nobel Peace Prize winner / Problem with karma / Intent matters*

**75**

**CHAPTER 9**

## Giving on Purpose (Myanmar, 2017)

*Giving alms / Meditating on giving*

**83**

**CHAPTER 10**

## The Gift of Tasting Ice Cream (Myanmar, 2017)

*A former monk on giving / Solitude / Thoreau's three chairs*

**89**

# Introduction

# The Trash Picker, the Slave, and the Garment Maker (The World, 2001–2018)

One of the most beautiful sights I've seen is an 11-year-old girl laughing in the worst place I've ever been.

She haunts me to this day.

Smoke and stench – fire and brimstone – surrounded her as she threw her head back, shoulders shaking. Her eyes closed to the hellscape of Phnom Penh's municipal dump. She had been sifting through previously picked-through trash looking for something of value. Treasure or trash? Discard or keep?

She and the other children earned a dollar per day, if they were lucky, by selling their findings while their parents picked through fresh trash brought by a parade of garbage trucks. Most of the trash pickers were former farmers.

*What must have life been like back on the farm?*

"Life in our village is tough," I imagined the parents saying. "Farming is no way to make a living. I hear there's this garbage heap in the city where we could work and even the kids could earn a dollar per day."

They packed up their belongings and moved to the city. My hell on earth was someone else's opportunity.

That thought coupled with the sight and the smell of the dump made me physically ill. I had to fight from puking. I didn't want them to see that what they did and where they did it disgusted me.

Until visiting the dump, I didn't realize that people lived in places like this.

The adults wore rags across their noses and mouths, their vacant, almost lifeless eyes searching through the trash.

But the girl …

The girl still had life and light in her eyes (see Figure I.1). I wanted to do something. I wanted to grab her hand, walk her away from the dump, and give her … an education? A chance? A future? But there were hundreds like her in this one dump.

What could I do? We live in a world where 1.2 billion people live on less than $1.25 per day. Where half the world's population lives on less than $2.50 per day.[1] Where 21% of American children live in poverty.[2]

*Figure I.1    The girl at the Phnom Penh dump (Cambodia, 2007).*

---

[1]United Nations Development Programme, "Sustaining Human Progress: Reducing Vulnerabilities and Building Resilience," Human Development Report, 2014 (February 2014) 19.
[2]Yang Jiang, "Basic Facts About Low-Income Children," National Center for Children in Poverty (January 2017).

I was just one man, researching my first book, traveling on my second mortgage. And she was just one girl.

I pulled out my Frisbee and tossed it to her. She threw it to a barefoot boy, who put down his burlap bag of trash treasures to catch it. I taught them how to throw a Frisbee and for 15 minutes we escaped into a world of throwing and catching, of laughing and smiling. Then they got back to work and I went to my $11 per night guesthouse and showered three times until the stench of the dump lingered no more.

But no amount of scrubbing could wash away the memory of the dump. Are awareness and empathy treasures that can enhance our lives? Or are they burdens that would be better off discarded because awareness without action leads to guilt and apathy?

———

When do we act? How do we act to make a positive difference?

I was faced with this same dilemma a few years ago when I traveled to Ivory Coast to meet cocoa farmers while researching my second book.

I never expected to meet a slave in my lifetime, but then I met a man named Solo who showed me a view of another world. He was from the neighboring country of Ghana and had followed false promises to a cocoa farm. He had asked to leave, but wasn't allowed to go. He told me the donkeys got treated better than he did because at least they were fed when they weren't working. He told me they do worse things to him than beat him. Solo called the guy he worked for "master."

For me hearing a human being call another human being "master," in this day and age, shook me to my soul. I knew modern slavery existed, but knowing about it and witnessing it were two completely different things. Sitting next to Solo, a living breathing slave and listening to his story, I felt compelled to act, to help, to make a difference.

I hatched a plan where I hired Solo as my translator away from the farm for the day. It worked.

At the end of the day, I paid Solo $40 and asked him where he wanted to go.

"Home," he told me. "To Ghana."

Solo's master figured out what was going on and sent me a text, threatening to have me arrested. Solo was trying to figure out a way home when we got separated.

But the slave …

Days later I learned Solo was back on the cocoa farm. Was he captured and taken back? Maybe. But it's more likely that he looked at the opportunities before him and chose to go back. Solo chose slavery.

When I learned Solo was back on the farm, I worried what repercussions he may have suffered from my actions. I acted. I did something, but I wish I had done nothing. Good intentions aren't enough; it's the results those intentions produce that matter.

I regretted not acting to help the girl at the dump. I regretted helping Solo.

━━━━━

I was a recent college grad when I met the man who made my favorite T-shirt outside the factory in Honduras where he worked. It was awkward. The T-shirt cost nearly as much as a day of his labor. There I was, skipping around the globe, and there he was in a sea of workers with a chain link fence and a long workday at his back, kind enough to stop and chat with me, puzzled as the security guard at the front gate had been.

*Why was I there?*

A degree in anthropology had inspired my curiosity and I left the flat fields of the Midwest to meet people who lived differently than I did. I'd save up money working a retail job or as a scuba instructor, and then I'd blow it all traveling. I started to write about my travels and would get paid a whopping $10 from publications for stories like spending the night alone in Castle Dracula in Romania. I could go anywhere in the world and have adventures worth writing about. It was the world's most expensive hobby.

I was looking for that next place to go, and my favorite T-shirt had a funny picture of a guy from a TV show in the early 1980s and these words: "Come with me to my tropical paradise." "So," I thought, "why not?" I put on the shirt and showed up at the factory half expecting the factory management to laugh at the randomness and silliness of it all and throw open the factory gates. They didn't, so I waited to the side of the factory to meet someone who possibly made my shirt.

When Amilcar stopped to talk with me, the randomness and the silliness faded, replaced by awkwardness and questions from a forgotten sociology course: Does this job provide a better life for you and your family? What are you paid? Is this one of those sweatshops?

Of course, I didn't ask any of these questions. I think deep down I didn't really want to know. Amilcar and I were the same age, but our lives were vastly different. I was traveling on a whim, following my curiosity wherever it led, and he was working in the factory that made my T-shirt. I looked at myself through his eyes as I had once looked at myself through the eyes of a beggar in Nepal, and I saw the privileges and opportunities of my own life. I wrestled with the fact that people make the clothes we wear, and we have it made.

I went to Cambodia where my jeans were made and while there I met the girl. I wondered what life was like for her and other rural farmers who were leaving the fields for factories, and I traveled around the world to meet farmers. That's when I met Solo on the cocoa farm. One person, story, and question flowed into the next.

I'm privileged, but I'm not Batman's alter ego Bruce Wayne by any means. In the 16 years of travel covered in this book, at times I earned a poverty wage, once I was unemployed, but mostly I earned a solid, but very unpredictable, middle-class income. Yet I received an education. I have access to health care. I have not known hunger or war, nor have my wife and kids. There are privileges beyond financial ones. Being a straight, middle-class, able-bodied, white dude in Muncie, Indiana, certainly comes with its own privileges.

I've traveled to some of the poorest places on our planet, and there are people I wish I could forget, like the girl trash picker, Solo the slave, and Amilcar the garment worker, but I never will. These are people who live in circumstances that have often paralyzed me to the point of inaction. But from the very beginning, I began to feel the responsibility of my privilege, and of the opportunities in my life that I have, that you likely have, that most of the world's people don't.

This is something I've been struggling with for years.

My global searches for connection have inspired me to try to be a better giver, activist, and global and local citizen. They inspired me to cofound a community storytelling nonprofit, The Facing Project, which has engaged more than 200,000 people nationwide. But still, when I think about the girl and Solo and Amilcar, I feel like I'm not doing enough.

Awareness without action feels irresponsible. I believe I have a responsibility to act, to do something, and I believe you do as well. If you make $52,000 per year, you are in the top 1% of global earners. Even if you live on $11,000 per year, which is below the poverty line in the US, you are richer than 85% of the world's population.[3] If you graduated from college, you are more educated than 90% of the rest of

---

[3]William MacAskill, *Doing Good Better: How Effective Altruism Can Help You Help Others, Do Work That Matters, and Make Smarter Choices About Giving Back* (New York: Avery, 2015), 18.

the world. If you are fortunate enough to have the education and time to read a book, you've probably been dealt a reasonably good hand in terms of privilege compared to the rest of the world. If you aren't convinced that you have a responsibility to make a positive impact with the opportunities you've been given and the privileges from which you benefit, part of my job is to convince you. I'll do that by introducing you to the experiences and people who've convinced me.

This book isn't about a middle-class, overeducated white dude, giving to the world or "saving the world" as overeducated white dudes are wont to do, but about the world inspiring and teaching that dude to be a better giver. And through my discovering the amazing opportunities I have to give and the benefits of giving and learning how to do so more meaningfully, I hope you will as well.

This book is about more than financial gifts. You don't have to have money to make an impact. In India I'll introduce you to a 26-year-old who lives in a slum and spent $6 on a soccer ball that led to 3,000 kids going to school. In Kenya, I met a group of former gang members who risk their lives promoting peace in the most violent slum community in Nairobi. They each had much more to give than money.

The scale and complexity of global and local issues can overwhelm us to the point of inaction, but I choose action. I'm choosing to make an impact and not just blindly accept that doing good or meaning well is enough, because it isn't. In a world where good intentions are no longer enough, where helping can hurt, how can I, a landlocked American with an average income and 2.54 kids (if a cat, hamster, and two goldfish add up to 0.54 kids) make a difference? We are about to find out together.

━━━━━

I'm not alone in my desire to make a difference. Ninety percent of Americans have donated money, goods, or services to causes.[4] Eighty-four percent of Millennials report that making a positive difference in the world is more important than career recognition.[5]

Trying to make a difference and actually making a difference are much different things. My volunteer opportunities haven't ended well. The boy I mentored through Big Brothers Big Sisters went to "kid jail." The cashier at PetSmart will ask me if I want to donate $1 for

---

[4]Robert D. Lupton, *Toxic Charity: How Churches and Charities Hurt Those They Help* (New York: HarperOne, 2011), 2.
[5]Bentley University Center for Women's & Business, "Millennials in the Workplace" (2011), 4.

orphaned puppies. What kind of jerk says no to orphaned puppies? Sometimes, me!

Ethicist Peter Singer believes, when it comes to giving of our time and resources, we are being immoral by not giving more. Singer believes that it is our moral obligation as Western citizens to give as much as we can to help save the lives of those facing extreme poverty and disease. In his eyes, we should be giving at least 10% of our incomes. Yet only 5.6% of Americans' donations go to global causes.[6]

Singer's work *The Life You Can Save* inspired a movement – effective altruism – that asks us not just to give more but to give better. In Kenya, I visited a nongovernmental organization (NGO) that is one of the darlings of the effective altruism movement. It simply gives cash, no strings attached, to people in poverty.

I address the aid debate highlighted by economists such as Jeffrey Sachs (if we gave more, we could end poverty) and William Easterly (we need to rethink aid and focus on development). Dambisa Moyo, who was born in Zambia and got her PhD from Harvard, said, "Aid has been and continues to be an unmitigated political, economic, and humanitarian disaster for most parts of the world."[7] *A disaster.* Yikes! When I read that it almost made me want to give up on giving.

I visited a village where the United Nations and Sachs tried to end poverty. I think you'll be surprised about what the villagers had to say. I spent time with one of the world's largest NGOs and the biggest proponent of child sponsorship in the world, and sometimes they even let me get out of the SUV to meet the people whom they help.

I think we need a balance of head and heart, and local and global giving. We need to question our altruistic motivations, measure our impact, and work with – not just for – those we help. We need to empower people and at the very minimum do no harm in our efforts to do good. We need to explore how we've received gifts, our gratitude or lack thereof for them, and how we are putting them to use. Giving is so much more than writing a check; it's a practice that connects us to our communities and the world and helps us find purpose and meaning in our lives.

I want there to be a "Good Person Equation," something to tell us how much we should give, volunteer, and engage in acts of local and

[6] Giving USA Foundation, "Giving USA 2017: The Annual Report on Philanthropy for the Year 2016" (2016).
[7] *Dambisa Moyo, Dead Aid: Why Aid Is Not Working and How There is a Better Way for Africa,* (New York: Farrar, Straus and Giroux, 2009), xix.

global activism and altruism. Actually, you'll see that at times I was quite desperate to fill the variables of such an equation.

Throughout the book I'll share Giving Rules that can help guide your giving. Think of them more as suggestions, my takeaways from the narrative you are reading.

> *Giving Rules: Gratitude first, then giving. When you look at your life, time, money, and talents as gifts, you will give more of them all.*

This journey is not about my travels around the world helping people – that would be pretty annoying – but it's about seeing the world and our lives through the lens of giving, and meeting people who have something to teach us about it. It's learning from a Hollywood executive who left a life of yachts and actress girlfriends for that dump in Cambodia where I met the girl. It's meeting a Burmese refugee who returned to see his country in a new way that changed his life. It's students time and again acting as agents of change, leading the way. It's sitting down with Gandhi's great-grandson and asking him, perhaps a little too desperately, how I should live my life.

We were born into relative prosperity and a wealth of opportunity. When faced with global poverty statistics and local harsh realities, it can be easy to feel guilt. This book isn't about how to absolve yourself of your first-world guilt. It's about helping you recognize your own privilege and the amazing opportunity that comes with it for each of us to impact the lives of people in our communities and around the world and our own through giving.

> *Giving Rules: We are products of the gifts others have given us.*

# Part I

## WHY GIVE (WHEN I HAVE PROBLEMS OF MY OWN)?

# 1

# Life After College (Nepal, 2001)

*The mission / The responsibility of privilege*

---

**AS A 22-YEAR-OLD RECENT COLLEGE GRAD,** I loved flying. Thirty thousand feet in the air, my book marked with a ticket to somewhere, was the only time in my life I knew where I was going and when I was going to get there.

I was on my way to Nepal – the next destination in a series of one-way tickets away from the expectations that surround a graduate who had moved back in with his parents. It wasn't that I had an issue with not knowing what I was doing with my life; it was that I had an issue with other people having an issue with it.

The maroon robe of the Tibetan monk in the seat next to me spilled over my armrest. He was in my space, and each time he moved his robe pulled at my headphone connection, interrupting the audio of the movie *Osmosis Jones*. Chris Rock was the voice of the white blood cell fighting infection on the streets of Bill Murray.

The monk would move; I'd sigh, and push my headphones in again. Occasionally we'd chuckle at the same point. I'm not sure if a white blood cell blowing his hair dry with a fart is physiologically correct, but it was humorous enough in a cross-cultural sort of way to make us share a moment.

We were on a flight from Bangkok, Thailand, where I had spent a few weeks island hopping. For less than 10 bucks a night, I rented beachside bungalows accessed by water taxis.

Before that I was budget backpacking through Australia.

This sounds luxurious, and in all of the important experiential ways it was, but I traveled on the cheap. Ate ramen. Camped in my tent. I knew my budget would run out before my desire to keep going waned.

My grandma, Frances Wilt, gave all of her grandchildren $5,000 when they graduated from college. This gift was why when my peers at Miami University were talking about the jobs they landed and how much they were going to get paid, I was shopping for a one-way flight away. Gone. I worked a few months swinging a hammer after I graduated to earn some money to add to Grandma's so I could be gone longer.

I graduated in 2001 with a degree in anthropology or, as one *Cultural Anthropology* textbook that wrote about me put it, "With only a bachelor's degree in anthropology, he set out on a global tour … "[1] But I didn't *only* have a bachelor's degree. I had the curiosity that earning that degree inspired and the tools to pursue that curiosity. As someone who grew up in the rural Midwest at a school that had a "drive your tractor to school" day, I wasn't exposed to a lot of cultural diversity or diversity of thought. College, specifically my anthropology courses, introduced me to cultures I had never imagined.

College students are filled with potential. Seventeen years of building a base of knowledge and skills on which to build a career. As a first-year college student there is pressure to declare a major, to decide what you want to be when you grow up. Senior year is when all of the education and potential success and world-changing rubber meet the road. The "I want to be [blank]" becomes an "I am doing it!" or "I am not doing it because … " Potential and expectations are realized or they aren't.

In the eyes of many, I had not realized my potential, and I had not met expectations.

I envied the future med students and teachers and anyone else who knew what they wanted to do. Their itinerary was set. They'd have to go to school for so many years and then start a career with benefits. I didn't even know what I was going to do when I landed in Kathmandu.

---

[1]Gary Ferraro and Susan Andreatta, *Cultural Anthropology: An Applied Perspective* (Belmont, CA: Wadsworth, Cengage Learning, 2017), 177.

I sort of hated arriving anywhere. I was more comfortable going – permanently in transit. My travels really didn't have a purpose and neither did I, but the monk next to me was about to change that.

*Osmosis Jones* ended. I took off my headphones.

We sat in silence. The monk chanted while turning the wooden beads of a necklace like my grandma praying the Rosary. A half hour before landing, our bond strengthened over stupid human tricks – a video of people spinning plates or juggling chainsaws, and one man who pulled a string out his ear after having inserted it into a small wound on his little toe.

"How to do? How to do?" The monk, whose name was Sange, laughed. His resting grimace turned into a face-swallowing smile.

"Is the airport close to the city?" I asked him.

"When you get to Kathmandu," Sange said, "where do you stay?"

I didn't have any plans or a guidebook or reservations, just an idea of wanting to go hiking in the Himalayan Mountains we were flying over.

"You come with me," he said. "If you good … stay longer … if not so good, we find you hotel."

We walked out of the airport and were greeted by signs held by his followers. There were flowers, and people came up to him with white cloths known as *khata*. They'd bow before him and then he'd place the cloths around their necks.

Sange was your exact mental picture of a monk – chubby, glowing smile, shaved head, and bright robes – but apparently, given the welcome, he was not an average monk.

I thought he must've been some reincarnated, black belt, sensei monk. Obviously, I didn't know much about Buddhist culture.

We went to Sange's brother's house, where Sange held court.

Young lamas filled a brass cup with Coca-Cola before a straight-faced golden Buddha on an ornately decorated shrine. All of this world is suffering, but Lord Buddha needed his Coke. They lit two sticks of incense, backed away from the shrine, bowed, and left.

I sat across from the shrine on the floor, a steaming cup of putrid, buttery, salt tea before me, jealous of Buddha, wishing I could get a swig of his Coke to wash down my heaping bowl of noodles.

At the head of the room, Sange greeted a steady stream of people coming to pay their respects. They called him Khenpo Sange or simply Khenpo. Think of the title Khenpo as a terminal degree in Buddhist teaching. The respect payers did double takes in my direction, bowed three times, and discussed matters with Sange. Conversations took place in Tibetan, Nepalese, Taiwanese, and, occasionally, even a little English directed at me.

Hours passed, each marked by a plastic cuckoo clock, which chimed out "Happy Birthday" pathetically as if its batteries were running low.

We sat and ate so much – he entertaining audiences, me bored out of my mind.

"Are you bored?" he'd ask.

"Just mindful," I'd respond instead of screaming.

When there was a lull in visitors, we'd chat. He asked about my travels in Thailand and I told him about a guy named Porn who said he would take me to the post office to mail a package and then took me unexpectedly to a whorehouse, which I promptly left. From his position at the head of a small gathering, he rolled in laughter.

My original intent was to go hiking in the Himalayan Mountains, maybe visit Everest base camp. When I told Sange this, he consulted his scrolls to see if it was a good day to start a journey.

"Not today," he'd say.

"Tomorrow?" I'd ask.

And then tomorrow would come, and we'd load into the SUV and see some sights before heading back home.

It was like I was being held hostage by hospitality.

At night we'd walk around the local stupa, a large multitiered structure with a dome in the center and a spire on top. He'd answer my questions about Buddhism. He never evangelized. His lessons were about understanding the world, not understanding a religion – a philosophy more than a faith. Sange was a Mahayana Buddhist. As he described it, our compassion and happiness promote compassion and happiness toward all sentient beings. All living things are connected, and our lives should be in service to them.

Khenpo Sange showed me a world and a worldview vastly different from the mental landscape of the flatlands of the Midwest.

He'd answer some of my questions by buying me books on our nightly walks to the stores surrounding the stupa. I read a lot. I wondered around the compound where monks would be lost in chants or creating intricate art using colored sand, only to wipe it away on completion – a reminder that everything is temporary and therefore attachment could only lead to suffering. Or something like that.

———

One evening Sange and I walked to the stupa with his nephew Dorjee. *Om mani padme hum*, a common Buddhist chant, droned from a speaker above. We were part of a mass of humanity walking clockwise around the local stupa.

As we walked the required three laps, we passed Internet cafés, tailors, bakeries, and souvenir shops. A legless beggar sat on a board with wheels and lashed out at my shin with her cane. She wanted me to give her money, but I had no money. I didn't need money. Sange took care of everything, even donating on my behalf when I lit 108 prayer candles.

Up to this point in my travels, I went the places tourists were supposed to go and saw what tourists were supposed to see. On the way to the stupa we had passed cows licking their calves, human and animal waste on the street, intestines covered with flies spread out on wooden tables, and a guy with a fridge strapped to his back. On the tourist path, I saw the world through my eyes; but in the eyes of the legless beggar, I saw myself through the eyes of the world, and it made me uncomfortable.

The thick smell of dirt and hot wax hung in the evening air as we finished our third lap and continued on to a fourth.

"I thought that we were doing three laps," I said.

"You do something once," Sange said, "it is not a big deal. Two times, it is a little more important. But three times it is really important. Three laps good. Seven laps better."

━━━━━

I felt the chanting as much as I heard it. A group of robed men sitting on the floor gave life to the damp morning air at 5 a.m. The incense slowly burned, releasing musky overtones in long, black, rising wisps of smoke.

My room sat high on the hillside, overlooking the comings and goings of life in the valley below. From a down cocoon of warmth and comfort, I unzipped my sleeping bag and entered a place and culture that I barely understood.

We were at Sange's monastery south of Kathmandu in the village of Pharping.

Breakfast was ladled out of a smoldering cauldron on a terrace cut in the hillside.

Soon the monastery and its ramparts were swarming with local villagers, pilgrims from Kathmandu, and brightly robed lamas. All were here to welcome Khenpo's teacher, His Holiness Penor Rinpoche, and to dedicate a new shrine at the lamasery to Padmasambhava, an eighth-century Buddhist master who was born out of a lotus and often depicted giving the "rock on" sign meant to repel demons.

"His Holiness is very powerful," Sange explained as we waited for his arrival. "When Chinese forced us away from our homeland, he was one of the last to leave. He left with many men and women. The Chinese follow them to the mountains with guns. They shoot and kill many people around His Holiness, but the bullets fall at his feet and their grenades do not explode until he has passed. The hike over the Himalaya is very difficult and others die of cold and hunger. His Holiness injures leg, which hurts him even today. Three hundred left Tibet; only 30 make it to India."

I tried to make myself useful during the preparation for His Holiness's visit. I helped lug a welder up the hillside, and, well, that's about all I did. Mostly I ate and played hackey sack and practiced kung fu kicks with the young lamas in training.

As the car of His Holiness Penor Rinpoche, the present-day reincarnation of a monk first born in 1679, came to a stop at the base of the monastery, the gathered crowd surged forward hoping to glimpse or touch him. A robed Secret Service emerged and cleared a tunnel for the short, squat holy man to limp through. *Khata*s were thrown at his head like panties at a rock star.

One by one we filed up to His Holiness, who was seated on an elevated throne. I knelt before him and presented him with a *khata*. He smiled warmly and placed his hand upon my head and ruffled my blond curls – I hadn't had a haircut in months.

The brightly colored walls, the smell of incense, the gold Buddha at the front of the room, the bulletproof monk with my friend Khenpo Sange at his side – it all was so exhilarating. It's not that I was caught up in the religious fervor and believed in reincarnation or bulletproofness; it was that I was a witness experiencing an ancient culture. I was a participant and I was an observer.

Participant observation is a research method employed by anthropologists in which a researcher isn't simply a fly on the wall scribbling in a notebook, but part of the action – sitting in prayer, lighting 108 candles, watching monks gift a gold Buddha Coca-Cola, and getting blessed by a smiling monk with a silk *khata* around my neck.

I felt like I was an anthropologist doing something I was meant to do, something important.

In my anthropology senior seminar we discussed a debate within the scientific community about how much an observer's presence impacts the data. The postmodern school of thought believes that when anthropologists go into the field, they bring back stories rich in context and meaning. The stories can't necessarily be quantified, but they can be appreciated for what they are: glimpses of people at a particular moment that provide value in the act of attempting to see, appreciate, and understand them.

If there is any anthropology occurring in my work, this is it. At least the authors of that anthropology textbook seemed to think so: "Employing an anthropological lens as a journalist and traveler, Timmerman enables us to see and feel the impact the global economy has on people ... "

It's weird now to be an example of applying anthropology. At the time, I was rudderless and felt like the classic example of what not to major in and what not to do with your college degree. I kept seeing anthropology consistently at the top of majors not to major in if you want to be a responsible adult.

Up until I met Sange, I was on the traveling circuit, ticking the boxes of all the things a backpacker should do. It wasn't until meeting him on the plane and his invitation and all the time he put into me that I had my first really amazing cultural experience. He showed me something so different from what I was used to. He made me fall in love with the world and writing about the people I met.

It's the age-old story. Injured traveler meets monk (see Figure 1.1). Monk takes traveler to lamasery in the foothills of the Himalayan Mountains, consults prayer cards, blesses traveler, and fills traveler's belly with rice and lentils. Traveler gets better – and 16 years later realizes the importance of it all.

*Figure 1.1 Khenpo Sange and the author.*

Sange had accepted me into his world and, although I didn't recognize it at the time, helped me discover what I was meant to do. My studies in anthropology weren't going to waste. He had given me the gift of purpose.

In hindsight, his impact is immeasurable on my life.

His wasn't the only gift to influence my trip. The trip was paid for in large part by Grandma's gift, and I wrote about it in the journal my Aunt Cathy gifted me.

In *The Gift: Creativity and the Artist in the Modern World*, Lewis Hyde encourages readers to "think of the gift as a constantly flowing river" and that we are the channels. The river shapes the channel and the channel defines the river. The time, talent, kindnesses, and resources we share – our gifts – don't stop; they are passed on and shared. They flow through us and connect us.[2]

Our lives are shaped by the gifts of others, people making small and large impacts that seem to embed into our DNA and change the course of our lives. Unless we recognize the people who have shaped our journey, we'll think we arrived on our own.

"I have a lot to be thankful for," I wrote in my journal on Thanksgiving Day when I was at Sange's monastery. "Over the last four months I have been living a dream, but also I have seen children in such poverty. I cannot imagine that they will ever have the gift of dreaming. When one has to dream about life's necessities anything else such as traveling seems superfluous."

I had witnessed global poverty, had a beggar whack me with a cane, and was wrestling with what it meant to live in this world of haves and have-nots. I didn't recognize all of this when I was 22 traveling alone. I had a long way to go, and probably still do, but I can see an awakening of gratitude and struggle with privilege in that entry. I began the search for the Good Person Equation. I left Nepal different.

My aunt had written a quote by Sue Ebaugh a few pages ahead of my Thanksgiving post: "Within our dreams and aspirations we find our purpose." "I am a better person for having met Khenpo Sange," I wrote in my journal. "And I will become better in the future."

We have to have gratitude for what has been given to us before we can give in an impactful way. If it weren't for Sange, my grandma, and so many other people, maybe even Osmosis Jones, I wouldn't have had the opportunity to follow my curiosity around the world to meet the people who've helped give my life purpose.

---

[2]Lewis Hyde, *The Gift: Creativity and the Artist in the Modern World* (New York: Random House, 2007). 9.

# 2

# One Night in a Slum Showed Me How Poor I Was (Kenya, 2010)

*Why should we care when we have our own problems? / My problem with missionaries / Giving thoughts and prayers*

**TO ME KENYA FELT LIKE AN ESCAPE.** Back home the world was shrinking.

The financial crisis of 2008 that had introduced chaos around the world first came to my attention in the monthly sales reports of my family's business, aka my day job. I had worked on and off for Timmerman Truss since I was in eighth grade. The American Dream my parents had built over four decades ended and the nightmare began.

The US economy neared collapse as the housing bubble, which had fueled the success of the business, burst. Our problem became everyone else's.

Main Street pointed to Wall Street's follies. Wall Street blamed Main Street's irresponsible borrowing. But on countless, nameless, and forgotten streets around the world, lives hung in the balance.

I lost my job along with my 40 coworkers. We weren't alone. Tens of millions of workers around the world also lost their jobs, but I became too lost in the epicenter of my own crisis to think of the impact it was having elsewhere. After two years of suffering meetings with bankers, lawyers, potential investors, and advisers, all hope of salvaging the business was gone, so I ran for the hills of Africa.

I had a wife who loved me and a 14-month-old daughter with whom I danced and laughed daily, but I felt like we had lost everything. We could barely make it to the next unemployment check and pay our health insurance.

We were not fine.

Unlike my father, I had another life.

A few times a month I traveled to universities that invited me to talk about the garment workers I met and wrote about in my first book, *Where Am I Wearing?*.

During the height of our depression I was visiting with a group of sociology professors talking about my book and one asked, "Why should we care about the people who make our clothes when we have so many problems right here?"

I was taken aback by the question, and even more so by my inability to answer it.

The room went quiet. I said something, but I don't remember what. The truth was I had become so focused on my own family's problems, I had forgotten why we should care about other people. It's natural; the closer to home our problems are, the harder it is to see a world beyond them. But I expected more from myself.

One day a friend sent me an e-mail highlighting the global impact of the financial crisis. As a result of the financial crisis, a substantial amount of people became food insecure[1] and 64 million people fell back into extreme poverty (living on less than $1.25 per day in 2010).[2]

The e-mail floored me. It reminded me how connected we all are and how local issues go global and global issues become local ones. I realized how small my world had become.

Why should we care?

We should care because our lives impact the lives of others around the world. It wasn't just our depression.

---

[1] Food and Agriculture Organization, "The State of Food Insecurity in the World" (2009).
[2] World Bank, "The MDGs After the Crisis" (2010).

It was like one of those Western movies where the drunk's head is dunked in the horse trough, and he's helped to his feet to refocus on a world and reality that was beyond the fog.

"I'm going to Africa," I told Dad one day as we sat in the factory the bank had shut down, and the factory which he laced up his boots and traveled to each day even though there was no work. My announcement sounded an awful lot like "I give up." I suspected that's what Dad heard, too.

Justin Ahrens, a friend who owned a design firm (and designed the cover of this book), was going to shoot a documentary for Life in Abundance, a Christian NGO that works with churches in impoverished areas to lift their communities out of poverty. He invited me to come to Kenya.

"Hmm," Dad said, his response to most news, whether it be the mail is here or the name of his first grandchild. "How long?"

"Not sure. Maybe six to eight weeks." We didn't project our lives that far out anymore. We lived in the tyranny of the moment, handling the crises as they came. In eight weeks, the plant could be up and running under a new owner or, more likely (and what eventually happened), the plant and all of its equipment would be auctioned off to the highest bidder in an afternoon.

No one knew what was going to happen. But I knew one thing: I was not myself. I felt helpless and hopeless – a victim of forces beyond my control.

My world had indeed shrunk.

> *Giving Rules: A world exists beyond your own problems. Even when you are in need, you have something to give.*

───

The night was dark and all that was Nairobi's Mathare slum was unseen: the valley lined with rusting tin shacks, the mother sleeping on a wooden bed with her foot on the floor to act as an early warning in case the nearby river happened to rise, the food scraps and plastic and cardboard and people in various stages of decomposition and degradation.

Behind a wall of sheet metal, a carefree whistle rose into the darkness along with an arm. A puddle seeped out forming tributaries of soap and islands of dirt.

Someone passed and said something in my direction.

"What did they say?" I asked James, one of the local boys who introduced me to life in the slums, as I took a break from helping the documentary crew.

"They say that you are easy to see."

I looked down at my arms covered in blond hair that all day had enticed the children of Mathare to pet me. They glowed.

You may have heard of the slum of Kibera, Africa's second largest slum, because it appeared in the movie *The Constant Gardener*. Mathare is Nairobi's other slum, home to more than 500,000, where only 5% of adults have formal jobs and 80% of kids don't go to school.[3]

James was 16. He had a crooked-toothed smile and the beginnings of a mustache. We small talked while waiting for his cousin, Thomas, to finish showering. Thomas was dirty from a pickup game of soccer that had begun with him expertly gliding past dusty clouds of stampeding defenders, and, after the sky opened, ended with him sliding and falling in the mud like a mere mortal.

I had watched the game with Thomas's younger brother, Moses. Moses was too shy to speak to me, but his smile, equal parts top and bottom teeth, and his eyes spoke volumes. When he beat me thumb wrestling he didn't say anything, just beamed. When he pointed out a rainbow, he burst with pride. When the downpour had started, it was Moses who brought a banana leaf for me to hold over my head as an umbrella.

"Thomas is taking a pretty long shower, huh?" I said to James.

"When it rains," James said, "the water is warmer."

The water wasn't actually warmer; it just felt like it, but it was not my place to correct James.

"Have you ever taken a warm-water shower?" I asked James.

"Only in the rain," he said.

The whistling in the shower stopped and Thomas, 17, emerged, bringing with him the clean smell of soap.

We spent the day cleaning Thomas's corner of the slum, a dusty alley lined with single-room apartments.

I expected to have a long walk ahead of us to fetch water, but it was the rainy season so the nearby cistern was full.

Thomas handed a few shillings to the girl sitting on a rock next to the spigot. Nothing in the slums is free.

"When the water runs out here," Thomas said, "we have to go a very far distance. When there's no water, you can tell. People look dirty. People smell dirty."

We started with laundry. Thomas laid out three plastic tubs – red, green, yellow. A pile of clothes sat in the first. Thomas picked up a bar of

---

[3]Mark Kramer, *Dispossessed: Life in Our World's Slums* (New York: Orbis Books, 2006), 69.

soap and started scrubbing, demonstrating to me how to rub the clothes on themselves in quick, short strokes.

While Thomas methodically scrubbed, I splashed about. Suds ran down my glasses. One by one we moved the pile to the middle bin and scrubbed the clothes some more. The last bin was to ensure all the soap was off, and then we hung them on a line to dry.

Never has a load of laundry encapsulated someone's life more. It was made up of Thomas's school and soccer uniforms. Without the soccer uniform there would be no school uniform. Thomas's mother couldn't afford the $300 per year to send him to school, but a coach had seen him playing one day and recruited him. He went to school for free.

Our last job was scrubbing the squat toilets hidden from view by doors on rusty hinges. The 11 other households in the alley shared the toilets, and each took its turn cleaning them.

Well-meaning foreigners aren't uncommon in Mathare. They roll up in vans to choruses of "How are you?" and chants of "*Mzungu! Mzungu!*" ("wanderer" or "white person" in Bantu). *Wazungu* (plural of *mzungu*) visit projects, some of which bring aid and hope, and others, like the incomplete bridge that spanned the river polluted to the color of orange Fanta, bring more questions from the residents: "Are you here to finish the bridge?" *Wazungu* wield clipboards and cameras. Kids fight for photographers' focus and do their best to please. Before posing, they ask questions like "Do you want me to smile or cry?" as if *wazungu* are interested only in emotional extremes.

> *Giving Rules: Your presence makes an impact. People are more important than photos.*

"I never knew white people could do this," James said.

"Huh?" I couldn't hear James as I scraped the coconut broom on the concrete surrounding the toilet.

"I thought white people were special," he said, "that white people were perfect. Now I know they aren't."

I wasn't an efficient clothes washer. I was a slow toilet cleaner. Being imperfect might just be the thing I'm best at.

The boys (see Figure 2.1) lived in a room half taken up by a homemade bunk bed. Sheets hid the rough concrete walls. The room breathed; as someone entered, the sheets inhaled.

There was no electricity, although Thomas was working on changing that. He had run wires from the main line on the street, but was waiting for things to settle down before he completed the installation.

*Figure 2.1    James and Thomas overlooking Mathare.*

The electric company had just raided Mathare, passing out fines to anyone "borrowing" service. Often the same electric company employees who disconnected the service had helped connect their neighbors' service while off-duty in the first place.

Thomas completed some minor repairs on a gas camping lantern and then a flame threw our shadows onto the walls. Life in the slums is a lot like camping.

Joseph, one of Thomas's friends, joined us and suggested we go for a walk. Thomas had his earbuds in, listening to Akon while reading a pocket guide titled *Physics Made Easy*. He told us to go ahead without him.

James, Joseph, Moses, and I headed out into the night. We joined the strollers browsing markets lit by candles.

A big box speaker sat alongside the road. We could feel it before we saw it. Why have a giant speaker if you aren't going to turn it all the way up? I could practically smell the black goo oozing from the speaker's center as it melted.

"It's a funeral," Joseph said. "You give them a few shillings and you join them in dancing. They will be out here all night."

It wasn't simply a celebration of life; it was much more practical, a fundraise for death to cover the expenses of the funeral.

At the end of the road there was an open space – darker than the rest and oddly empty. At first I thought nothing of it. James, Joseph, and I were chatting and I looked to find Moses. He was a few feet away, standing still. He stared across the street into the void and his shoulders quivered just enough to reveal he was sobbing.

"What's the matter with Moses?" I asked.

"Bad things happened here," Joseph said. "After the election in 2007 was decided for the Kikuyu, the Luo caused trouble. At first it wasn't in Mathare. Then one night it was. There were homes there. Let's go."

Moses and Thomas lost a brother in the postelection violence. Luo gangs attacked those belonging to the Kikuyu tribe. The Luo gangs went into Mathare and asked questions in their native tongue. Those who answered in Luo were left alone, but those who didn't had their houses torched, and were burned, beaten, or killed. That night neighbors and friends sought shelter with Thomas. He could speak Luo well enough to fool the gangs. He answered the life-and-death questions correctly.

Moses turned away, hiding his tears with shadow.

# 3

# We Aren't the Heroes (Kenya, 2010)

*Toxic charity / Fair trade travel*

**GOING INTO THIS TRIP WITH A CHRISTIAN NONPROFIT,** I knew that faith would be front and center and, at some point, mine would be called into question. I had this idea that faith-based NGOs dangled food in front of the hungry and said, "Pray to our God and we'll give you seconds."

I had actively avoided missionaries since meeting a retiree at an Internet cafe in Honduras. He was from Florida and came to spread the Word after his wife died. He ran a school for girls, was getting ready to head back to Florida, and was faced with the tough decision of which 18-year-old he was going to bring back to the States to marry. *Nice, huh? Not bad for an old man, huh?* He didn't say this, but that was his demeanor. I hated him.

Since then I had traveled to several remote places where the only foreigners were soldiers for a God or a government or greed – all on missions I wanted nothing to do with. I'd cross the street to dodge a conversation.

So, yeah, I was prejudiced toward missionaries, but somehow decided on spending a week with them. *Were they missionaries? If so, did they think I was too?*

I wasn't sure what to do. Do I stay in the closet and hope I'm not called on to bless the food or share some spiritual insight? Or do I step off the plane, drop my bags, strike my best smiling, pointing, winking Buddy-Jesus pose, and announce, "The heathen has arrived!"?

The days were hot and exhausting, but it was always the moments when we stopped to pray that made me sweat the most. When would it be my turn to lead the prayer?

The last time I prayed, I think I was praying for a puppy dog. It had been a while.

After we had settled into our accommodations and completed a few days of shooting, I was outed. One of the members of the group asked me, "Where do you stand on the whole faith thing?"

I was honest. After that I could relax when it was time to pray because I wouldn't be asked to lead.

There was plenty to pray about. We met mothers and fathers who prayed that today they would find a job so their children might be able to eat tomorrow. Work was hard to come by, and wages in the slum were down 20% while food prices had increased 133%. It wasn't just food costs on the rise. Everything was more expensive. Cooking fuel was up 30–50%, forcing women to search for firewood and charcoal in the nearby woods, exposing them to increased chance of being assaulted or raped.

One prayer stood out above all the rest. I was in a small shanty with Rosa, a single mother who was a Christian already, a few of her six kids, and Bruce, a youth pastor from Chicago. Rosa's greatest fear was that one of her children would step out her front door and be washed away when the rain turned the alley into a flash-flooded slot canyon.

Bruce asked us to bow our heads and then began to pray. By the end of the prayer, my eyes were watering. It wasn't some transcendent, spiritual experience that hit me; it was rather the beauty and importance of Bruce's words, and the language of prayer. The compassion and the honesty with which Bruce prayed touched me. I don't sit down with strangers or loved ones and express how thankful I am for them, how much hope and love I have for them. I don't actually take the time to let those thoughts and feelings breathe. When tragedy strikes, there are those of us who offer thoughts, like me, and those who offer prayers, like Bruce. My "I'll be thinking about you," actually means, "I might think about you if my scattered brain wanders in that direction at random, but otherwise I probably won't." Buddhists practice Loving-Kindness meditation where you focus positive thoughts on a particular person – say, an uncle who drank too much at your birthday party and made a fool of himself.

The positive thoughts don't magically make your uncle less of a doofus, but do impact the way you feel about your uncle. Good thoughts push out the bad.

Later Bruce told me he thought he had messed up the prayer, and that he didn't know how to pray in a context like that, but for me Bruce's heartfelt prayer was like showering in the rain – it was warm and I didn't want it to end.

Too often folks like me with a secular point of view dismiss faith-based nonprofits, as if their compassion isn't as pure as ours: "We're not trying to win souls or real estate in the afterlife; we're trying to help our fellow man just because we're nice like that." People slap a "Good without God" on their Prius and drive around with conscious-clean airs of moral superiority. But those who are affiliated with a religion are more likely to give, and not just to a congregation, but to other types of charitable organizations. Sixty-two percent of religiously affiliated households give to charities, compared to only 46% of unaffiliated households.[1]

When you wade into these waters, someone will always bring up Robert Lupton's book *Toxic Charity: How Churches and Charities Hurt Those They Help.* Lupton, a critic of secular aid as well, estimates that $2.5 to $5 billion is spent annually on religious mission trips, but trips "seldom yield appreciable improvement in the lives of those being served." He makes the case that "[w]hen relief does not transition to development in a timely way, compassion becomes toxic." Aid can lead to dependency and rob those being served of their dignity and motivation to improve their own lives.

There is a right and wrong way to do aid. Improper aid is done to people, not with people. Judith N. Lasker, author of *Hoping to Help: The Promises and Pitfalls of Global Health Volunteering*, refers to volunteer trips that represent aid done to people as "New Colonialism" in which volunteers extract experiences, build their resumes, contacts, and social capital.[2]

"Throughout the world, there are many, many places that get excellent, dedicated medical care from church-group missionaries," Lasker told the *Chronicle of Philanthropy.* "I don't want to diminish that. I don't want to neglect that. But if you have to listen to a sermon or go

---

[1] Giving USA, "Giving USA Special Report on Giving to Religion," givingusa .org/just-released-giving-usa-special-report-on-giving-to-religion/ (12 March 2018).
[2] Rebecca Koenig, "Author Urges a Rethink About Medical Volunteerism Abroad," www.philanthropy.com/article/Author-Documents-Pitfalls-of/236465 (March 12, 2018).

to a movie or pray before you can get treated, I have a real problem with that...My impression is that most faith-based groups do not do that. Many faith-based groups and people that I've talked with strongly oppose doing that. They feel their religious faith motivates them to make the world a better place and serve the poor."

When evangelizing is involved, it's an attempt to take advantage of people's poverty to colonize their souls. Gandhi said, "To a man with an empty stomach food is God." I would worship whatever god you offered me if my kids were hungry and you had some pancakes.

> *Giving Rules: If you are a person of faith, let it motivate you but don't impose your beliefs on others.*

Mission trips, and any volunteering experience, done improperly can often be more about the volunteers than those they are helping. There are the classic stories of churches being painted six times in one summer by well-meaning volunteers on short-term missions. Imagine the church. Imagine the people. Do you imagine them all wearing matching shirts that say the group's destination alliterated with a verb to produce slogans: "Help Haiti" and "Save Senegal"?

We aren't the heroes in the lives of others. We aren't the Batmans. We aren't even the Robins. When we are at our best as volunteers and as givers we are the Alfreds, Batman's loyal butler, giving people the asked-for tools, resources, and knowledge to create their own change; we help people help themselves. Unless we are bringing a specific skill to a task that the local people can't complete on their own, we should see ourselves less as helpers and more as Fair Trade Learners, a term coined by Amizade, a Pittsburgh nonprofit that takes volunteers from high schools, universities, and community groups on global service trips. This approach plugs volunteers into the work of local nonprofits with an established relationship in the community, and considers that there should be at least an equal benefit to the local communities as to the volunteers.[3]

If you are volunteering internationally, look for established organizations with ongoing local efforts to which you can contribute. You are there to learn and to champion. The biggest change your presence is likely to make in a community is that you can show people you care.

---

[3]Eric Hartman, Cody Morris Paris, and Brandon Blache-Cohen, "Fair Trade Learning: Ethical Standards for Community-Engaged International Volunteer Tourism," *Sage Journals* (June 10, 2014).

You can listen to them. It's about setting proper expectations – your own and the expectations of those with whom you will be interacting.

Lord knows I was a crappy documentary crew member because I kept wandering into shots like I had stumbled out of a memory care unit. Forget the silver screen; I was a Silver Alert. Life in Abundance working with local communities through churches, and the filmmakers using tools and skills not possessed by local people, seemed to meet all the standards set by Lupton in *Toxic Charity* and the idea of Fair Trade Learning. The documentary the team put together toured churches and raised more than $300,000 for Life in Abundance's work.

After seeing Life in Abundance in action, I came to appreciate how, when done responsibly, faith-based organizations can efficiently work with the people they serve because they have an automatic connection.

> *Giving Rules: Our gifts should give others dignity, not take it. Giving isn't about you.*

———

In Mathare, I recognized the stress on the faces of the fathers. I had seen it in my bathroom mirror and in the face of my own father. Yet in the slum, it was life and death. I saw how connected we all are. I also saw community as a coping strategy, a very foreign strategy to me. For the first time in a long time, I saw a world beyond the walls of my own problems. The night I spent in the boys' room, I stared up at the ceiling in a forgotten slum shanty, unable to sleep.

I had seen an unfinished bridge started by well-meaning *wazungu*. I had heard about broken-down and unfixable wells that NGOs had constructed out of materials that weren't readily available. All were acts of good intentions done by people who were visitors. The locals remained.

Thomas and James slept. I was wide awake thinking about the risk that Thomas took to protect his neighbors and how I barely knew any of mine back home. Inspired by Thomas, I knew that if I wanted to become a better giver, I needed to start where I lived.

Lasting change isn't achieved by temporary visitors, but by locals.

# 4

# Confessions of a Volunteer Addict (Indiana, 2010)

*Benefits of volunteering / 100-hour rule / Make where you live interesting*

**I KNEW SOME OF THE STORIES OF THE WOMEN IN THE CIRCLE.** There were stories of bad luck, deaths, diseases, and abuses that led them into poverty or kept them there. We sat in a church basement on cold folding chairs and listened to Steve Selvey, the building commissioner, talk about some of the conditions he had seen people living in.

"We have a lack of quality low-income housing," Steve told us. "Two weeks into my job, I got called out to a house … " He paused and stared at the floor. It seemed as if he were setting up a long story that would include details like where the house was and what it looked like. But then he sat back and got right to it. "A mother was holding her child and she forgot to put the rubber glove on that her landlord gave her to safely flip the light switch. They were both electrocuted."

The room went silent. A breath would have been as loud as a gunshot.

"Now, now," he said, not in a consoling way but in a "I should have said *shocked* instead of *electrocuted*" way. "They were treated and released."

We all breathed a sigh of relief.

"I think it's immoral to [as a landlord] take money and not provide simple services," Steve said.

He told us more stories of similar circumstances, where people paid to live in places that weren't safe, and that didn't have water or electricity.

This wasn't Kenya or Nepal, or some developing nation I visited; this was my hometown, Muncie, Indiana. There was an American flag in the corner. The odd thing was that I wouldn't have been at the meeting hosted by TeamWORK for Quality Living, a local nonprofit that helped people in poverty, if it weren't for having traveled to places like Kenya.

After a decade of travel, I was a global citizen, which is to say I was a citizen of everywhere and somehow nowhere. I barely knew my neighbors in Muncie, Indiana. The more I traveled, the more I realized that the people who make the biggest impacts on the lives of others make them where they live, where they can wrap an arm around someone, offer a hug or a cup of coffee, or, in the Midwest, a casserole during a time of need.

I needed to be a better local citizen and neighbor. I had lived in Muncie for a couple of years and didn't know anyone really or how to get involved.

I had heard about TeamWORK for Quality Living on the local NPR station. The organization was looking for volunteers, so I attended an informational session and learned about poverty in my own community.

Poverty in places like Kenya and Nepal, although extreme, didn't make me feel as uncomfortable as poverty in my own community. It was easier to look someone in the eye in a slum in Kenya and hear his or her story than it was to hear the story of someone living in poverty in Muncie whose kids may go to the same school as mine, whom I might pass in the grocery.

Of course I knew poverty existed in my community, but I never really thought to see life in Muncie from the point of view of those who lived in poverty. I had put much more time and heart into thinking about those living in global poverty.

I think this is for several reasons.

I looked at Muncie as just a place I lived. It wasn't my community. It wasn't a place I had responsibilities or, at least, accepted them for anyone else other than my own family.

When I met Amilcar, the guy who worked at the factory where my T-shirt was made in Honduras, it changed the way I saw the world. I realized that there were people who were invisible to me. If I hadn't thought about the people who made my clothes, who else wasn't I thinking about? To see poverty in my hometown up close and hear the stories for the first time was to admit I hadn't really seen my fellow citizens who lived in poverty.

There was also the fear that it could be me. Half of Americans don't have access to $1,000 in cash. There are a lot of unexpected problems that total more than a grand. Poverty, like death, is something that is all around us, but we like to pretend it doesn't exist and could never happen to us.

Most cultures have prejudices toward the poor. I've noticed this when I travel. I've had translators in China and Cambodia who wondered why I would want to talk to people who worked in a factory or lived in a slum. I've had plenty of translators and friends who've said things like "They talk uneducated," and they do things because "they don't know better." For many of my translators, the poor in their country are as invisible to them as the poor in my own had been to me. Researchers found that tourists on slum tours in India looked at slum residents as a positive part of a community and culture, while they perceived the homeless in their own communities as lazy or addicts. We are harsher critics of the poor in our own communities.[1]

The narrative of the American Dream where if you work hard you will succeed lends itself to an undercurrent of the inverse: Those who don't work hard aren't successful, as if poverty is solely a condition of lack of effort.

We fear poverty; we are made uncomfortable by poverty. We judge people. We ignore people. We put the responsibility on the poor and not on ourselves, until we meet them.

Gregory Boyle, a Jesuit priest, founded Homeboy Industries in Los Angeles that employs former gang members. He writes about his experiences and the need to build community with all members of society in his book *Tattoos on the Heart*.

> Our locating ourselves with those who have been endlessly excluded becomes an act of visible protest … The powers bent on waging war against the poor and the young and the "other" will only be moved to kinship when they observe it. Only when we can see a community where the outcast is valued and appreciated will we abandon the values that seek to exclude.[2]

---

[1] Bob Ma, "A Trip into the Controversy: A Study of Slum Tourism Travel Motivations" (2010), 23, 24.
[2] Greg Boyle, *Tattoos on the Heart: The Power of Boundless Compassion* (New York: Free Press, 2010), 177.

As I volunteered with TeamWORK in my community, I realized that proximity over time leads to compassion. The group ran the Circles program, a model that matched a person living in poverty, known as the captain, with two to four volunteer allies. The allies helped the captain however they were able except monetarily. The group hosted weekly dinners at which I often couldn't tell who was a captain or who was an ally. The ground rules of the dinners encouraged us not to talk about things that would divide us from one another. In our conversations we weren't our jobs, and we tried to avoid topics that would place us on the socioeconomic hierarchy, because we were all equal; it was just some of us faced tougher economic circumstances than others.

*Giving Rules: Proximity over time leads to compassion.*

At first it was challenging to have conversations that didn't begin with "What do you do?" or mention an activity that would identify me as middle class. This made me realize how the majority of conversations in my life were with people who've had very similar experiences to my own. I traveled around to see the world and its diversity of culture and thought, but in my own community I lived in a bubble.

Twenty-one percent of citizens of Delaware County, Indiana, where Muncie is located, live in poverty, and 26% are the working poor who struggle to meet basic needs on a monthly basis.[3] Not seeing these individuals or understanding their situations, knowing their names, their hopes, and their dreams was to ignore almost half of my fellow citizens.

Getting engaged as a volunteer with Circles helped correct that.

It wasn't always easy. When you volunteer you go into the experience with certain expectations: I was going to be matched with someone who lived in poverty, and then that person would get out of poverty, and I would be matched with someone else. So one by one I'd help people out of poverty. It's laughable to think about now.

*Giving Rules: Give with no expectations.*

There are many social, economic, structural, and psychological factors that keep people in poverty. Abuse of some sort played a part in so many of the captains' stories. They bore scars I was in no way

---

[3]United Way of Delaware County, www.invitedtoliveunited.org/alice (March 12, 2018).

capable of healing. To receive certain financial assistance from the government, you can't have more than a few hundred dollars in your checking account or a net worth more than $2,250.[4] *How can you get out of poverty if you can't save for life's challenges?* If you start to earn an income that by definition is not at the federal poverty level, your assistance drops and you were able to meet the basic needs of your family better when you didn't have the job and relied on assistance only. This is known as the cliff effect.

One day my captain, a single mother of three, asked me to help her set up a budget. We factored in her assistance and by the end of the month she was still short.

My chest got tight. "Oh my God," I thought. "What is she going to do?" She lost money every month and had no savings to make up the difference.

She sensed my panic.

"It's okay," she reassured me. "I'm used to it."

*Would I have her strength, hustle, and calm resolve if faced with the same circumstance?*

I had several captains through the years. Their challenges varied. I felt unqualified because there were so many things I couldn't do. But there were things I could do. I could listen. I could take dinner to a kid after school. I could make an introduction to someone who could help put together a business plan. I could take her daughter to the daddy-daughter dance at the elementary school. I could meet for coffee and talk about zombie TV shows or anything that didn't have to do with income or budgets or getting out of poverty. I could show up at the hospital when a baby was born, or when things seemed so hopeless that pills seemed the only way out.

I also became a Big with Big Brothers Big Sisters. It was only a four-hour commitment every month, and I spent it with my little brother tossing a football or going to basketball games and movies. The majority of kids in the program waiting on Bigs were boys, yet there was a lack of male volunteers.

It was a common problem. In the US, only 21.7% of men volunteer, compared to 27.8% of women.[5]

*Giving Rules: We all need to volunteer more.*

---

[4]Indiana Family & Social Services Administration, "Do I Qualify for SNAP?" www.in.gov/fssa/dfr/3099.htm (March 12, 2018).

[5]Bureau of Labor Statistics, "Volunteering in the United States, 2015" (2016).

I was matched with my Little when he was eight. In no time he was a teenager and had other things to do and a busy social schedule. His mom worked nights, so often he was left to his own devices. I can only imagine what hijinks I would've gotten into as a teen if I were left alone most nights.

One night he and a friend were walking through a neighborhood when his friend grabbed a backpack out of an unlocked car sitting in a driveway.

The cops got them and my Little spent months in juvenile detention.

His mom called me and broke the news. He screwed up, for sure, but the punishment seemed to outweigh the crime.

"If that were me," I thought, "my parents would've hired a lawyer and I wouldn't have spent a night in detention."

But he wasn't white or middle class. He didn't benefit from the privileges that I did, and that seemed like its own injustice. I visited him at the Youth Opportunity Center, a remarkable residential program for kids in trouble. We played Scrabble. We talked. Sometimes we just sat in silence. I told him this moment didn't define him.

He got into alcohol and weed and dropped out of school or was kicked out; I'm not sure.

I told a potential landlord that he was a good kid and needed people to give him a chance. When another landlord was done giving chances, I stored his couch, TV, and random garbage bags of clothing in my barn.

He became a father at 18. I held his tiny son in his apartment, stared into his blue eyes, and wondered about his future.

He loved his son as much as I loved mine. I was proud of the dad he was and wanted to be. We don't choose our brothers and we can't control their actions or decisions, but, no matter what, they are still our brothers.

My volunteer opportunities didn't go as I imagined. I'm not sure how much of a difference I made, but the experiences volunteering made a difference in me. This is a cliché point, but it's unavoidable: When you volunteer, you often get more than you give. When people say that, they are often referring to the "warm glow" of giving, as if volunteering and giving back, addressing real problems in your community, is supposed to be easy. It's not.

There were plenty of times I wished I hadn't volunteered and that I didn't know about the inequality and injustice in our community, that I wanted to live permanently in my privilege bubble and not look out. But volunteering made Muncie feel like home.

At the TeamWORK dinners, I got to know people from all walks of life, including the captains, state senators, nonprofit leaders, and county commissioners. I started to care more about local issues because I knew people impacted by them. For the first time in my adult life, I became part of a community, and being a part of that community has been one of the most rewarding things I've experienced.

Unfortunately, community involvement and civic engagement have eroded for decades.

Think about a community organization. Imagine walking into the room where members meet and shaking their hands. Now, what's the average age of those in the room?

I seemed to be at least 25 years younger than most of the other TeamWORK volunteers, and the same goes for the other organizations I've visited.

One of the best books I've read about this erosion is *Bowling Alone: The Collapse and Revival of American Community* by Robert Putnam, a political scientist at Harvard. Putnam writes about the decline of memberships at community organizations and churches, voter turnout, newspaper subscriptions, and a whole host of other areas. He documents that more people are bowling, but fewer people are bowling in groups.

Volunteering is in decline, too. In 2015, only 24.9% of Americans above the age of 16 volunteered, which was down from 28.8% in 2005.[6] On average, Americans volunteer only 15 hours per year. That's less than 20 minutes per week.

How much should we volunteer? In terms of a variable for the Good Person Equation, this is an easy one: 100 hours per year. Research shows that people who volunteer 100 hours per year are happier, are more satisfied, and live longer.

Adam Grant writes about the 100-hour rule in his book *Give and Take*:

> One hundred seems to be a magical number when it comes to giving. In a study of more than two thousand Australian adults in their mid-sixties, those who volunteered between one hundred and eight hundred hours per year were happier and more satisfied with their lives than those who volunteered fewer than one hundred or more than eight hundred hours annually. In another study, American adults who volunteered at least one hundred hours in 1998 were more likely to be alive in 2000 ... This is the 100-hour rule of volunteering. It appears to be the range where giving is maximally energizing and minimally draining.[7]

---

[6] Bureau of Labor Statistics (2016).

[7] Adam Grant, *Give and Take: Why Helping Others Drives Our Success* (New York: Viking, 2013), 173, 174.

*Figure 4.1    The author (back left) with students from Ball State University.*

Volunteering is a life hack at getting connected to a community (see Figure 4.1). And not having a strong community is worse for your health than smoking. Susan Pinker pointed this out in her book *The Village Effect: How Face-to-Face Contact Can Make Us Healthier, Happier, and Smarter.*

Neuroscientists have discovered that feelings of isolation leave a "loneliness imprint" on every cell impacting us biologically and psychologically. Pinker writes:

> Women with breast cancer who have expansive, active, face-to-face social networks, for example, are four times as likely to survive their illness as women with sparser social connections … Fifty-year-old men with active friendships are less likely to have heart attacks than more solitary men, and people who have had a stroke are better protected from grave complications by an in-person social network than they are by medication … [P]eople with active social lives recover faster after an illness than those who are solitary – their MRIs show greater tissue repair – and … older people in England who participated in social gatherings kept their memories longer … And it's not just about pensioners. When the daily habits of nearly 17,000 utility workers in France were monitored throughout

the 1990s, researchers discovered that their degree of social involvement was a good way to predict who would still be alive at the end of the decade.[8]

**Giving Rules: Volunteer 100 hours each year; you'll be happier and live longer.**

Volunteer to connect with your community, but quality of volunteering matters as well.

I worked summers at my parents' wood truss manufacturing plant swinging a hammer, pushing a broom, and cutting and stacking boards. But I am by no means a carpenter. When I built a bookshelf in shop class in high school, the cuts were rounded and it was a rocking bookshelf, which really isn't a very desirable quality for a bookshelf. My father, on the other hand, can build anything. If Dad and I both showed up to volunteer at building a home for Habitat for Humanity, Dad's skills would be put to much better use than mine. The Financial Accounting Standards Board calculated that the current value of a volunteer hour is $23.56. But a volunteer hour from Dad working on a construction site is much more valuable than one from me.

Volunteers should seek out opportunities where their specific skills and training could be put to use. Besides adding more value to your community, you'll also find the experience more rewarding and it's more likely you'll keep at it. Often this is the thing that the world already pays us to do. A student approached me once after a talk at his university, and he said that he wasn't sure how he could make a difference because he was studying accounting.

"Do you know how many nonprofits need a good accountant?" I told him. "Like, all of them!"

The best way to volunteer is making use of special skills, talents, or knowledge, or doing something an organization would have to pay someone else to do. If you are a body or a number volunteering to do a basic task, look at it as a social function or an opportunity to learn new skills yourself that may allow you to make a bigger impact as a volunteer later.

Volunteer for organizations that make a proven impact (I'll write more about this in later chapters) and rely heavily on volunteers. Big Brothers Big Sisters is a great example of one that meets both requirements. Kids who are successfully matched with a Big are 46%

---

[8]Susan Pinker, "Susan Pinker: Why Face-to-Face Contact Matters in Our Digital Age," *The Guardian* (March 20, 2015).

less likely to use drugs, 27% less likely to start underage drinking, and 32% less likely to hit someone. Big Brothers Big Sisters is a program that works and one that can't function without volunteers.

> *Giving Rules: The most valuable thing a person has to give is time to someone else.*

I've put together a list of sites to help you find local and international volunteer opportunities at www.kelseytimmerman.com/glocalvolunteer.

Volunteering is a great way to make connections and to discover how you can best make a difference in your community.

———

On more than one occasion I've had someone in Muncie whom I was meeting for the first time say, "Dude, why are you here?" I'm not sure how to take this.

Is it a compliment? Are vagabonding, traveling authors too interesting for Muncie?

Or is it an insult? Who in their right mind, if they could live anywhere, would choose the Midwest or Muncie? There's a bumper sticker that I've seen in town that reads: Is Muncie Necessary?

My wife Annie stopped working at an outside job 10 months after Griffin, our second child, was born. That's when it dawned on us: We could live anywhere. I could do my job from Key West, California, or Colorado. We had a brief discussion about where we wanted to live and the result surprised us both: We wouldn't want to live anywhere else.

I think a lot of this had to do with volunteering in the Muncie community, which allowed us to plant roots. Muncie is big enough to have plenty of opportunities to get involved and small enough where you can make a difference.

A few years ago I wouldn't have written this. I made up a slogan for the Midwest: "A Great Place to Leave!"

I remember something Mom used to say to me when I was faced with yet another long summer afternoon in which all the baseballs, soccer-balls, basketballs, swords, lawn darts, and laser guns were strewn about the yard. I would complain to her, "I'm bored!" and she would respond, "Only boring people get bored," which didn't help, really.

But I get her point. The day is what you make of it, and so is your community. I've decided to stop complaining about where I live and instead actively try to make it better and more interesting.

All of that started with seeing home differently and seeing myself as part of the community. I love Muncie. I love Indiana.

If we aren't getting involved in our communities, we are isolating ourselves from those who live in our community, vote in our community, breathe the same air and drink the same water as we do, pay taxes that support our community's schools. It's bad for our mental and physical health and for our communities.

I easily volunteered 100 hours per year from 2010 to 2013. I was happy to give my time and was frustrated with the injustices and struggles I saw. But after a few years of volunteering, I found a way that I could better put my skills to use for the Muncie community. It led to me volunteering more than 1,000 hours per year the past few years, and recruiting 7,500 others to get involved as well. It wasn't swinging a hammer. It was telling stories. I cofounded The Facing Project, a community storytelling project that I write about more in a later chapter. There would be no Facing Project if I hadn't volunteered. If it weren't for volunteering, I wouldn't have discovered this purpose that has become such an important part of my life.

The best projects are locals helping locals – they are the superheros. You are a local somewhere. Get involved. Be a part of your community. You'll be a better local and you'll also be a better global citizen, because you can't identify the good locally led programs in other countries until you've been part of one in your own.

*Giving Rules: Volunteering can help you find purpose.*

# 5

# What Can One Person Do? (Cambodia, 2017)

## *Leaving Hollywood for a dump in Cambodia / The White Savior Industrial Complex*

**THE GROUND WASN'T EARTH.** It was something sinister, gelatinous, a sponge that could compress a few inches or leg-swallowing feet. Black sludge oozed out between my toes and covered my flip-flopped foot as I shifted my weight.

I never forgot the smell or the hopelessness of this place. It's something that can't be washed away with a decade of showers. And as much as the sight and the smell of the Stung Meanchey municipal dump in Phnom Penh were unforgettable assaults to the senses, it's the people who picked through the trash I never forgot.

I wrote about visiting the dump in my book *Where Am I Wearing?*:

Two thousand farmers turned freelance scavengers live here and earn less than $1 per day collecting recyclables. They live in makeshift shacks at the edge of the dump. They pay rent to live in the shacks. They chose to come here, seeking a better life. I wonder if this is it … what amount of hunger and suffering and desperation did they experience before choosing life here?[1]

Before I left the dump, I stopped to play Frisbee with kids picking through older trash, including the girl I mentioned in the Introduction.

The disc hangs in the warm, smelly breeze. She alternates between stretching her arms out in anticipation and holding onto her bucket hat. Her eyes are bright and sparkle when she flashes her perfect smile. She doesn't make the catch, but is quick to pounce on the disc as it wobbles to a stop … She tosses the Frisbee, and it blows behind her. One of the boys says something to her, and she throws her head back and laughs. She still has the innocence long ago lost by the adult scavengers below.[2]

Ten years ago when I visited this dump, I walked away.
But the girl …
That laugh and smile in that place, that hell. I regretted not doing anything to help her or a boy who had an infected cut on his foot. I left but in some sense I never left.
*Why didn't I act?* I have my excuses.
I was broke. I was 28, about to get married, and the air-conditioning and furnace in our new house unexpectedly went kaput. I didn't have enough money to help. But couldn't some minor first aid supplies help the boy's foot? Couldn't $20, almost a month's wage for these kids, make a difference? I could afford that.
I was just one person. The immensity of the need at the dump and in the world was paralyzing.
Nearly half the world lives on less than $2.50 per day,[3] and 10% live in extreme poverty – less than $1.90 per day. And both of those numbers are already adjusted for purchasing power. So, imagine that I gave you $1.90 at the beginning of each day and told you to survive in Chicago.[4] Hundreds of thousands of people live like this and I couldn't help everyone, so I decided to help no one.

---

[1]Kelsey Timmerman, *Where Am I Wearing?* (Hoboken, NJ: Wiley, 2012), 130.
[2]Timmerman, *Where Am I Wearing?*, 132.
[3]United Nations Development Programme, "Sustaining Human Progress: Reducing Vulnerabilities and Building Resilience," Human Development Report, 2014 (February 2015).
[4]World Bank, "Poverty: Overview," www.worldbank.org/en/topic/poverty/overview (accessed April 27, 2018).

Also, I was a white American and all too aware then and even more so now of the white savior complex – the guilt that comes with having an education and a car and a relatively comfortable American middle-class lifestyle, and the hubris to think that I would know how to fix a problem somewhere I couldn't even ask where the bathroom was in the local language, let alone understand cultural nuances.

Nigerian-American writer Teju Cole wrote about the White Savior Industrial Complex in a series of tweets:

"The White Savior Industrial Complex is not about justice. It is about having a big emotional experience that validates privilege."

Those tweets became an essay in *The Atlantic* where he criticized *New York Times* columnist Nicholas Kristof, who often writes about global poverty:

> I do not accuse Kristof of racism nor do I believe he is in any way racist …
> His good heart does not always allow him to think constellationally. He does not connect the dots or see the patterns of power behind the isolated "disasters." All he sees are hungry mouths, and he, in his own advocacy-by-journalism way, is putting food in those mouths as fast as he can. All he sees is need, and he sees no need to reason out the need for the need.

Cole would have us look beyond the war to American foreign policy, beyond the famine to our farm bill, beyond an economic collapse to the actions of the International Monetary Fund. Beyond the people at the dump in Cambodia to the fact that the US secret bombing campaign made it one the most heavily bombed countries in the history of the world, and destabilized a nation, making way for the Khmer Rouge and a genocide led by Pol Pot.

Cole continues:

> The White Savior Industrial Complex is a valve for releasing the unbearable pressures that build in a system built on pillage. We can participate in the economic destruction of Haiti over long years, but when the earthquake strikes it feels good to send $10 each to the rescue fund. I have no opposition, in principle, to such donations (I frequently make them myself), but we must do such things only with awareness of what else is involved. If we are going to interfere in the lives of others, a little due diligence is a minimum requirement.[5]

---

[5]Teju Cole, "The White Savior Industrial Complex," *The Atlantic* (March 21, 2012).

So as a broke, helpless, potential white savior, awakening to the complexities of helping, I left the dump and didn't think I'd ever step foot there again.

*Giving Rules: You'll have more regret about the times you didn't give than the times you did.*

———

My foot disappeared into the muck and came out with a sucking sound.

"Watch your step here," Scott Neeson, whom some locals have nicknamed the mayor of Stung Meanchey, said as he gave me a tour of the dump and surrounding community. "It's a bit swampy."

Scott Neeson is a former Hollywood executive who helped bring to life movies such as *Star Wars*, *X-Men*, *Braveheart*, and *Titanic*. In 2003, he took a sabbatical to Asia after leaving 20th Century Fox International and before starting a new job at Sony Pictures Entertainment.

"It was just a holiday; I was trying to recharge," Scott said. "I had no charitable intentions or history of giving. In fact, I was fairly cynical about charities."[6]

He was in Cambodia to see Angkor Wat and asked a friend to show him the real Cambodia, which led him to the dump. While there he saw a kid working alone and instead of turning his back and walking away, Scott acted.

"I couldn't tell if it was a boy or a girl; she was skinny and swathed in rags. I called over my translator and within 20 minutes we'd found the girl's mother, and I'd arranged to get them a house, money each week, schooling for the girl, and medical treatment for her younger sister who was ill with typhoid and on her last leg. That's when the hook was in. I'd saved a child's life and it felt great."

*Giving Rules: Often it takes less time and money to impact a life than you would spend on an evening out at your favorite restaurant.*

He founded Cambodian Children's Fund (CCF) in 2004, planning to balance his Hollywood career with the work at the dump. One day he was standing in the dump and got a call from the agent of a celebrity whom Scott inferred we would know. The celebrity wasn't happy with

———

[6]Madeline Ross, "Rewriting Their Story," *Hong Kong Tatler* (June 2015).

the in-flight entertainment options offered aboard the private jet Scott had arranged.

"My life wasn't meant to be this difficult," the celebrity said in the background.

"I was standing there in that humid, stinking garbage dump with children sick with typhoid," Scott recounted, "and this guy was refusing to get on a Gulfstream IV because he couldn't find a specific item on board. If I ever wanted validation I was doing the right thing, this was it."[7]

Scott was standing in the dump where a kid's life could be changed with a little bit of money and time. It would be convenient to say here that this was the moment that created Scott Neeson, Humanitarian, like a superhero origin story involving spider bites or gamma rays. But that wasn't the case.

"There was never a single point," Scott admitted. "I was in the middle of the dump. It was all reactionary. When I confront a problem I want to solve it." The decision to move wasn't an epiphany or a sudden moment. He commuted for a year between Hollywood and Cambodia before making the move.[8]

The phone call was one of many moments.

So Scott stopped solving movie problems and got to work solving dump ones.

"The trash heap is still burning," Scott said as I accompanied him on his nightly walk through the community. "Before, in places it would be like lava."

At first I thought he meant the consistency of lava, but he actually meant the heat, too.

"Once I was wearing rubber boots and sunk down into it. It melted my boots to my skin. I still have a scar," he said, pulling up his pant leg. "You can see a slight discoloration there."

It had been a while obviously. The scar had disappeared, faded more than the memory. The dump closed in 2009, not because of how hellish a place it seemed to be, but because of a very unexpected reason: real estate.

"Land prices here are like LA's," Scott said. "A thousand dollars per square meter."

---

[7]Tibor Krausz, "Scott Neeson Left Hollywood to Save Children Rooting in Cambodia's Garbage Dumps," *The Christian Science Monitor* (August 10, 2012).

[8]Scott Neeson, from Reddit Ask Me Anything (AMA) thread, www.reddit .com/r/IAmA/comments/2apwof/im_scott_neeson_a_former_film_executive_who_ gave/ (July 15, 2014).

A giant purple-and-white house overlooked the dump. A builder built it on spec when land prices started to go up. It sat empty.

*How can land be valued so much in a place where people are valued so little?*

The dump was a 100-acre scar on the landscape still seeping smoke. When I was at the dump 10 years ago, I reasoned that the fires had been lit intentionally to burn down the trash heap, and maybe that was partly true, but decomposition of organic matter creates heat and spontaneous and deep burns occur.

Death fuels the fire and the fire never stops.

Nothing happened now where people had picked trash, dump trucks had dumped, and excavators had dug. The peaks and valleys of trash, shaped by gravity and erosion like any mountain, were empty. But people lived on the edges, still on strata of trash.

"There are so many drugs," Scott said as we approached a home on stilts. "These guys are the worst."

A man sat in the doorway with a ponytail that went straight up. Scott said something to one of the kids inside. A man in the back stared at me. It seemed that Scott wanted to show them respect, that he was here and he wasn't afraid of them.

"I'm a little uncomfortable," Scott said, as we left. "Some of the people here wouldn't think twice before shooting me in the back. It's safer for me than the Khmer staff."

Two guys in blue jeans and button-up shirts accompanied us. They floated ahead and behind us, disappearing and reappearing. One would be walking with us and then we'd turn a corner and he'd be walking at us. This was Scott's security detail, and the bulges at their hips let me, and others, know they were armed.

Drugs have become a big problem in the community and one Scott and CCF have worked to fight.

The drug of choice was yama, meth laced with rat poison and caffeine. The rat poison thins the blood and increases the high and the caffeine makes the high last longer.

"There's some now." Scott nodded to a woman holding a plastic bag with a white substance in her hand.

———

There was some question of whether or not I should join the antidrug march a few days later. CCF wanted it to be as local as possible. One foreigner in the background could lead to the perception that the locals weren't the driving force. But no amount of "foreign ideas" could've turned out more than a thousand community members.

Men and women, grannies and kids stood in two straight lines holding blue banners.

Once the group started marching, a woman grabbed a bullhorn and tried to get the line pumped up and a chant going. It never really took. Every once in a while as they marched someone would yell out and fists would go up.

There was a joyful energy to the march, even though what they marched for was a serious problem tearing up families and the community as a whole. People who had been subjected to the bane of drugs in their community were taking a stand, speaking out. The joy was that their voices were being used and heard. They were empowered, proactive.

The rising hill of grown-over trash was in the background. It was why we were all there. That was where this community began, where CCF began. Trash brought us together.

They marched as a community, but it was hard to get much more transient than many of these people's lives. They left their homes in the villages to live in temporary structures next to strangers. They were united in their circumstance.

> *Giving Rules: Look for ways to support locals helping locals.*

A boy in a tiger shirt pulled up his too-big pants as he stood next to his mom. Later he'd smile at me and then flip me the bird.

A guy picked up the bullhorn and did a better job than the first woman at getting people fired up. A chant almost took shape for a few moments. More hands and fists rose toward the sky.

"That's one of our *tuk-tuk* drivers," CCF's staff photographer, also named Scott, said, pointing to him. "He's usually shy, but give him the bullhorn and … "

The cheer died down, and, a beat after it, a squeaky little voice shouted out. It was a little girl holding a granny's hand. Everyone laughed and smiled.

Another little girl walked up and grabbed my right hand. She was barefoot. Her hair was disheveled. She smiled at me, revealing one black tooth.

I stopped scribbling notes and instead of recording the moment I was in the moment. The girl's bare feet matched my steps.

We arrived at the open field where the culminating rally was taking place. TV cameras recorded the marchers. I stepped to the side and ducked behind a bus and made my way over to Cath, the donor relations manager at CCF. Cath had worked for six years for the very wealthy on their private yachts traveling the globe. She was looking for a job with more purpose and got a job in Brisbane with the Cerebral Palsy League. One Sunday eight years ago she saw a story about CCF and was so moved by the story she wrote them a note congratulating them on their success. Six years later she was casually looking for another job, saw an opportunity to work at CCF, and left Australia. That was almost two years ago.

"I've never seen Scott this nervous," she said.

Scott stood next to the community outreach manager, Hoin, reading paragraphs printed in a giant font on a few pages. Hoin spends as much time in the community as Scott, and if Scott finds someone who needs immediate attention, Hoin is his first call. Scott read and then jotted down a few notes.

Scott took the stage followed by the police.

"Scott!" people yelled.

He smiled nervously, coughed into both of his hands, walked to the side of the stage and, like a farmer, blew his nose out into the weeds and then wiped his hand onto his jeans. So Hollywood.

The crowd was still shuffling in, and a guy wearing a SlipKnot T-shirt drove in on a motorbike stacked with pink chairs 10 feet above his head.

I did a rough estimate and put the crowd at between 1,700 and 2,000 people.

"Thank you," Scott said in Khmer, as the six television cameras in the front aisle focused on him.

He read from his papers and turned to look at Hoin and the police to see if he said a word right. They nodded, and Scott celebrated.

His paragraphs were punctuated by the clapping of the audience.

The girl with the tooth came and held my hand again. Other kids followed suit. They petted my blond arm hair. Too far. Kids always pull you in. They asked me my name and favorite color and favorite fruit.

When Scott was done, the police took turns talking and then they took questions and comments from the audience.

"Look at that," Cath nodded. "She's picking lice out of her head."

A girl, maybe eight, sitting in the back sifted through the hair of a younger girl looking for lice. When she found one, she held it between her fingers and crush it with her thumbnail. When I looked back later, the girls had switched.

"A lot of us have had lice," Cath said. "Scott never has, which is strange because he's always head to head with the kids."

The microphone for the audience made its way to a lady in a green shirt. She yelled rapidly into it, her voice cracking with emotion. When she paused the crowd erupted in applause.

A little boy to the side of the stage played in the mud with a plastic Coca-Cola bottle, floating it like a ship on a great waterway. Imagination knows no bounds. A bit later I looked over and other kids had joined him.

Another lady gripped the microphone with two hands as if her life depended on it, and maybe it did. She started to cry as she spoke. The emotion in her voice distracted the kids from their play and they ran to get a better angle to see her.

Scott leaned toward her from his seat on the stage, scribbled something in his notebook, and leaned back as Hoin translated something he didn't quite understand.

I asked Cath if Scott had any kids. She told me he didn't, "not even a partner." She didn't think he ever would. It was the same for Hoin. They were married to their work. Scott has thousands of kids.

A little girl took my pen, wrote the word "dog" and then turned the letters into a drawing of a dog. Not to be outdone, the girl who held my hand did the same with "butterfly."

After the talk, the audience applauded and dispersed. The media and some of the kids waited around with Scott.

Scott sat on the stage and the kids came up to him. Hugs and head ruffles. Scott told me the audience really put the police on the spot, something they would've never done in a different environment. One woman asked how someone could be arrested for selling drugs and then be back in the community four days later. Another asked what happened to the drugs when they were taken by the police.

Cath told me the community needed education about drugs. One father got addicted to them when someone gave him a drug when he was sick. He thought it was medicine. He was able to work harder and longer and had more energy. But eventually it started to dominate his life.

Scott gave an interview to the camera in English, and Hoin translated: "Drug dealers are breaking up our community."

*Our community.*

"Our mission is to get it out of our community," Scott said. "Police have arrested more than 400 people. CCF helps community members get rehab, but if they sell drugs, especially to our kids, we have them thrown in jail."

As Scott talked there were kids around his legs. A girl in bright yellow, impossibly clean sandals stood next to Scott, supporting him. He gave her a side hug as he talked.

The reporters wanted to talk with a kid, and Scott gave them permission.

Scott bent down to encourage a little girl in a pink dress whose father was an addict. Her friends gathered around her. She talked for at least five minutes.

A 12-year-old girl spoke to the cameras. Her father was an addict, too. A Christian organization had given her father a *tuk-tuk*. Scott told me this, laughing. He went on a three-month bender road trip. He'd pick up fares and then score some drugs. Eventually he came home and was out of the picture. Now his wife drove the *tuk-tuk*.

"I think she's the only female *tuk-tuk* driver in all of Cambodia," Scott said.

Scott seemed exhausted but still picked up kids and shared a bit of their stories with me. He was about to head off to the province of Kompong Cham, a five-hour drive. He was taking a young girl who had been regularly raped by her father. She reported him and he went to jail, which doesn't always happen. In the past, the police would take a bribe (or fine) from the perpetrator and split the money 50/50 with the victim's family. There was a lot of victim blaming of this little girl, especially by the neighbors, and she didn't feel comfortable visiting her home on her own.

A black Toyota truck backed up – Scott's ride. One of Scott's security guys opened the truck bed.

Scott surveyed the kids around him. "Now, I owe *you* a coloring book and *you* … "

# 6

# Happiness Isn't Having a Lot; It's Giving a Lot (Cambodia, 2017)

*The Hero's journey / What* The Matrix *teaches us about happiness and purpose / Four pillars of meaning*

---

**"COME IN HERE," SCOTT SAID TO ME.** "You've got to see this."

Scott greeted a family during his nightly walk and then asked to come into their home. It was a ground-level home with a dirt floor. The ceiling was so low that Scott and I had to stand like exhausted basketball players, hands on our knees. The wall was lined with awards – mainly for one girl, Soklin, but her siblings were also following in her footsteps. Each award was framed and signed by Scott. One of the awards was dated 2009.

From kindergarten to university, the Cambodian Children's Fund (CCF) has 2,295 kids enrolled in its education program, maintaining a 96% annual retention rate.

"This is what it's all about," Scott said. "This one girl is going to lift her family out of all of this." He pointed to a picture of her that he gave the family when he "found" her.

"Someday she'll mention this place to her kids and grandkids and they won't believe that she came from the dump or ever lived in a place like this."

The rain picked up and a family invited us onto their front porch. A drunk man wiped off the bed for us to sit. A family – mother, father, three kids, and a grandparent – lived there. The kids weren't old enough to be in school.

"I pick garbage," the drunk guy said.

There was no more work at the dump, so the man commuted three hours, pulling a wiry wagon mounted on bicycle tires to the city in the wee hours of the morning. This was a common practice since the dump closed. Families would load their kids in wagons and pull them in the dark. Every year a few kids were killed in accidents where cars ran into them. CCF started a day care program to give them an alternative. This man's kids spent the day watched at CCF's day care center run by "grannies" who were also included in the CCF program. Each day they cared for 112 children under the age of 6.

"Sometimes the solutions are so simple," Scott said, almost regretting that it took as long as it did to land on the idea of the day care program. "It costs next to nothing to run the program – a granny in a room with a hammock … These are the solutions you don't think of unless you are in the community on a regular basis."

The rain let up and we took a few turns to meet the grannies. The grannies play a special role. They act as mothers, foster and otherwise, and they are sort of the heart of CCF.

The grannies had heard the bullets of the Khmer Rouge, had felt the shock waves of the bombs dropped from US planes, and had survived when so many had not, and they remembered a time before the genocide. CCF pays them $8 per week along with five kilograms of rice to babysit young children, and to mentor the older ones and educate them on Khmer culture and customs of which their parents may know nothing. In turn, groups of student leaders are matched with a granny to check on her two or three times per week.

"These women are the only ones with knowledge of what life was like before all the troubles in Cambodia," Scott said. "It worries me that children are growing up without values, without knowledge and morals. These women can help change that."

The Khmer Rouge led by Pol Pot and inspired by Mao and Lenin came to power in 1975, and attempted to create a purely agrarian society. They moved people from the city to the fields. Teachers, professors, doctors, lawyers, monks – anyone with an education – were rounded up

*Figure 6.1    Scott with the granny.*

and executed. No one is sure how many were killed in the genocide, but most put it around 2 million, or about 25% of the population.

"You know," Scott said, "when I first started coming here, I was told not to be affectionate, that it was against their culture. The grannies told me that was bullshit. The Khmer Rouge left an entire generation or two less affectionate – probably for survival reasons."

A 95-year-old granny welcomed us into her home (see Figure 6.1). There were eight framed pictures hanging on the wall of her with Scott, including one in which he was handing her the "granny of the year" award. She couldn't stand straight and her torso was bent 90 degrees, parallel with the ground. A kneeling Scott was taller than she was by a few inches.

"We thought she was going to die. We took her to the hospital. She thought it was time to go so she stopped eating. That was two years ago. So I visited her every day in the hospital for 10 or 12 days."

Scott met her in 2005. She had lost both of her kids to the Khmer Rouge. Another photo on her wall was of Scott posing with his laptop on which her picture is the wallpaper.

We ducked under the granny's neighbor's house across the street and Scott told me about the violence that this house had witnessed. The mother cut the daughter with a fishing knife. The CCF team took her to an American surgeon, who had to clean out fish scales. Scott came by once while the husband was beating the wife. He said it looked like the husband was on the outside of the house trying to pull a cat through a hole in the wall, but it was his wife's hair.

The daughter received some vocational training through CCF and is now in the garment industry.

The whole time Scott related this story to me he examined the kids, checking everyone's status, rubbing a few heads, and passing out hugs. He talked about horrible, dark things – the worst humanity has to offer – while showing those in his presence nothing but warmth and compassion.

"She's off to a Tony Robbins conference in San Diego," Scott said gently, placing his hand on the shoulder of a teenage girl. "It's a leadership conference for kids from around the world. After the conference, the student leaders will lead their own leadership conference based on what they learned for their fellow students."

To think this girl, who lived in the shadow of a dump in a world made of nails and scrap wood, would fly in an airplane and walk the streets of pristine San Diego gave a fella hope.

Another family poked their heads out of a shack.

"They're new," Scott said.

They had recently moved. They had a bright-eyed 11-year-old daughter who had never been in school. "She'll have some catching up to do," Scott said.

A naked little two-year-old boy rounded the corner.

"I keep giving him clothes and he keeps shedding them off," Scott said, laughing.

The family moved from the provinces, rented this land, and constructed their own home. Scott said CCF hasn't been able to accept them into the program because the organization didn't want to contribute to urbanization. CCF didn't want people moving to the city and the dump to join the program. It ate at him. I could tell he was considering responsible ways to help them.

*Was this girl out of reach?*

After winding our way through alleys, once again, we were on the edge of the dump. It was dusk and the surrounding lights lit the bottom of rain clouds, giving the smoking dump a strange sepia color, like walking through an old-time movie. Frogs had started to sing in the aftermath of the rain, welcoming the night.

"There's a guy that sits in the middle of the road over there and talks to himself," Scott said, pointing up a hill. "At first I thought he was talking on his mobile, but he's not. He's there every day. The strange thing ... he takes Sundays off."

Scott laughed. It seemed like there was nowhere else in the world he'd rather be. He seemed happy.

"This is my pride and joy," Scott said, showing me another school, which looked like a set of a Nickelodeon show. It was brightly colored and the walls were painted with kid art.

The entrance to the school faced the old dump.

"Scott!" the kids hollered and ran up. One little girl had rice stuck to her face and arms. Another little girl carried around a sticky handful of noodles.

The 130 student leaders run the feeding program, which feeds 800 children each day. He introduced me to one of the teenage leaders.

"She worked in the dump," Scott said. "Now she's studying physics."

The dance teacher invited us into a room where the students, all girls, lined the wall. They danced a traditional Khmer dance in unison that mimicked rice planting. They gracefully twisted their hands and waved their fingers. While they danced, paper cranes attached to two strings that crisscrossed the room flew above their heads.

Scott obsessive-compulsively scrolled through the 168,000 photos of kids on his phone.

"I've probably taken a million, but I've deleted some," he told me, still scrolling.

"Here!" He held up his phone and positioned it so a girl sitting on the floor across the room was beside it. The before-and-after shots. Before: The little girl in the photo was standing on the trash heap wearing one sandal, staring directly into the camera, a blank look on her face and her finger in her mouth. After: The smiling girl was sitting in a well-lit classroom and laughing as two of her classmates danced.

When you look at each of these kids you see a personality, an individual with an individual future that isn't set in stone. Before CCF, we all knew what they were going to be when they grew up. They were going to live in the dump and pick trash.

At the end of the performance, the entire class turned toward Scott and smiled. He looked up from his phone and bowed.

> *Giving Rules: Giving is an opportunity to make an impact and a connection; it shouldn't feel like a burden.*

---

When I was at the antidrug rally, I had an odd realization watching Scott on stage: From a distance, his blond hair and sharp features looked a bit like a future me. When you meet Scott or come across his story, you can't help but be challenged by it and ask yourself, "What have *I* done? Who am *I* helping?"

I turned away from the dump. He moved there.

*Are we all just one experience from dedicating our lives to something?*

He had a Porsche, a yacht, movie star girlfriends, and an annual salary of a million dollars, and then he chose to come here.

"The reason I'm almost obsessive-compulsive when I go [into the community] is because an extra 10 minutes can literally change the life of a child, especially now that we have a process. Remember that shack with the kids? They started school today. It's so sweet! Ten minutes to stop in their house changed their kids' lives. I don't mean to be immodest. That's just a magical thing when you have the power to do that."

Scott has purpose, but not everyone does.

"Even billionaires I met," Scott said. "God ... oh my goodness it gives me nightmares to think what their lives must be like ... I believe that the happiest you'll be is when you find your groove and settle into it. I believe in the philosophy of Joseph Campbell."

Joseph Campbell was an American mythologist who wrote about the common themes and journeys of mythical heroes. Campbell wrote:

> People say that what we're all seeking is a meaning for life. I don't think that's what we're really seeking. I think that what we're seeking is an experience of being alive, so that our life experiences on the purely physical plane will have resonances with our own innermost being and reality, so that we actually feel the rapture of being alive.[1]

I told Scott about a conversation I had with my friend Jay, who has had a great business career but told me that he was desperate to make a difference but not sure how.

"He's lucky because he feels that desperation," Scott said. "The people I feel badly for are those who it hits them way too late in life ... For me it wasn't about glamour, glitz, Porsches, boats, and material goods. The American dream got screwed up in the 1990s when it became about materialism and superficial stuff."

Scott is close to right. In the mid-1960s 86% of first-year college students reported their top priority was "developing a meaningful philosophy of life," but in 2016 it had fallen to 46.8%. The top priority has become "being very well off financially."[2]

---

[1] Joseph Campbell, *The Power of Myth*, (New York: Knopf, 2011), 4, 5.
[2] Kevin Eagon et al., "The American Freshman: National Norms Fall 2016," Higher Education Research Institute, UCLA (2017).

Scott had all the money and all the things that money could buy. He lived a life that 82.3% of first-year students in 2016 would indicate to be "very important" or "essential" to them personally. Yet he learned what many of us are supposed to know already, but don't believe: Money doesn't buy happiness.

But of course it does to a certain extent. It's just that it will buy only so much happiness. Economist Angus Deaton and psychologist Daniel Kahneman found that earning an income beyond $75,000 per year would not add significantly to an individual's happiness.[3] Scott had earned way more than that. There were things Scott missed such as spending time on his boat.

In Cambodia, Scott doesn't appear to be living in happy circumstances. He works too much, and worries that he might get shot in the back. He confronts people about raping children and deals with the aftermath. He has a folder of photos on his phone from the Child Protection Unit – a partnership between the police and CCF. Each photo is accompanied with a horrible story. Scott scrolled through his phone and landed on a picture of a smiling girl who could've been one of the dancers.

"Attempted murder and rape. Guy tried to drown her. Held her underwater. She swallowed really nasty water and got a lungful of pneumonia and another infection. But we got them. These two really nasty people. They've gone away forever. Ah … horrible stuff."

How is this happy?

Recently the Dalai Lama wrote an editorial in *The New York Times* addressing our need to give to others:

> … [R]esearchers found that senior citizens who didn't feel useful to others were nearly three times as likely to die prematurely as those who did feel useful. This speaks to a broader human truth: We all need to be needed … Americans who prioritize doing good for others are almost twice as likely to say they are very happy about their lives. In Germany, people who seek to serve society are five times likelier to say they are very happy than those who do not view service as important. Selflessness and joy are intertwined. The more we are one with the rest of humanity, the better we feel.[4]

---

[3] Belinda Luscombe, "Do We Need $75,000 a Year to Be Happy?" Time.com, ti.me/Pok8UM (September 6, 2010).

[4] The Dalai Lama and Arthur C. Brooks, "Dalai Lama: Behind Our Anxiety, the Fear of Being Unneeded," *The New York Times* (November 4, 2016).

Life in Cambodia helping kids and families of the dump is Scott's groove, and it is full of meaning and purpose for him.

Emily Esfahani Smith, author of *The Power of Meaning: Finding Fulfillment in a World Obsessed with Happiness*, argues that long-term happiness is achieved through meaning. She writes about a thought experiment put forward by Robert Nozick, a Harvard philosopher:

> Superduper neuropsychologists could stimulate your brain so that you would think and feel you were writing a great novel, or making a friend, or reading an interesting book. All the time you would be floating in a tank, with electrodes to your brain. Should you plug into this machine for life, preprogramming your life's experiences?

Basically this is a *Matrix* situation in which you'd always feel happiness and not know struggle or loss or pain – just a lifetime of hunky-dory bliss.

Sounds horrible, doesn't it? Unplug me and let's attack our robot overlords.

Smith writes:

> Most people would say no to a life of feeling good in the tank … the happiness we find there is empty and unearned. You may feel happy in the tank, but you have no real reason to be happy. You may feel good, but your life isn't actually good. A person "floating in the tank … " has no identity, no projects and goals to give his life value. "We care about more than just how things feel to us from the inside," Nozick concludes. "There is more to life than feeling happy."

Researchers from Florida State University who compared happiness and meaning found that "[h]appiness without meaning characterizes a relatively shallow, self-absorbed or even selfish life."

"Leading a meaningful life by contrast," Smith writes, "corresponded with being a 'giver,' and its defining feature was connecting and contributing to something beyond the self."

Smith breaks down meaning into four pillars:

1. A sense of belonging: Do you matter to others and do others matter to you?
2. Purpose: Using your time, talents, life experiences, and skills to make a contribution to others and to society.
3. Transcendence: "moment where you are lifted above the hustle and bustle and you feel your sense of self fade away."
4. Storytelling: The narrative of our lives that we tell ourselves.

Meaning isn't something that we find in ourselves, but only in putting ourselves and our gifts to work for others. This is true in our daily lives of abundance, or in the most extreme conditions you can imagine.[5]

Viktor Frankl, an Austrian neurologist and psychiatrist, wrote about his time surviving the Holocaust and life in concentration camps, including Auschwitz, in his book *Man's Search for Meaning.* Frankl acted as a therapist to his fellow prisoners, helping them find meaning in the senseless tragedy they all faced.

"Being human," Frankl wrote, "always points, and is directed, to something, or someone, other than oneself – be it a meaning to fulfill or another human being to encounter. The more one forgets himself – by giving himself to a cause to serve or another person to love – the more human he is."[6]

> *Giving Rules: Forget self-help; if you want to help yourself, help others.*

———

Shortly after Father's Day, I watched as Scott handed out student awards at another CCF school. He called the names of the award winners. At the end, after he'd passed out all the awards, the teachers presented Scott with a special Father's Day poster signed by the kids. That began a procession of kids placing candy necklaces around Scott's neck and presenting him with handmade drawings. One read: "I will always bliss you."

Once the program was over and Scott was loaded with art, half the kids left and the other half gathered around him for hugs. Scott picked them up, hugged them, and joked with them. He didn't stand and look down at the kids. He stooped to their level or bent down to look them in the eyes.

The first time I saw Scott with the kids I wondered if it was all an act. But after days and hours spent with him, he never approached them differently. It was too exhausting to be an act. These kids lit him up.

After the awards ceremony, we walked with Hoin, CCF's community outreach manager, to CCF's new high school. Local officials have taken to calling Scott the mayor of Stung Meanchey. Scott thinks it was meant to be a dig, but now accepts the title with pride. If Scott is the

———

[5] Emily Esfahani Smith, *The Power of Meaning: Finding Fulfillment in a World Obsessed with Happiness* (New York: Broadway Books, 2017). 10–11, 14–15, 41–42.
[6] Viktor Frankl, *Man's Search for Meaning* (Boston: Beacon Press, 2006), 110, 111."

mayor of Stung Meanchey, Hoin is the deputy mayor. Hoin just earned his PhD in social work, but doesn't like to talk about it. He has been with CCF for six years and turns Scott's interactions in the community into actions. He gets kids enrolled in school and doctor appointments arranged.

At night the dump disappeared into darkness. Overlooking the darkness, the Neeson Cripps Academy glowed. The school was nicer than my high school and certainly Hoin's. Inside a physics classroom Hoin held up his phone showing his childhood schoolhouse that looked like a blue barn.

"This is a very cool evening," Scott said. "Chemistry, Photoshop, and 3-D printing. This is engineering. They are writing programs to tell the robots where to go."

Robots swept up pieces of paper. Two boys cheered as their robot neared its goal before taking an abrupt turn into the wall.

"Back to the drawing board," Scott laughed.

We left the school and got in Scott's truck. When the driver turned the key, the lights washed over a girl stuffing plastic into sacks.

"This girl here, she works seven days per week, 7 a.m. to God knows when," Scott said. "She wants to come to school, but she can't come to school because she's indentured … she's been here for three years and I see her every single day. I don't know when she stops."

Scott saw the girl, and he wanted to do something. He wanted to help. But he wasn't quite sure how to do it yet.

———

I talked with several former CCF students who had graduated from college and who had worked in the dump when I visited 10 years ago.

Chuun has a degree in English, is working on his master's, and now works in a library. His favorite book character is Sherlock Holmes. When he thinks about the day on the dump he found the body of a boy, he cries. Soeurn wants to be a flight attendant; actress Heather Graham came to her wedding, and she remembers she was selling baskets to support her family when she met Scott. Choh remembers sleeping on the dump with his family and being worried about a truck running him over. Now he makes films.

Whenever someone writes about Scott, they talk about the change in his life: what he gave up, and what he does now. It's a remarkable story, but nowhere near as remarkable as the kids who have lived and worked on the dump who are now programming robots, learning physics, graduating from college, and hoping to work in Hollywood someday.

———

But the girl …

I was interested in CCF and Scott, but one of the main reasons I wanted to come back was to find the girl who had laughed at the dump when we played Frisbee 10 years ago. I thought it would be impossible. She lived in an insecure, impermanent world and I didn't even know here name. All I had were two pictures that I thought I'd show Scott's team once we had established a rapport. Even then, I thought they would laugh at me or question my intentions. But in the first conversation I had with Scott on the phone before traveling to Cambodia, he asked me whom I had met and whether I had any pictures of them. Maybe they could find them.

Hoin found her. Her name is Ratana.

"I'm here to see Hoin," I said, walking into the lobby of one of CCF's offices.

Women and children waited in the lobby. It had the feel of a medical clinic or a government assistance office. I've had to wait in those offices, too. You sit there and you are admitting, "I need help. I can't do this alone." I've applied for Medicaid for my son who is on the autism spectrum. I've filed for unemployment. There are all the forms and income statements and interviews where people sometimes look at you like you are trying to pull one over on them. It can be demoralizing.

The steps to Hoin's office were narrow and the ceilings low, so I had to watch my head. I entered and sat on his leather couch.

Hoin always seems deep in thought.

"Okay. She is coming," he said.

"Who?"

"Ratana."

*What? I thought we were going to meet her somewhere. But I'm not ready. I needed to emotionally prepare for this.*

She walked through the door and it took me a few moments to subtract 10 years from her face – from a woman to a girl. Maybe this wasn't her. I had talked about her on countless stages, her laugh projecting on screens behind me. I had looked at her picture hundreds of times. I had memorized her face and her smile. And there she was, next to a baby-faced teenager and a little boy (see Figure 6.2).

*Figure 6.2    Ratana in 2017 with her husband and son who is holding a picture of her from 10 years earlier.*

"I remember you," she said. "You walked right by me [in the lobby]."

"Sorry," I said.

She had smiled at me in the lobby and I don't think I had smiled back. I was running late and didn't know she was coming to the office. I was suddenly ashamed. But who else had I walk by and ignored? There were other families. What does it matter that I met her 10 years ago? Why is it that I care more about her family?

"No problem," she said. "My face is completely different."

Her face was fuller and pockmarked with acne scars.

"The day you met me, my mother was in the hospital after an accident and my two older sisters were studying. I was the only one making income for the family at that time."

A car had hit her mother on a rainy day while she rode a motorbike to the city to sell shoes. Ratana had lived a relatively normal life in the countryside, her family working as farmers, until the accident.

"Before the accident we weren't in financial trouble," she said.

There was no safety net, no insurance, nothing, so her family sold the farm to afford treatment for her mother and moved to Phnom Penh.

"I was in school before working in the dump. I studied through grade 5. I started working in the dump at grade 3. I would study in the morning and work in the afternoon."

I've been told I ask enough questions to sink a boat, whatever that means. But for some reason I was at an awkward loss of what to ask her next.

Hoin's phone rang and he stepped out of his office to take it.

"This is my family," I said, showing her photos of Annie, Harper, and Griffin.

"Beautiful," she said in English.

I handed her son a blue Frisbee like the one I had tossed with Ratana years ago on the dump. He shyly took it and Ratana forced him to say, "Thank you." His name is Run. Run's baby-faced father is 19 and seemed proud of his family although slightly confused about what was going on.

Hoin returned to translate.

"What do you remember about that day?" I asked.

"I didn't know the reason you were there. I once saw someone there to distribute food and I was really hungry."

She was hungry and I played Frisbee with her and took her photo.

"I also like getting photos," she said, as if sensing my guilt. "I'll never forget it. When I saw you I tried to get close to you."

She worked at the dump until 2009 and moved into a resident home at an NGO until it ran out of money. She met her husband at school. Now she sold coffee and he sold fruit at a market.

I asked if she ever thought about working in one of the many garment factories.

"At that time I was not able to work in a factory because my family needed money quickly, so I worked as a scavenger. At a factory you have to wait until the end of the month [to get paid]."

She had been too poor to work in a garment factory.

I asked her to compare her life now to before.

"The situation of my family hasn't improved much. We still support my mother."

Ratana received medical care from CCF during her labor and delivery. In 2016 the CCF medical team completed nearly 30,000 free consultations and treatments in the Stung Meanchey community, including caring for 131 expectant mothers. Since 2010 the program hasn't lost a mother.

Before our meeting Hoin's team had her fill out an intake survey.

"Does it look like they'd be a candidate?" I asked.

"Their income is $157," Hoin answered. "Their expenses are $163 per month. In this case, there is almost a balance because they are supporting [her mother]. But when their son is six, it will be a problem because school will be another expense, so they can send him to a CCF school."

I asked Hoin if there was anything I could do to help them now, for taking the time to chat with me. He assured me that his team had taken care of them, paying them $15 and giving them 30 pounds of rice.

"How do you make ends meet?" I asked, thinking about the $6 they were short each month.

"We adjust."

The poor often have a strong network of support among each other, which, unlike a bank account, is inexhaustible. That's what Ratana leans on to adjust. Lewis Hyde, author of *The Gift: Creativity and the Artist in the Modern World*, warns us, though, that when we mythologize the poor's affluence – "they always smile and seem happy" – we ignore the realities they face and why they face them.[7]

Ratana was the little girl who laughed in the worst place I've ever been. Her attitude is a testament to the human spirit. But there's nothing funny about what she and the other kids like her have had to go through and the future she might have had if that attitude could've been focused on education instead of survival.

"What are your hopes for Run?" I asked.

"I want my son to be a medical doctor," she laughed.

I thought about the boy at the dump we had played with and the cut on his foot. There was no medical attention. The seemingly disposable people of the dump died of preventable diseases. The thought of her son becoming a doctor ... it was possible.

"Your laugh and your smile ... I never forgot," I said. "I'm honored to see you again."

---

[7] Lewis Hyde, *The Gift: Creativity and the Artist in the Modern World* (New York: Random House, 2007), 23.

"I remember you picked up some plastic trash for me," Ratana said.

"I remember being there and wanting to do something, but I had no idea how. I'm so thankful that there are people like CCF who are helping," I said, but Hoin didn't translate.

"Thank you so much," she said and gave me a hug and a pat on the back.

She left.

# 7

## Giving Is Complicated: Ethnic Cleansing in the Most Generous Nation on Earth (Myanmar, 2017)

*Change starts with students / Problem with empathy / World Giving Index / Problem with orphanages*

**THE REVOLUTION STARTED WITH STUDENTS.** It was August 1988 and the Burmese students had had enough.

Advised by astrologers, the military-controlled government of Myanmar, also known as Burma, voided currency notes that weren't divisible by the number nine. I understand this makes no sense at all, so let me be even clearer. The government took advice from people who took advice from celestial bodies. The astrologers told General Ne Win, the leader of the military junta, that his lucky number was nine. General Ne Win consulted with his astrologers and got rid of the 100, 75, 35, and 25 kyats currency notes, leaving only the 45 and 90.

Overnight, students had less money to pay for tuition. It was one among a string of senseless decisions. The military also forced farmers to sell their products for less than market value to increase revenue to the government.[1]

On August 8, 1988, also known as the 8888 Uprising, hundreds of thousands of students, monks, civil servants, and people from all walks of life took to the streets across the country, protesting against military rule, demanding democracy.

"When the Army shoots," General Ne Win warned the public, "it shoots to kill."[2]

Troops gunned down protestors at City Hall and even at Shwedagon Pagoda, the most sacred Buddhist pagoda in Myanmar. Hundreds, if not thousands, of protesters were killed.

Yet, still the students and the others protested.

Tim Aye-Hardy was a student among the protesters.

"I was involved in the beginning and then I was kicked out of school," Tim told me in his office in Yangon. He wore a fedora and seemed dressed for a laid-back but classy bar in Southern California. "[The school] asked me to sign an agreement: 'You will not be involved in any future movements or any politics if you want to come back to school.' I never signed the document. I was like, 'The school system sucks already. I'm not giving up my rights just to go back to school.'

"They tried to arrest me. Tried to keep your mouth shut by killing some students, arresting them … It was a bit risky during military time. Even if you go out on the streets and they have any suspicion, they just grab you. So we were very careful. Everyone was watching everyone."

Later that month, Aung San Suu Kyi, the daughter of the founding father of Burma, took the stage in front of a giant crowd at Shwedagon Pagoda to call for democracy and elections.

"It is the students who have paved the way to the present situation where it is possible to hold such a rally. The occasion has been made possible because the recent demonstrations have been spearheaded by the students and even more because they have shown their willingness to sacrifice their lives."[3]

---

[1] Kate Woodsome, "Burmese Way to Socialism Drives Country into Poverty," *Voice of America* (October 24, 2007).
[2] Hans Hulst, "U Aye Ne Win: Rewriting History," *Frontier Myanmar* (August 8, 2015).
[3] Aung San Suu Kyi, "Speech to a Mass Rally at the Shwedagon Pagoda," *Freedom from Fear and Other Writings* (London: Viking, 1991).

By October, the government had squashed the protest and continued to make Myanmar one of the most isolated countries on earth.

"Even in the US if you look at the movements," Tim said, explaining his mind-set during the protest, "it's the young people. More open-minded and less responsibility. Nothing to worry about, right? No jobs. No kids. No one depending on them. So … let's do it!"

Tim was right. Students have been at the forefront of many protests in the US, as well. UCLA students protested apartheid and forced the university to withdraw $3 billion of investments from South Africa. Students protested the Vietnam War, placing flowers in the ends of guns held by riot police. Four black students from North Carolina Agricultural and Technical College refused to leave their seats at the "whites only" counter in a store in Greensboro, inspiring nationwide sit-ins.[4] Students from Marjory Stoneman Douglas High School in Parkland, Florida, less than a week removed from a mass shooting that killed 17 of their classmates and teachers, reinvigorated a national discussion on guns and school safety. Students often become a nation's conscience, questioning injustices accepted by societies. The student protests in Myanmar had life-or-death consequences.

"A lot of students left," Tim said. "[Some] went into the jungle and picked up arms. Some of them became refugees. So I was like, 'What do I do?' A lot of my friends left or [were] killed or in prison."

During all of this turmoil, Tim accompanied two monks to the US embassy to help translate for their visa interviews.

"Don't you want to go to the US?" someone at the embassy asked Tim.

"I had no idea what the hell the US even was," Tim said. "I wasn't expecting it. I found [out] that I was leaving to the US three or four hours before the plane left. I went straight from the embassy to the flight. I called my mom right outside the embassy to pack something and to meet me at the airport … She was very upset. She was like, 'How could you do this? You should've at least let us know ahead of time so we could've had a proper good-bye.'"

His mom packed his school backpack and met him at the airport.

"I didn't even know what she packed until I got to the US."

Tim left Myanmar on a flight to Thailand. He bought his first pair of blue jeans during a layover in Bangkok. When he landed in Los Angeles, he had $12 the US embassy had given him.

---

[4]Lilly Rothman, "History Has Good News for Today's Student Protestors," *Time* (November 15, 2017).

He wouldn't return to Myanmar for 20 years, a period of time that would see something like democracy come to Myanmar, a chaotic opening to the outside world, and two mind-bending superlatives:

Myanmar is the most generous nation on earth. And it is also home to the longest-running civil war and an ethnic cleansing.

How can these truths exist in one country? That's what I came to Myanmar to find out.

━━━━━━

For the fourth year in a row, the UK-based Charities Aid Foundation (CAF), which seeks to connect donors to effective charities and to promote giving, found that Myanmar was the most generous nation on earth in its World Giving Index. The rankings are based on three areas: the percentage of respondents who have donated, volunteered, or helped a stranger in the previous month.

In the 2017 CAF report, 91% of respondents donated money, topping Indonesia by 12%.[5] Much of this giving goes to monks or to build Buddhist holy places, but not all of it. For instance, there was the couple who owned the Airbnb where I stayed. They had owned a fishing business before retiring. One day at lunch (their bed and breakfast also had lunch and dinner), Mr. Swan turned his laptop toward me to show a nearly complete retirement home for men. There were eight buildings, a cafeteria, an office, and a meditation room. They donated $26,000 of their own money and got others to chip in nearly $700,000 for construction and operations.

"How many donated?" I asked.

"So many people paid," he responded. His sister-in-law gave him $9,000. Another friend gave him $2,500. He scrolled through his Facebook page showing person after person giving him money. Each photo was taken at their in-house Buddha shrine next to their TV, the bills displayed on a silver platter.

"Why do people give so much?" I asked.

"They believe in me," he said.

> *Giving Rules: Support the giving of friends and family. Sometimes we give without question to causes that aren't our causes because they are important to people who are important to us.*

---

[5]Charities Aid Foundation, "CAF World Giving Index 2017: A Global View of Giving Trends" (September 2017).

In the 2017 CAF report, 53% of people in Myanmar said they had helped a stranger, which ranked them 57th in the category.[6] I was a stranger who had declined an umbrella from my hotel – a bad idea during monsoon season. When the rain came, the air was more water than air. I stopped at a stand on the sidewalk beneath an umbrella and bought some bananas, but really I was just getting out of the rain. The banana-seller nudged her son, who was playing a game on his phone. He got up and gave me his seat and went inside to get another for himself. So there we sat – three people selling bananas in a monsoon.

I was an absolute clueless stranger riding the train that circled the capital. A man who washed himself next to a clay pot of water pointed me to the track. I asked a girl reading an engineering book if I was on the correct side of the track. She said I was because she was too polite to tell me "No." People in Myanmar don't like to say "No." A man with an umbrella on the way to work informed me of my error and helped me get on the right train.

The train cut through people's lives. Women did laundry. Kids squatted to pee. People sold stuff, laughed, lived. The train was an old Japanese model. The engine didn't have a door – just an engineer standing there, wind rushing through his hair. On the train a guy held up a brain scan to the light entering through a window. Young men broke out into infomercials as they sold medicine, pencils, and durian.

A sort of democracy had come to Myanmar in 2010. Aung San Suu Kyi, who won a Nobel Peace Prize in 1991 for her resistance to the military government, had been released from house arrest and became the first state counselor, which is like a prime minister. Myanmar opened to the world and investments poured in.[7] Now as people traveled on old Japanese trains, they took selfies on modern Chinese phones. In 2011 Myanmar had the second-lowest population of people with cell phones, and now 90% of the country's people have access to phones and Facebook.

But the military still retained a lot of power, and Aung San Suu Kyi was often criticized for balancing the military's power with human rights. Her power was relative to the military's, which had drafted the constitution and was beyond civilian and political oversight. And relative power rules relatively. Journalists could be thrown in jail under law 66(d) that prohibited the use of the telecom network to

---

[6]Charities Aid Foundation, "CAF World Giving Index 2017."
[7]Evan Osnos, "The Burmese Spring," *The New Yorker* (August 6, 2012).

"extort, threaten, obstruct, defame, disturb, inappropriately influence, or intimidate."[8]

In October 2017, you could find statistics on the Charities Aid Foundation home page showing why Myanmar was the most generous nation on earth, but you could also find an appeal for aid to assist the Rohingya, a minority Muslim population in Myanmar. Rohingya militants had attacked an army base and 30 security posts, and the military responded with force.

US Senator Jeff Merkley visited the Rakhine state, the home of the Rohingya. One hundred and twenty thousand people have lived in camps there for five years, and in another part of the state only one in eight Rohingya were left in the community.

"Many refugees have suffered direct attacks, including loved ones, children, and husbands being killed in front of them, wives and daughters being raped, burns and other horrific injuries … " Merkley said. "We are profoundly disturbed by the violent and dispropor-tionate response against the Rohingya by the military and local groups."[9]

The United Nations called the action of the military a "textbook case of ethnic cleansing."

Six hundred thousand Rohingya were driven from the most generous nation on earth and into Bangladesh.

CAF addressed the incongruence in the introduction to the World Giving Index 2017:

> Inevitably, such an achievement will be contrasted with reports about the ongoing suffering and contested rights of the Rohingya people. At this point, it is important to remember that the World Giving Index measures only the charitable activities of the general population within a country, and does not take wider issues affecting society into account. As such, we make no attempt to rationalise negative or mitigating factors in the World Giving Index.[10]

Humans aren't equal opportunity givers. We give shelter and money to some, and persecution and death to others.

---

[8]Shwe Yee Saw Myint and Aung Hia Tun, "Myanmar Detains Two Newspaper Offi-cials in Defamation Case," Reuters (November 11, 2016).
[9]Alexandra Wilts, "Treatment of Rohingya Muslims Has 'All the Hallmarks' of Eth-nic Cleansing, Says US Senator," *Independent* (November 21, 2017).
[10]Charities Aid Foundation, "CAF World Giving Index 2017."

Psychologist Paul Bloom points out that this is the problem with empathy, which he calls a "poor moral guide" that "grounds foolish judgments and often motivates indifference and cruelty." Bloom argues that empathy is a spotlight of compassion and requires proximity or familiarity. We care more about those who are in our spotlight than those who are outside it. We'll have compassion for and make decisions based on that compassion in favor of those in our spotlight even if it is harmful to those on the outside. Bloom says we need to have more rational compassion.[11]

Empathy can fuel tribalism, racism, and nationalism and lead a nation, regardless of how generous, to deny the existence of a people while at the same time actively eliminating their existence.

———

In the 2017 CAF report, 51% of respondents had volunteered in the past month, ranking Myanmar third.

I met an English professor, Htoo Htoo Wa, who told me "more and more I think the meaning of life is to help people."

Htoo Htoo Wa brings his students to an orphanage every three months. They hold a fund-raiser before they go. This time, instead of a class of students, he took me.

The house was in a decent neighborhood with paved roads, but it in no way looked like an orphanage except for the sheer quantities of everyday items. We stepped over 20 pairs of scattered flip-flops and onto a front porch where 26 umbrellas hung from the walls.

Thet Naing Oo, "the person in charge," according to the orphanage's one-page description, greeted us (see Figure 7.1). Despite having 19 kids under his roof, it was obvious he spent some time getting his hair just right. He may have been wearing makeup and was arguably the best-dressed man I had seen in Myanmar.

He invited us to sit in standard-issue sea foam plastic chairs in the living room. There were kids everywhere – behind him, beside him, in the adjacent kitchen, upstairs in a loft that overlooked the living room. The kids were silent and used each other as furniture, sitting back-to-back, and younger kids in laps.

Htoo Htoo Wa, who taught at a Christian university, told me to be sensitive to the issue of Thet Naing Oo "being a gay," since "homosexual acts" could land you in prison for 10 years in Myanmar.

———

[11]Paul Bloom, *Against Empathy* (New York: HarperCollins, 2016), 2–3.

*Figure 7.1    Thet Naing Oo and the children of The Good Samaritan*
*Orphanage.*

"These kids saved my life," Thet Naing Oo said. The kids stopped picking at each other to listen. "I'm gay."

"Have you been discriminated against?" I asked.

"I dressed and lived like a woman in the 1980s. I faced so much discrimination, I thought about suicide."

It was obvious that he identified with the kids who were cast out. Some of these kids were born to mothers who were sex workers who died from AIDS. One of them lost his family to Cyclone Nargis in 2008.

Thet Naing Oo has been their father since they were babies, adopting the first kid in 2001.

The government doesn't officially recognize The Good Samaritan Orphanage because Thet Naing Oo doesn't own the home or have enough resources in his bank account, but for 15 years he has supported up to 30 kids.

The orphanage doesn't assess its impact beyond food in kids' bellies and kids in school. It doesn't file tax records that show its financial stability but it's obvious that the orphanage has made a difference in the lives of these children and this man.

"How many of you have changed a diaper?" I asked the kids.

All the hands went up but for one, David, who is six. No matter how old you are it's awkward to be reminded that people you know changed your diaper. David hung his head in embarrassment.

Htoo Htoo Wa dismissed the children and they scattered into the kitchen, upstairs, out the front door. Within a few minutes some kids were eating dinner. Htoo Htoo Wa told me that in some families like this they allow the kids to eat only one egg. Thet Naing Oo makes them eat two.

A boy hit another boy playfully in the nuts at a small kitchen table that seemed to magically appear. The home is immaculately well kept. Everything is in its place. Off to the side of the living room there was a room neatly stacked with boxes from floor to ceiling.

"In 2006 I contracted HIV," Thet Naing Oo said. "At that point I had five children … It became AIDS and I was dying. I even wrote my own obituary. My blood count was low . . . It was the kids and my responsibility to support them that made me fight and seek treatment."

Thanks to antiretroviral medicines from Doctors Without Borders, he has been able to live a healthy life.

"What would you tell one of the kids if they told you they were gay?" I asked.

"Lydia!" he hollered. "I would show them how to live a healthy life."

A shorthaired, stocky teenage girl walked over and stood by him. Lydia.

"Lesbian," he said, touching her shoulder, and then he told me how her father left her mother when she was seven months pregnant with Lydia. He remembered the story because he lived it. He signed the papers to become her legal guardian.

The rest of the kids looked on. A girl in a penguin shirt stretched up to touch the top of the door frame. I pictured a smaller version of her trying and failing and then one day getting it. Kids grow up whether they have parents or not – whether they are loved or not.

"You give so much," I said. "What advice do you have for other people who want to make a difference?"

"Feeling sorry is not enough," he said. "Not every person can do or wants to do. I'm doing this because I love children."

***Giving Rules: Feeling sorry is not enough.***

———

I cursed at the ATM. My Facebook friends were too generous.

I had shared about The Good Samaritan Orphanage on Facebook and ended the post with this: "Thet Naing Oo gives more than most, and sometimes those who give the most need the most help. I donated $40 to him. If you'd like to offer some support, tell me how much you'd like to give in the comments, and I'll make sure he gets it."

They donated more than $1,000, which is $1.4 million kyat. It took me seven transactions at the ATM due to the maximum withdrawal limit – hence the cursing – before I had a bank-robber stack of money.

I couldn't believe the generosity of my friends, but I also couldn't believe that I was taking $1,000 to an orphanage. I set out on this adventure with the belief that those who can give have a moral responsibility not only to give, but to give in the most effective way possible. And I was giving to an orphanage? Orphanages have a horrible track record of abuse and inefficiency.

In his book *Little Princes*, Conor Grennan recounted volunteering at an orphanage in Nepal when he discovered the "orphans" had parents who were looking for them. A man had come through remote villages promising to take kids from the village to Kathmandu to get an education. The kids were placed in orphanages where foreigners would pay money to volunteer to help them. The orphanages were businesses that profited from pity produced by children living in impoverished conditions.

I knew that the United Nations Children's Fund (UNICEF) was against orphanages and warned about their spread as tourism increased.

"Myanmar could see an exponential increase in the number of orphanages over the coming decade, especially in tourist destinations," Aaron Greenberg, UNICEF Myanmar's chief of child protection, warned *The Guardian*. "Such an increase in orphanage care could violate the rights of tens of thousands of Myanmar children. We need to act before orphanages dot the landscape."[12]

Seventy-three percent of children in orphanages in Myanmar are not orphans. Children in orphanages are more likely to have developmental delays and exposure to violence and exploitation. UNICEF cites that "75 studies targeting more than 3,800 children across 19 countries found that children in orphanages had on average an IQ 20 points lower than their peers in families."

---

[12] Oliver Holmes, "'Orphanage Tourism': Fears of Child Exploitation Boom as Myanmar Opens Up," *The Guardian* (September 29, 2016).

So, yes, I couldn't believe that I stuffed 1.4 million kyat in my messenger bag and hopped in a cab to head back to The Good Samaritan Orphanage. *What was I thinking?*

Okay, I guess this is what I was thinking:

A former monk told me I should do it. (You'll meet him soon.)

Htoo Htoo Wa, an English teacher, not someone selling a tour, introduced me to the orphanage. And Robert Sterken, a senior Fulbright scholar and author of *Teaching Barefoot in Burma*, introduced me to Htoo Htoo Wa.

Htoo Htoo Wa regularly visited the orphanage with his students who fund-raised for the orphanage, and he donated his own money as well.

Neither Thet Naing Oo nor Htoo Htoo Wa ever asked me to give.

Htoo Htoo Wa was critical of the standard of living that Thet Naing Oo provided for the kids. He thought it was too high. Thet Naing Oo had turned down a donation of used clothes. Not for his kids. Htoo Htoo Wa thought Thet Naing Oo could send the kids to cheaper schools, yet he still gave.

The Good Samaritan Orphanage was not a tourist orphanage. In fact, we had trouble finding it the second time, and it was apparent that Thet Naing Oo didn't focus enough on fund-raising, nor was he any good at it.

It was a Sunday morning when I showed up with $1,000 to attend church with Thet Naing Oo and the kids. I wasn't sure what to expect when I gave him the money I had folded up into a city map of Yangon. Thet Naing Oo owed the bank $450. School was free up until the 10th grade. He said that sometimes he hoped the ninth graders didn't pass into the 10th grade because he couldn't afford it. Four of the kids were in 10th grade now and their tuition was 40,000 kyat per month. The amount of money in the map was enough to take care of a few of his problems.

He didn't count it. He didn't get emotional.

*Giving Rules: A gift should be given without expectation.*

Only 6.2% of people in Myanmar are Christian. Visiting any church for the first time always makes me nervous; I never know what I am walking into. Thet Naing Oo was a born-again Christian, and my translator, Kyaw, was an atheist.

*This could be interesting.*

It wasn't a church with a steeple; it was just someone's house. A blind man who spoke English told me that it was nice to see me. The pastor donned a blue shirt with long sleeves and a *longyi* and told me he had been to Boston. He asked me to sit beside him in one of the four seats at the head of the room.

The kids sang hymns from laminated pages. Lydia closed her eyes, threw her head back, and full-throated every note. One of the teenage guys sounded like his voice was changing from a boy's to a man's beat to beat.

During the service, I noticed Thet Naing Oo counting the money.

They read from loosely bound Bibles. No one handled spitting cobras. There was a reading. My translator translated the sermon.

It was Father's Day. I had forgotten. They asked me to speak.

*Crap.*

I stood.

"It is an honor to be here on Father's Day with so many fathers, and also with one father of so many," I said, motioning to Thet Naing Oo. "My father worked as a farmer and he worked in construction building buildings. He taught me how to work hard and how to treat people with respect. My father showed me these things; he didn't always tell me these things because he is a man of few words. Those are the big examples that my father gave to me. I'm thankful for those gifts.

"I have two children. I have a daughter who is eight and a son who is six. I remember the first time I saw my daughter; it changed the way I saw the world. I started to see the world through the eyes of a father. And suddenly I had far less time to make a difference, but more of a reason. And that is the gift my children gave me.

"Again, I am very honored to be here. Thank you so much. I cannot imagine being a father to 19. Being a father to two is a lot of work. Being a father of 19 takes a special kind of person. It is great to meet all of you. This experience today and meeting all of you is my Father's Day gift, and I would like to thank all of you for that."

Thet Naing Oo thanked me for the donation, wrote out an official certificate, and thanked me again. Now, the certificate sits on my book-shelf in my office, a reminder that every kid deserves more than pity, and that giving can change the lives of others, and in some cases, it may save your own.

*Giving Rules: Giving to others may save your life.*

# 8

# Seeing Differently to Make a Difference (Myanmar, 2017)

*A not-so-noble Nobel Peace Prize winner /
Problem with karma / Intent matters*

---

**AS NIGHT FELL, THE LIGHT EMANATING** from a shipping-container-turned-classroom in the parking lot of the Yangon train station penetrated farther into the growing darkness. Rows of tiny heads faced the front of the converted shipping container sitting on the bed of a green truck. The heads followed the movements of their teachers.

The male teacher tapped a boy on the head with a role of paper he made ever tighter by fidgeting with it.

It seemed voyeuristic watching the class through the glowing windows – two-dimensional characters, distant others – while I stood invisible in the dark. A girl raised her hand, said something to the teacher, and walked out the back of the container classroom.

She glanced at me and then ran off to a tree on the edge of the property where she squatted to pee. When it poured rain, I used the tree as an umbrella; she used it as a toilet.

I wasn't alone in my voyeurism. A few kids played in the parking lot, stopping to watch the class of 16 kids. A boy stood on a post behind the

*Figure 8.1    Tim Aye-Hardy standing in front of one of myME's mobile
classrooms.*

classroom and posed like Peter Pan to get a better glimpse of what was
going on. Not growing up is a luxury most of these kids will never know.

These kids have jobs. They work 10- or 12-hour days in teahouses
spread throughout the city, and then at night they attend this mobile
classroom run by the myME: Myanmar Mobile Education Project,
founded by Tim Aye-Hardy, who had returned after 20 years in the US
(see Figure 8.1).

I had eaten at a teahouse first thing after arriving on an early-morning
flight. Kids and teens navigated the crowded room of plastic tables and
yelled out orders. The walls were open to the street and everything was
wet. I had assumed all the kids were family members.

"'We treat them like family,'" Tim said, mimicking the teahouse owners. "But the reality is that [the teahouse owners] pay crap and let them
sleep on the floor. [They] don't even feed them properly … These kids
work 12 or 13 hours every day. No weekends off, no holiday. If they get
lucky they can go back to the village maybe once per year for the Water
Festival. They make … $35 to $40 per month and all of it is sent back to

their families … These kids have a lot on their shoulders. They are also forced to drop out of school by their own parents."

When Tim arrived in Los Angeles 20 years ago, courtesy of the US State Department after the 8888 Uprising, he had nothing. He lived five months in a monastery with the monks he had helped at the consulate, and then he got a job at a gas station and enrolled in a community college.

"I almost got kicked out. I got a notice: 'Your GPA is 1.9.' I was like, 'What the hell is a GPA?'"

He had come from an educational system where you had to take one test per year and it wasn't important whether you went to class or not.

"I was 19. I'd go out with friends partying – just hanging out with some gang members."

Tim was a friend with the Crips and the Bloods, the Puerto Rican and Filipino gangs. He drove a low-rider with tinted windows and a 12-inch woofer in the back. His friends would steal the latest Alpine or Kenwood speakers and removable-face cassette players for him. He carried a gun, had friends who were arrested, and he lost friends in drive-by shootings.

"[You] don't have any friends, you know? [Gang members] feel pushed out and left out. It becomes like family – so close. I'm not sure how many are still alive."

Tim graduated and went on to get his bachelor's degree at Cal Poly Pomona.

"I studied computer science because I couldn't speak or write English real well."

His timing was impeccable. Programmers were in such high demand that a company hired him six months before he graduated. They paid him an annual salary of $50,000 to go to class, which was so much more than the $4.25 per hour he made at the gas station. They even gave him a pager, which was the ultimate status symbol in the 1990s.

"I was a big deal," Tim laughed.

Tim's work took him to San Diego, where he got his master's degree and considered pursuing a PhD, but got involved in the Free Burma movement that opposed the military rule in Myanmar. He led and spoke at demonstrations, and even worked with UNESCO on human rights issues. He moved to New York City, and the teenager who had shown up with $12 and his school backpack now had become a programmer with a six-figure job, a BMW, and an NYC lifestyle. But he never stopped fighting for Burma and monitoring what was happening.

After Tim left, the government squashed the 8888 Uprising. Aung San Suu Kyi was elected state counselor in 1990 while under house arrest, but the government refused to concede and maintained control. Later the government referred to her as a "genocidal prostitute."

By 1992 General Than Shwe had come to power. To give you an idea of his commitment to the people of Burma, he considered buying the Manchester United soccer team for a billion dollars as a gift to his grandson, who was a soccer fan. By the mid-2000s, Transparency International ranked Burma tied with Somalia as the most corrupt country in the world, and *Foreign Policy* magazine listed General Than Shwe as the third worst dictator in the world behind Kim Jong-Il and Robert Mugabe.

The people felt unheard and under the thumb of the government. In 2007, tens of thousands of monks led antigovernment demonstrations that were met by lethal force. The army killed and arrested monks and civilians alike.

Cyclone Nargis hit in May 2008, killed 138,000 people, and left an estimated 2 million homeless. The government refused outside aid in the immediate aftermath. The government wouldn't even allow Burmese organizations to help.

"At that time," Tim told me, "ordinary citizens tried to help others by providing drinking water, rice, clothing. They would get turned away or put in prison. Jail for 35 years for providing water to people who needed it."

Zargana, one of the best-known comedians in Burma, joined the Nargis rescue effort and was threatened. "I want to save my own people," Zargana told the *International Herald Tribune*. "That's why we go with any donations we can get. But the government doesn't like our work. It is not interested in helping people. It just wants to tell the world and the rest of the country that everything is under control and that it has already saved its people."

The Free Funeral Society (FFS), founded in 2001 by actor Kyaw Thu (not my translator at the orphanage), risked arrest to help those who were impacted by Nargis. Early on, FFS simply provided funerals for those who couldn't afford them. From there the organization worked its way backward: Why are so many people dying? Poor health and lack of access to health care. So they built a clinic. Why are so many people sick and in our clinic? Poor living conditions and lack of education. They started a school.

"My work at the organization has taught me a lot," Kyaw Thu said. "As an actor, I used to crave publicity and chased money and fame, but now I want nothing but to help those in need. The people's tears are your tears. The people's happiness is your happiness."[1]

This wasn't a sentiment shared by the government. Anyone helping just made them look bad and reminded everyone of the government's shortcomings. Where government fails to care for people, people often fill the gap. That's what I saw at the orphanage, and that's what I saw in the efforts of my Airbnb hosts to build a retirement home for men. That's what I saw in Tim's myME project to educate teahouse children.

The government was feeling the heat by 2010 from the citizens and the international community, which was calling for prosecution of war crimes. General Shwe passed leadership to Thein Sein, who became the nation's president as the generals traded in uniforms for civilian clothes and laid a plan for democracy. Thein Sein watched episodes of *The West Wing* to learn how government and an executive branch should work.

Elections were held, and the opposing party won 43 of 45 contested seats in parliament. Three days after the election, the US lifted sanctions and Burma was open for business.

Tim had left Burma wearing a *longyi* and returned wearing pants.

"[My] first trip was just to visit to see how the country was … [i]t was a bit of a culture shock. All of these buildings. People everywhere. When I left this country, when you went onto the street you could hardly find cars or people. It was so isolated no one really knew anything about other countries. The informers and spies were everywhere. People who don't even say anything about government or [are not] questioning or criticizing … they disappear the next day. Even within your own family members you don't even know who's who. You don't talk about any of those things. When you talk about it people just start to step away from you. People don't even listen because even listening you could end up in jail. So that was the situation when I left. When I came back everyone was talking and speaking. Posters of Aung San Suu Kyi everywhere. Human rights. Democracy."

Tim was planning on starting a technology company in Yangon and then returning to New York.

---

[1]Buena Bernal, "Myanmar's Kyaw Thu: The People's Humanitarian," www .rappler.com/world/regions/asia-pacific/104636-2015-ramon-magsaysay-awardee-kyaw-thu (September 3, 2015); Cherry Thein, "Free Funeral Service Society Overcomes Stigma," *The Myanmar Times*, www.mmtimes.com/special-features/ 154-ngos-aid/3366-free-funeral-service-society-overcomes-stigma.html (November 26, 2012).

"Instead, I found a bunch of kids working on the street and I was like, 'What the hell is going on? Why aren't they in school? Where did they come from?' You start asking questions and people start looking at you like, 'Where have you been, man? What's wrong with you? Are you missing something?'

"Yeah, like 20-plus years, an entire generation," Tim would tell them.

If Tim hadn't seen the outside world, he might not have asked these questions. Change needs to be locally driven, but sometimes we don't even know what change we need or what questions to ask. Tim is in the unique position of being from Myanmar, a local, but seeing his country with an outsider's point of view.

> *Giving Rules: We have to see differently before we can give differently.*

"We do this because we know the kids should be getting their rights," Tim said. "The kids should be getting education for a better future."

The World Giving Index measures three very specific things: volunteering, donating, and helping a stranger. It doesn't measure who is helped or why they are helped. It doesn't define what giving means. Tim told me that the teahouse and home owners who employ children believe they are giving [to the kids].

"For them, they are doing charitable work by giving these kids places to sleep and something to eat. They don't realize they are part of the problem. We provide basic education ... Now these kids are ready to move on, but the owners are like, 'You can't take them.' They are owned. Some parents take an advance on salary – six months to [a] year – so the kids can't leave. They have to stay and pay off [the advance]. It is bonded labor. It is even slavery."

So when someone from Gallup rolls up to your house and asks if you've given money or time or helped a stranger in the past month, you could answer all three positively and yet you could own a slave. In fact, you might even consider that to be one of the ways you gave. You could be a soldier participating in an ethnic cleansing. You may have just killed someone before breakfast, but you donated to the Buddhist temple last week, so you are marked down as a giver. The World Giving Index doesn't capture the intent or effectiveness of the gift. It isn't some measure of overall compassion in which acts of love are subtracted from acts of hate across an entire population. This is why Myanmar can be the most generous nation in the World Giving Index and also home to an ethnic cleansing. But that doesn't mean the index doesn't have value.

"The value of the index is looking at the whole data set," Adam Pickering, international program director for the Charities Aid Foundation (CAF), told me. "We publish this and we can sit back and watch different news sources pick it up around the world. In some countries it's a huge story. And you watch debate rage. Why has [giving] gone down? Why has it gone up? And the causes behind it … You see people asking questions that they should be asking anyway, introspection of how generous our culture is and how [they] might try to motivate us to be more generous."

> *Giving Rules: Organizations and individuals should constantly evaluate their giving and adjust as necessary.*

Tim has strong opinions about giving in Myanmar.

"You need to look at the culture and religious expectations," Tim told me. "Culturally, society and your family expect you to behave in that way. The intention … a lot of people give but a lot of it goes to Buddhism-related activities. People tend to put more money to more prominent monks, temples … Now, people are just like, 'If you give money to the monks, you get a better return.' That's why people [in Myanmar] don't give to people at the bottom. People believe that if you are poor and ugly and disabled, [it's] because of bad karma, bad deeds you have done in a past life. Now it's your time to pay for those. They don't feel so much sympathy because they are paying for their consequences. 'I'm rich. I'm healthy and beautiful because I did good things in my previous life.' That's how they think."

For Tim, six months in Burma became three years, so far. He thought he could get the project started and then turn it over to his staff, but he's not there yet. The project is bigger than he thought it would be, with eight buses, and 3,000 child workers from 53 teashops enrolled in classes. He's working with his team to develop myME boxes – small computers that will cost less than $35 and can download educational curricula and resources for free. The Myanmar Ministry of Education has created a Department of Alternative Education that is partnering with myME to spread educational access to the 10% of kids who don't have it, like the kids on the bus.

I watched as the kids stepped from the shipping container converted to a classroom in the downpour. A woman approached with a young girl at her side and stopped. I thought for a moment that she was there to pick up her daughter after school, but she wasn't. That's not reality here. These kids' parents weren't around.

As I watched the kids scatter into alleys lit only by the Coca-Cola sign atop the train station, I thought about a video myME had sent me.

Tim had traveled back to the village with a 12-year-old boy in the myME project and a camera crew from Al Jazeera.

"I'm happy to go home," the boy told the camera. "When I get to the village I will eat and sleep, and see my aunts and uncles. They will feed me snacks and we will talk a lot."

And then he watched as the reporter interviewed his mom. She said he earned enough to allow them to pay off the debt they go into to buy rice.

"It's not that I want them to work," his mom said. "Well, yes, I want them to because we aren't doing well. If we were doing well, I wouldn't let them. Kids shouldn't be far from their parents. They could be corrupted. I let [him] work only because we're not doing well."[2]

The boy began to cry and the reporter asked him what was wrong.

"It bothers him because he wanted to do more," Tim explained. "To provide more to get out of this situation. But now he can't fulfill that, so that's why he's sad."

Four barefoot girls left the bus, leaving school, and stepped into the muddy parking lot splashing with raindrops. One girl popped open an umbrella and held it so the others could join her.

"I'm not regretting all this," Tim told me. "Here I'm getting some things I can't buy no matter how much money I have … People say, 'You are doing such an amazing job,' and I'm like, 'Nah, man, we all can do this. I'm just happy to be here.'"

---

[2]Al Jazeera TV, "Tea Shop Child Goes to School" (February 2014).

# 9

# Giving on Purpose
# (Myanmar, 2017)

*Giving alms / Meditating on giving*

**"ARE YOU READY?" VAJIRA,** a Buddhist nun from Chicago, asked.

"I think so," I responded.

I was nervous. The thought of meditating for six hours and being alone with my thoughts terrified me.

Sometimes I will walk into the bathroom, realize I left my phone downstairs, and then go get it just so I don't have to be alone with my thoughts. When I mow the yard, I listen to audiobooks. When I shower, I listen to podcasts. When I drive, I constantly have someone else's thoughts entering my head to avoid being with my own.

If I had nothing to think about, what would I think about?

So that was scaring the hell out of me. And it also didn't help that my friend, Janja Lalich, a cult expert, was really against the idea of the meditation retreat.

"Too much self-involvement," she wrote to me. "That doesn't change the world, which I believe is your mission."

I would never state my mission so boldly, but I do hope to encourage you (and myself), as Gandhi put it, "to lose yourself in the service of others." And meditation seemed to be the opposite of that. How would so much self-reflection lead to connecting more with others? But giving plays such a large part in Buddhism and so does meditation, so I decided to try it. The Charities Aid Foundation (CAF) speculated that Myanmar's position atop the World Giving Index had a lot to do with Buddhism. Nearly 90% of Burmese are practicing Buddhists, and almost all of them follow the Theravada branch of Buddhism, which heavily emphasizes the practice of giving, known as *dana*.

Buddha used his teachings on the value of giving (*dana*) as the foundation for all of his other teachings. Only after his audience realized the virtue of giving would he move on to lessons on morals, karma, and the Noble Truths. For Buddhists, giving is an act of selflessness and is the best weapon to combat greed and selfishness. It's the first step on the path to enlightenment. If I wanted to learn about the heart of Myanmar's culture of giving, I had to experience Buddhism in Myanmar.

Vajira, a wispy nun, invited me to her monastery in Yangon.

She said the minimum time they allowed yogis to meditate was 10 days. I talked her down to six hours, negotiating my way to a fast-food enlightenment.

Still, six hours alone in silence? I wasn't sure I could survive.

I was also concerned about my ability to lean in to the experience. I was afraid my writing mind would try to document it the whole time.

Vajira led me across a brick courtyard and up to the men's meditation room where three men sat in silence.

"That's going to be us!" my mind screamed.

With wood beams and wood floors, the room reminded me of the one in *The Matrix* where Keanu Reeves (Neo) fought Laurence Fishburne (Morpheus) after proclaiming, "I know kung fu." I guess that made Vajira my Morpheus.

"I'm trying to free your mind, Kelsey. But I can only show you the door. You're the one who has to walk through it." I imagined Vajira saying this, wearing futuristic glasses.

And then she showed me the door next to the meditation room and instructed me to sit on a bamboo mat before a chair. Sobhita, the monk who was my teacher, entered and sat in the chair.

"Have you meditated before?" he asked as Vajira translated.

"Yes," I said. (I had a meditation app on my phone and after six months had completed the first 10 free lessons.) "Kind of."

"For how long?"

"Ten minutes," I said, doing the math that 10 minutes was one-36th of six hours.

"How many days are you here for?"

"Just one," I said, worried that he was going to kick me out for being too American. Instead, he taught me how to walk.

"Think left, right, left." He narrated his walk from side to side with his hands laced behind his back. "Always thinking," he motioned from his head to his feet. "And then, up … ," he lifted his right foot, " … and down," and then did the same with his left. There was even the more advanced "up, forward, down."

When he got to the end of his path, he said, "Standing, standing."

"That always feels good," Vajira chimed in.

"Always know your path," Sobhita said.

I wanted to assign great meaning and wisdom to the phrase "always know your path" because wisdom came from places like this and people like him. But what he really meant was the equivalent of a guy on a corner yelling at a car too close to the sidewalk, "Hey, jackass, watch where you're going." He wasn't speaking about a path on some higher level of consciousness, but the path on the floor.

And then he showed me how to sit and concentrate on my breathing. Rising. Falling.

At first I had my legs crossed over each other. "Not good," he told me. "Your legs will hurt. Like this … " He showed me that his legs were crossed but not stacked. "And then if you need to move, first thinking, 'I want to move. I want to move.' And then move. Think, 'moving, moving.' Slowly." He lifted up his legs and switched positions.

"You understand?" he asked.

"Yes," I said. "I think so. What if I have to go to the bathroom?"

"You go," he said, outlining the path with his finger around the outside of the room. "But always noting."

*Peeing peeing peeing. Pooping pooping pooping*, I thought, trying not to giggle. *Giggling giggling giggling*.

He led me into the men's meditation room and had me place my bamboo mat and pillow next to a pillar. Three men were 20 minutes into an hour of walking meditation, which would be followed by an hour of sitting meditation and so on until I was done or my brain exploded.

I began walking. *Right, left, right, left. Standing. Standing.*

I had to walk so slowly because my mind wasn't quick enough to note any faster movements. If Janja saw me, she would think I was a shaved head from cult status.

So I found my path and I walked. One guy's path walked out the door and back. Another's paralleled mine. But I didn't pay them too much attention because thinking about walking took all I had.

*Right.*

I felt the weight transfer to my left foot as I picked up my right, and then my right landed, heel slightly before the ball of my foot.

*Left.*

Sometimes my weight would shift and I'd have to compensate with my body not to fall from my path, but this was not something that the observer would have noticed. These are only the small shifts and adjustments that one can notice in oneself. I was feeling pretty good about the process, but realized that my thinking about how things were going was my not thinking about the act of walking.

There were two clocks in the room, and I did my best not to watch them, but I checked them every 15 minutes or so and sometimes much more often. When all you have is time and your thoughts, it's easy to lose track of both. Time slowed down and time sped up. It's like when you are a kid and the days are so slow, yet somehow you become an adult so fast with kids and a mortgage. One minute of play is gone in a flash, and other moments of grief or loss or at the dentist are unending, inescapable, unbearable black holes where time ceases to exist.

*Standing. Standing.*

When the clock chimed, we all slowly made our way to our sitting places.

*Sitting. Sitting.*

Sitting required so many movements. And the distance to the floor was a journey much longer than I remembered. I sat on the cushion, my legs in front of me folded but not crossed like Sobhita had shown me. I straightened my back.

*Rising. Falling. Rising.*

This was much more difficult than walking. I'd note a few breaths and then my mind would disappear. Months later while listening to a podcast in the shower, I heard an experienced meditation practitioner say that it was okay to be distracted because it was the refocusing that matters. He compared meditation to weight lifting in that refocusing is picking up the weight. That's the practice. That's the work.

The warm air became a blanket and the stillness a bed I wanted to curl up onto and fall asleep. I nodded and then jerked awake. No one falls asleep lifting weights!

"Did the guy in front of me nod?" I thought. "Dammit, stop worrying about him."

*Rising. Falling. Rising. Pinching. Pinching. Pinching.*

I thought pinching the meat of my thumb would release endorphins or whatever. I thought about slapping myself in the face. That's what I do when I'm driving tired, attempting to fool my body that it's under attack and needs to be alert. But it's so hard not to take the slap unexpectedly without turning your cheek to soften the blow. Besides, what would the other meditators – two yogis and one monk – think? Mind over matter is easier said than done. I suppose the point of this type of meditation is to lose your mind in your matter, to be mindful of the machinery of your own body.

Pinching didn't work, so instead I decided to meditate as hard as I possibly could. My brow furrowed as I stared daggers at the eight-foot gold Buddha in the glass case at the front of the room. There were flowers and offerings and shrines in there with him and a spinning neon light that would be in a casino or on the wall of a stoner's dorm room. I meditated so hard I was like a Jedi in *Star Wars* attempting to keep a heavy falling object from squashing his Padawan. The weight of the mental effort affected me physically. I was sweating. A headache was on its way.

And it went on like this for hours until I stopped trying. My easy gaze fell on the knot of a mosquito net tied in front of me, dancing mindlessly like a jellyfish on the light breeze.

The mat kept my feet off the bare floor. But my anklebones and my knees hurt. It was all-consuming, until it wasn't. I'd note the pain *hurting hurting* and then it would be gone and once again I would focus on my breathing. The urge to scratch would come, I'd note it, and then it would disappear.

Not every itch needs to be scratched. Not every stimulus requires an immediate reaction.

The jellyfish swam and blurred as my vision tunneled. I entered the tunnel and was able to look around without losing my focus.

It was in this pain and in this tunnel alone that a phrase came to me: "other people first." I have no idea why or where it came from. In hindsight it seems kind of forced, too convenient. Giving was on my mind; after all, that's why I was there. I think it was sort of like the last television show you watch before bed creeping into your dream. It's not like it's some original phrase.

Einstein said: "We know from daily life that we exist for other people first of all, for whose smiles and well-being our own happiness depends."

There's also the counter quote: "That's the problem with putting others first; you've taught them that you come second."

Rising. *Other people.*

Falling. *First.*

It became my mantra in a meditation that wasn't supposed to have a mantra.

*Giving Rules: The more kindness and time you give yourself, the more of each you'll have to give to others.*

# 10

# The Gift of Tasting Ice Cream (Myanmar, 2017)

*A former monk on giving / Solitude /
Thoreau's three chairs*

———

**A FEW DAYS BEFORE MY MEDITATION EXPERIMENT,** I went to an art gallery to talk to a man with an interesting insight on Buddhism's impact on the culture of giving in Myanmar.

I walked up the stairs, drenched in sweat, thus retaining my title as Myanmar's sweatiest man.

The gallery had an exhibit entitled "Give Peace a Chance," and the art was informed by the lyrics of John Lennon. Lennon's " ... and no religion too" seemed fitting, considering the man I was seeing. Pyay Way was a former monk (see Figure 10.1). The exhibit featured several canvases, including one with a large grenade and a white dove. In one corner a blindfolded baby doll sat in front of a pile of amputated and headless action figures.

Pyay Way was up another flight of stairs above the exhibit, showing paintings to an indecisive husband and wife from England. There were so many paintings from which to choose. Some were on wood frames

*Figure 10.1     Pyay Way, a former monk, standing in his art gallery.*

stacked against the wall 60 paintings deep, allowing only for a narrow walkway. Others were rolled up and stashed on shelves.

The couple wanted a painting to hang over their sofa. Pyay Way swished through pictures on his iPad. When he found one that interested them, he somehow would find the corresponding canvas.

It was like an episode of *House Hunters* where people say subjective things as if they were facts and you kind of hate them for it. As if they know. As if they are art experts. Some of the paintings were so big they required the husband and me or Pyay Way to hold them up while the wife commented. Then they would trade places and the husband would make annoying comments.

"The teapot is a little big."

"I'm not sure what the artist is trying to say."

They settled on a painting … they thought. It was of stacked logs that had brightly colored ends – pink, red, purple, green.

*But wait. What's that?!* There were two smudges. The husband said he could touch it up. Pyay Way called the artist. The artist said they weren't smudges, but butterflies.

The couple craned their necks at the smudges, eyes inches from the canvas.

Suddenly the smudges were gorgeous and this little scene in the art gallery just gave this $700 painting a bit more story and flavor.

Even after pulling up a picture on their phone of the wall in their house, they couldn't decide, so they went to lunch. Thank Buddha, I could finally chat with Pyay Way alone.

I was desperate to ask him one question, but it was an awkward one to lead with so we chatted about his gallery and the paintings and he told me why he had left the monkhood.

"Curiosity," he said. "I lived in a monastery most of my life. All the friends and teachers at the monastery were all the same. Then when I went to India to study linguistics for my master's, the society there was totally different.

"I went to a university with five thousand students. There were only six monks there. No religious studies department. Honestly, I didn't want to study religion because I had studied Buddhism my entire life. The life at the university was totally different from my life in Myanmar. It totally made me change a lot.

"It was the first time I had been that far from Myanmar. Suddenly I realized that travel broadens your mind and perspective. I had new ideas [about] what I wanted to do with my life. I was no longer content to just be a monk."

Most kids born in his village went to school only through fourth grade, but to the delight of his family, friends, and village, he had entered the monkhood. With their financial support, he was able to travel and pursue his education. Once he decided to leave the monkhood, he was afraid to tell his sponsors, who had given him so much.

He left and didn't tell anyone for six months. When they finally tracked him down, they said they still wanted to support him. They helped him think about what he could do. He had started to hang out with artists and writers and had a passion for supporting his friends and buying their art. He had an idea that he could open a gallery.

"I did not have a place to stay, money, business acumen, or a job. I had to face the world as a new person. I fell in love for the first time and got my heart broken. I learned how to wear normal clothes. Sometimes I got drunk and learned how to cure a hangover. Life is never easy, but there are always people in your life that help make life a little bit easier. I truly appreciate all those who have helped me through support and encouragement."

As a monk he knew the concept of *metta* – loving-kindness. But his family and supporters reflected this back to him. That was their gift to him, and, as we've seen with other gifts so far, it is a gift only if it is passed on. That's exactly what he did when he started his gallery.

"I was running the gallery like a monastery where people meet and do good things. I think that's because I simply don't know any other way. I created a space, a forum for exhibitions, open mic events for those who feel unrepresented and don't have a voice."

He has built a community of 81 artists. Some do well and can buy cars and apartments. They also help support the others who struggle to sell a painting a month.

Pyay Way takes a lower commission than most gallery owners: 25%. He said he could take more, but he doesn't. He has enough.

I asked him about giving in Myanmar. He thinks it is hard to separate religion from culture, so it's not fully accurate to say that Buddhism is the reason the nation is the most generous. He was also very critical of why people give.

"If you want to experience giving in Myanmar, most people would say come to a celebration at a pagoda. Every village, every town has some kind of donation ceremony. They want to give at a ceremony. But actually, giving anything is *dana*."

"Like you giving your time to me right now?" I asked.

"Exactly … When people talk about *dana*, in their mind they think about material things. *Dana* is about everything. It doesn't need to be material. Your time. Your knowledge. Anything. Many people give because they want more [in return]. The reason you do *dana* is to ward off your greed … it makes you a more generous person."

I took a drink of water and prepared myself to ask the question that I was really not sure I wanted answered. I false started a few times. I felt like it might be more of a confession than a question.

"I've seen a wide scope of human existence," I said, "and then I come back home and see the privilege of my own life and I kind of want to crawl into it and just be with my wife and two kids and not think about the rest of the world. But then I think about all the suffering and the opportunity to help mitigate it that exists. Because I've seen what I've seen, I feel driven and compelled to try to make a positive difference in the lives of others. To some extent I think this is guilt-driven. Is that a bad intention?"

I'm not sure what I expected from him. Maybe he'd give me some way to repent. Maybe he'd pull out a piece of paper and write out the Good Person Equation, or maybe he'd let me off the hook totally.

"Intentions are important," he said. "It's not bad everyone has different things to do. Looking after your family is a good thing, because you are also responsible. Even looking after yourself is good … If you are a good person you are good for society. If you can't take care of yourself and your family you can't help anyone else. To be a good person, you don't have to be a monk or priest. Of course, if you become a monk you have less responsibilities; you have more time to do good things for society. It's not a bad thing to have kids or a family, but you have less chance to do more things for other people."

*Giving Rules: Give because not everyone can. We can't all give equally and we can't give equally throughout our lives.*

Too often we focus on what we don't have to give, instead of focusing on what we do have to give. Pyay Way showed me that giving can be as small as a monetary donation and as big as a discussion over a cold bottle of water.

"What's the best way to experience the culture of giving in Myanmar?" I asked him just before I left.

"Here, a lot of people are very generous. The thing is most donate to a monastery or pagoda. Actually, according to Buddha's teaching, it's always better to donate to the place that really needs more. There are thousands of people [in need]. People ignore them and build another pagoda. If we have extra money, that is fine. For me, I would give to an orphanage. And if you have more time, meditate."

———

*Other. People. First.*
And then the tunnel closed and I was back to *Rising. Falling.*
*Right. Left.*
I changed my path out onto the veranda in search of water – or, as I'd later write in my notes, "in search of the writer," which seemed profound in a Freudian sort of way. I found the water. *Drinking. Drinking.* I was conscious of the muscles that were involved.

"How's it going?" The voice broke the silence.

Vajira stood next to me, and I thought it was some kind of test. Before the meditation began she told me that if someone were to speak to me, I should ignore them and act like I didn't hear them.

I hesitated and then responded, "Good." I felt the word crawl out the back of my throat and smash into my teeth. I smiled.

*Smiling. Smiling.*

"Was I enjoying this?" I wondered.

She smiled back and left.

Soon I started to smell food and noticed the other meditators were gone. I hadn't even noticed them leaving, which probably said more about them than me. Now I was self-conscious, which means I wasn't noting.

"Please. Eat." A woman staff member appeared and pleaded with me to go to lunch.

I turned to follow her, still noting every movement as I had been told. She walked so fast. How could I possibly think about walking that fast? For social pressure reasons, I stepped up my pace a bit.

When we entered the room, I saw I was the last one in. The room was full of quiet eating, whispered conversations, and metal spoons on metal plates and cups on tables. I got my plate, filled it, and then was directed to a table with another foreign yogi.

I visited a forest monastery a few days before and witnessed other foreign yogis with shaved heads walking and eating as slowly as if they had recently suffered a stroke. It was so odd then, now that was me. Eating took a lot of thinking – so many movements all at once to note. I tried to pick one each time to note. *Scraping, lifting, chewing, swallowing.* I've never sat at a table with someone else and never looked at them. A staff member brought us upside-down Styrofoam cups in metal bowls. The other yogi waved it off.

"Is that ice cream?" I thought.

*Hoping. Hoping.*

After I cleaned my plate, I turned my focus on the Styrofoam cup, which was, in fact, ice cream. I lifted the cup and the contents slid into the bowl. The first bite was an explosion of flavor. The ice cream contained nuts and spices. I tasted every molecule. I felt the cold melt into the warmth of my mouth.

*Tasting. Tasting.*

When you focus on ice cream, you realize how amazing it is. You savor it. This is not my typical ice cream experience in which I scoop a bowlful, get to the couch and realize I got way too much, and then a few minutes later wonder where all of it went while pondering seconds.

Happiness is focusing on a single bite of ice cream.

What else have I been missing out on?

Sherry Turkle makes a case for the importance of solitude for society in her book *Reclaiming Conversation: The Power of Talk in a Digital Age.* She writes, "A love of solitude and self-reflection enables sociability."

When Henry David Thoreau sought the solitude of Walden Pond, he wrote that in his cabin were "three chairs – one for solitude, two for friendship, and three for society."

"These three chairs," Turkle writes, "plot the points on a virtuous circle that links conversation to the capacity for empathy and for self-reflection. In solitude we find ourselves; we prepare ourselves to come to conversation with something to say that is authentic, ours. When we are secure in ourselves we are able to listen to other people and really hear what they have to say … [S]olitude reinforces a secure sense of self, and with that, the capacity for empathy."[1]

Turkle writes about how much we hate being alone with our thoughts, and points to a study in which people were asked to sit in a room by themselves with no phone or anything to read. The only thing there was to do was to self-administer an electroshock. Before the experiment started, the subjects were asked if they would consider shocking themselves. They all said no. But after six minutes alone with their thoughts many of them began doing just that.

If we want to be more generous, better, and more compassionate givers, we need the self-awareness of what is important to us and what we have to offer.

Yes, this practice had me focusing on the smallest and most elemental of things – breathing and walking – but what if I applied 10% of that level of consideration to how I move through the world and interact with people? We shouldn't be mindless robots not noticing, not thinking. Not rote machines stuck in routines. We need to witness life and all of its diversity.

We give without thought. Our intentions matter – not on some cosmic, karmic level, but in how the act of giving impacts us. We are guilted into supporting a cause because someone corners us on the street or it's someone to whom we can't say no. So we give. And then we complain when the updates arrive in the mail or in our in-box on how the organizations are using our gifts and the work they are doing.

We need to live and give more intentionally.

We automate our giving because we can't be trusted to remember to give. But giving is something that should be felt.

We have to see the light in ourselves. The joy of ice cream first and then we are in a position to help that light in others shine brighter. Before

---

[1]Sherry Turkle, *Reclaiming Conversation: The Power of Talk in a Digital Age,* (New York: Penguin, 2016), 10.

we give, we have to have gratitude, and then we are ready to put other people first.

I didn't say any of this to Vajira when she returned for me at the end of my six hours. I just told her about the ice cream.

"Now you know more than before," she said.

*Giving Rules: Live and give intentionally.*

# Part II

## WHAT CAN I GIVE?

# 11

# Science of Do-gooding (Kenya, 2017)

*Effective altruism / The cost to save a life /
Should you give your kidney? /
Extreme givers*

**I THREW MY CELL PHONE,** dropped my laptop bag, and ran as if my life depended on it. Part of me wanted to throw up or scream or both, but I needed to focus all of my energy on running as fast as I could.

Nothing else in my life mattered in that moment more than running.

Moments ago, the kids had followed me into the garage. Before I helped them into the car, I realized that I had forgotten my wallet.

Griffin, who was 4, is on the autism spectrum, and has a deep curiosity to explore places where he shouldn't be – all of our cabinets, no matter how high, the top of the refrigerator, the inside of a stranger's unlocked car, the tub of the dryer. You could say he's part spelunker or mountain goat. In autism lingo, he's also an "eloper" – here one second, gone the next.

I had been pretty sure he wouldn't bolt for the road and that I had enough time to grab my wallet off the counter and get back outside before anything bad could happen. I had assumed wrong.

Griffin wasn't in the garage. He wasn't playing outside the garage. He wasn't on the swing. He usually takes two strides and does this little skip, as if he's too footloose and fancy free to run full out, so he runs joyously. Not this time. He was running at a dead sprint down our long driveway to the road.

Dead. That's what he would be if I didn't get to him, I thought as I ran. But he was already two-thirds down the driveway, and I wasn't gaining on him fast enough. The fencerow to the east of the drive would block the oncoming traffic from seeing him.

He made it to the road. I didn't catch him in time. But luckily we live on a crumbling, country road in Indiana with very little traffic.

Griffin sat in the middle of the road and laughed. I was emotionally wrecked for three days.

Now I want you to imagine that you are standing on my driveway by the garage and you are holding your computer and phone. You see Griffin running to the road and you know he's a kid who won't stop. Let's add a few certainties: (1) You'll have to drop your phone and laptop to pursue him, and they are certain to break if you do, destroying more than $1,000 of electronics; (2) there isn't a doubt in your mind that you can catch him, but only if you drop your phone and laptop; (3) if you don't catch him, he is certain to be hit by a speeding vehicle.

What do you do? Do you save Griffin?

I bet you would. I bet you wouldn't think twice before sacrificing $1,000 of things to save a young child.

This thought experiment is one similar to, although not as philosophically pure as, one ethicist Peter Singer put forward in his "drowning child" scenario in his essay "Famine, Affluence, and Morality" in 1972. In a later essay, he writes of how he uses the scenario in his classes:

> To challenge my students to think about the ethics of what we owe to people in need, I ask them to imagine that their route to the university takes them past a shallow pond. One morning, I say to them, you notice a child has fallen in and appears to be drowning. To wade in and pull the child out would be easy but it will mean that you get your clothes wet and muddy, and by the time you go home and change you will have missed your first class.
>
> I then ask the students: do you have any obligation to rescue the child? Unanimously, the students say they do. The importance of saving a child so far outweighs the cost of getting one's clothes muddy and missing a class, that they refuse to consider it any kind of excuse for not saving the child.

He then asks his students a few more questions:

> Does it matter if there are others around who could save the child but are not acting? The students agree that it doesn't.
>
> Does it matter if a child in similar life and death circumstance that could be prevented with your actions was in another country? The students agree that our obligation to save the child is the same: If our actions can save a life, then we ought to act.[1]

I think most of us agree with that. But here's where it gets challenging. Singer argues that there are children around the world who are dying preventable deaths, and most of us are doing nothing to save them. On average, Americans give 2% of their income to charity, and only 5.6% of that goes to supporting global causes.[2] That's less than $70 to helping save a kid's life, or $930 less than the laptop and phone you dropped to run after Griffin.

Singer's philosophies rooted in practical ethics formed the foundation of effective altruism, "a philosophy and social movement which applies evidence and reason to working out the most effective ways to improve the world."[3] Like Paul Bloom, who argues for "rational compassion," Singer basically thinks that our hearts are idiots that misguide us at times from doing the most good we can.

I dove deeply into researching effective altruism while researching this book, reading works by Singer (*The Life You Can Save* and *The Most Good You Can Do*) and Will MacAskill's *Doing Good Better*, and visiting websites like www.givewell.org to learn about the most effective and transparent nonprofits. GiveWell has crunched the numbers and determined that the most effective way to save a life is the mass distribution of malaria bed nets. The Against Malaria Foundation calculated that for $3,400 the organization could save a life. That number struck me because I had just paid a contractor nearly that same sum to pour a concrete floor in my barn.

When I was a kid in the 1980s, actress Sally Struthers was in a series of commercials for Christian Children's Fund. Honestly, I don't even

---

[1] Peter Singer, "The Drowning Child and the Expanding Circle," *New Internationalist* (April 1997).
[2] Giving USA Foundation, "Giving USA 2017: The Annual Report on Philanthropy for the Year 2016" (2016).
[3] Peter Singer, *The Most Good You Can Do* (New Haven, CT: Yale University Press, 2015), 4, 5.

know any of Struthers's other work because these commercials were so unforgettable. In one she walked through a slum in a designer jacket with 1980s shoulder pads and 1980s hair and said, in a quavering voice, "Every year 10 million third-world children won't live to see their third birthday and another five will be gone before their fifth birthday. Those who do live beyond that ripe old age for this part of the world will grow up in dung heaps like this." And then under her breath as she walked out of the shot she said, "Happy birthday."

She talked about "this god-awful misery" and then motioned to kids innocently playing behind her. She held a girl and said her "heartbreaking" cry was the result of being so malnourished that her teeth were falling out. Watching these commercials now, I get the sense that many of the people in the videos had no idea what was happening or, if they did, they asked the filmmakers, just like the kids in Mathare had asked, "Do you want me to smile or cry?" Often, kids don't like being held by strangers, especially strangers wearing 1980s designer sunglasses.

According to Struthers, the kids who weren't crying were so starved they were too weak to cry or so dehydrated from diarrhea they had no tears left. And then she walked toward the camera in leather cowboy boots and asked us to give 70 cents per day, only the cost of a cup of coffee, to end this problem. She made it seem as though if we all just stopped drinking coffee we could end poverty.

Is Singer's "drowning child" thought experiment that different from Struthers's plea?

Sure, $3,400 is more than the cost of a cup of coffee, but for what you get – a life saved – it's amazingly cheap when you think about it. If you saved my son's life or ran into a burning house or dove into a pond to save a child, you'd be a hero. You might even make the nightly news. Compare this to the cost of saving a life in the US. On average, the US government will spend $7 million on infrastructure improvements to save one life.[4]

The TV ads would have to be updated. I could almost picture Sally Struthers, with her 1980s big hair and designer sunglasses, walking out in her boots from behind my barn and saying: "For the cost of one concrete barn floor in rural Indiana, you can save a life."

*Did I value my concrete barn floor more than saving a life?*

It was an uncomfortable thought to have and one that began to make me look at everything differently. Did we really need cable TV?

---

[4]William MacAskill, *Doing Good Better* (New York: Penguin Random House, 2016), 46.

Do I really need an office to work out of when I have a perfectly good kitchen table at home? Could I give up these luxuries to save money to give to fight extreme poverty?

Our society judges people on what they have, not what they give. When we give to a charity, we may receive a thank-you note. Giving is seen as going above and beyond; it's not expected. No one is shamed for not giving. This is partly because most of the time giving is done in private, but it shouldn't be.

Giving inspires giving. Your generosity can act as an example for others. Sure, it can seem like bragging, but is that much different than sharing photos of your new car, or vacation, or fancy dinner, or many of the other life luxuries that so many of us share?

We stand on the sidelines and don't give to a cause or an emergency because we don't see anyone else jumping in to help. This is called the bystander effect. We assume someone else will help the child in the pond, and, in fact, the more bystanders standing around watching, the less likely we are to come to the child's aid. Bill Gates and Warren Buffett joined The Giving Pledge, in which billionaires publicly commit to giving more than half of their wealth away. They've inspired 175 of the world's wealthiest individuals to sign on, and to commit to giving away more than $365 billion. For the rest of us nonbillionaires, there is the Giving What We Can pledge (www.givingwhatwecan.org), where you can publicly commit to donating 10% of your income to effective organizations. As of March 2018, 3,335 members have pledged to donate more than $1.5 billion. Peter Singer has inspired 19,323 people to sign on to his pledge at www.thelifeyoucansave.org. Singer has a calculator that determines, based on income, what percentage you should give starting at 1%.

We should be less humble about our giving than our consuming. We should be more public about our giving than our consuming.

I'm a little uncomfortable admitting this, but the more I read of Singer, the more I started to judge not just my own consumption habits but those of others: the TV, the car, the new grill. This wasn't a healthy way to look at the world or at people, and it started to drive me a little nuts.

> *Giving Rules: Giving isn't some additional duty we squeeze into our lives; it should be a central focus of our lives.*

Twenty-seven thousand children die of poverty every day – from hunger or preventable and treatable diseases. What am I doing about it? Singer's book *The Life You Can Save* introduced these tough questions to me. It felt like a rabbit hole that I might not escape … some people never do.

In *Strangers Drowning*, Larissa MacFarquhar writes about Julia Wise, who is so obsessed with earning and saving money to give that she couldn't even bring herself to buy a candy apple at an orchard. Did she really need a treat more than the antimalarial bed nets the cost of the candy apple could purchase? In 2012, Julia and her partner Jeff spent $12,107 on their own living expenses and donated $49,933.[5]

Julia's altruism seemed reasonable compared to that of Charles Gray. Gray thought that no one should consume more than his or her equal share, and he was sick of the "high consumption, throwaway society" in the US. In the 1970s, he decided to live on something he called the World Equity Budget – dividing global income by the total population – and then reduced the amount further to allow for a growing population. He lived on an annual budget of $1,200 by dumpster diving for food and life's necessities. He scavenged for lumber, appliances, books, and luxury items such as ice cream and exotic fruits and vegetables.[6]

Gray believed the money that one saved by living on the World Equity Budget should be paid back to the global poor as reparations for the abuses and injustices they have suffered.[7]

His wife, who was a pretty extreme altruist already, giving away half of her inheritance, told him it was either her or the budget. He chose the budget.

Many of the people MacFarquhar writes about give so much it disconnects them from society, and pushes them away from friends and families. When people take Singer's philosophy to the extremes they ask themselves questions such as: Why haven't I given away my extra kidney?

> *Giving Rules: Giving shouldn't disconnect you from people; it should further connect you.*

One effective altruist crunched the numbers and found that there was a 1-in-4,000 chance of dying as a result of donating a kidney.

---

[5]Larissa MacFarquhar, *Strangers Drowning* (New York: Penguin Press, 2015), 74–78.
[6]Charles Gray, "The Nuts and Bolts of Living on Less," www.aislingmagazine.com/aislingmagazine/articles/TAM19/Less.html (1989).
[7]Charles Gray, "Repaying Our Debt to the Poor," www.aislingmagazine.com/aislingmagazine/articles/TAM25/Repaying.html (1989).

So, not donating your "extra" kidney means that you valued your life 4,000 times more than that of a stranger.[8]

I cited this argument to my wife Annie, who emphatically told me, "No, you are not donating a kidney." I think she's got dibs on it.

Not all effective altruists go to the extremes of MacFarquhar's subjects, but they commit to doing far more than most of us. They examine how they give money, time, and their careers.

At its simplest terms effective altruism says it is "about answering one simple question: how can we use our resources to help others the most? Rather than just doing what feels right, we use evidence and careful analysis to find the very best causes to work on."[9]

Americans spend less than two hours per year evaluating their giving decisions. What if we looked at giving as an investment in a company or even a toaster we were going to purchase? We'd want to know how the company has performed in the past and how it is expected to perform in the future. We'd read the reviews for the toaster. Is it worth the price?

Elie Hasenfeld was working at a hedge fund in Connecticut. He and his friends had some extra money that they wanted to donate, and started to evaluate charities as they would an investment.

Most of us are inherently bad at evaluating charities. We don't put much thought into the subject whatsoever and, when we do, we want to know how much the executive staff gets paid, and how much of our donation will go to programs versus overhead. We want to know things like how many meals are served and how many kids are taken care of. Elie and his friends wanted to go deeper. Eventually they founded GiveWell.org, a charity evaluator that looks at cost-effectiveness, impact, transparency, outcomes, and what additional funding would enable the organization to accomplish. GiveWell chooses "evidence-backed, thoroughly vetted, underfunded organizations" and lists them on its site.

I knew if I wanted to learn more about effective altruism, I needed to see one of GiveWell's top charities in action.

The Against Malaria Foundation is the darling of the movement. It's the one everyone pointed to, offering the most cost-effective method of saving a life – for only $3,400! Yet there was another organization, GiveDirectly, that does something pretty unique. It gives money directly to people in poverty. That's it. No strings attached. No need to repay it.

---

[8]Peter Singer, *The Life You Can Save* (New York: Random House, 2009), 130–131.
[9]www.effectivealtruism.org (March 12, 2018).

No telling a recipient how to spend it. It's a unique model, sometimes controversial, and one that would teach me a lot about giving.

———

"What are those flowers on the side of the road?" I asked John Okinda, an associate field manager with GiveDirectly near Kisumu, Kenya.

"You like them?" John replied, looking down the nameless dirt road lined with bright yellow flowers. "They are a noxious weed, actually."

The road narrowed to a bumpy path. We pulled off near a pavilion with a shiny blue metal roof. A jump rope whooshed through the air, and a little girl pulled up her dress to her shins as she jumped it. The rope kicked up a tiny cloud of dust with each revolution.

John made a call, and soon a man in boots with a tucked-in shirt led us down a path to his home. He was a hat and beard short of looking Amish. He welcomed us into his living room and sat in a chair like a laid-back king on a throne made from branches.

His name was also John, like my translator. Farmer John had lived on and off his 1.25 acres for 30 years. As a young man he left the village for work in the port city of Kisumu, met his wife, Margaret, and a year later they had their first child. The trip back down memory lane seemed to be one he hadn't taken for a while. His wife sat on a couch beside him with two of their daughters (see Figure 11.1).

"I like living here so much," he said in a baritone voice as smooth as the polished concrete floor at our feet. "The soil is fertile, there is plenty of water, and wild fruits like avocado, mangoes, and guava. I grow pineapples, too."

But the majority of Farmer John's income comes from maize and millet that he sells, earning $112 per harvest. It's not enough.

He's a subsistence farmer, so he feeds his family with what he produces, but he doesn't have a lot leftover for anything else like school fees, medical expenses, and transportation.

It was especially not enough when his wife and daughter both fell ill.

"My daughter had a mental condition and she was also bitten by a wild dog. She had to be admitted into the hospital. My wife was diagnosed with ulcers and typhoid and at some point, she developed some mental problems. She doesn't remember anything. She wasn't talking and she wasn't eating until she was admitted. Even now she hasn't healed completely. She still has memory lapses. She isolates herself."

Margaret blinked as if she were trying to bring the world into focus but couldn't quite do it.

*Figure 11.1    Farmer John (left), his wife (beside him), his daughter Beryl
(fourth from left), and family.*

Farmer John's mother also got sick and racked up medical bills before
passing away. He had to pay for a funeral, and he had to send his wife and
daughter to Kisumu where they would stay in a hospital for a month. Not
to mention that he still had to support his household of eight. He considered reaching out to his neighbors, family, and friends for donations,
but he was too proud. He worried that they would laugh at him.

"My last resort was to sell my land. But then GiveDirectly came in
and spared the land."

GiveDirectly identifies poor communities using publicly available
data. Then they send a team door-to-door to learn more about the
families. Farmer John received two payments that totaled roughly
$1,000 transferred to him electronically. He accessed the funds through
his phone or he could collect cash through mobile money agents in his
village or nearest town.

"I used my first transfer on two things," John said. "I used it to plaster
the house to make it look the way it is now. And a huge chunk of it
went to pay my wife's and daughter's medical expenses. The bill was over
[$300]."

John used his second payment to buy a solar lighting system, seeds, fertilizer, and labor to till his field, to pay more medical bills, and for his mother's funeral.

"What did you think when you learned about GiveDirectly and the lump-sum payments?" I asked.

"I first heard about this program in 2015 from some of the ladies who were born here and live in Alego [one of the first places GiveDirectly dispersed funds]. I was interested. The ladies shared both positive and negative information about GiveDirectly. They said that the people who received the money made the most of it – they spent it wisely. But there were also people who were apprehensive about GiveDirectly and did not enroll in the program for various reasons. But I focused on the positive things."

I get the skepticism. What would you think if someone showed up at your house and told you that they were going to give you a year's worth of living expenses? I'd think it was a scam.

This is how many in the village reacted. There were rumors that the Illuminati or devil worshippers were involved, and that people had accepted the money and then a family member had died.

But there was no catch. Families could spend the money however they wanted, and they didn't have to pay anything back.

GiveDirectly is one of GiveWell's favorite charities because of its scientific approach. The organization puts forward a theory: What if we cut out all the people, process, and overhead typically between donor and recipient and just gave people money? And the impact has been measured and documented by third-party researchers conducting randomized controlled trials, considered the gold standard for evidence.

One such study found that for every $1,000 given, income increased by $270, assets by $430, and the amount spent on nutrition increased $330.[10]

"I welcome GiveDirectly. My daughter is bright, and she performs very well in school," John said. "Beryl, get your report card."

A chicken roosting on a wheeled suitcase in the corner started squawking, and Beryl picked it up and threw it out the door. She placed her report card and a gift she had received from the school for her good work – a math book – onto a table in front of me. She was ranked number one in her class.

---

[10]Johannes Haushofer and Jeremy Shapiro, "The Short-Term Impact of Unconditional Cash Transfers to the Poor: Experimental Evidence from Kenya," *Quarterly Journal of Economics* (April 25, 2016).

"What would you like to study?" I asked.

"Mathematics."

"What would you like to be?"

"A pilot."

Farmer John, sitting with his legs crossed as if he had all the time in the world and none of the worry, laughed deeply and proudly. Beryl had once been inside a plane on a school field trip, but had never flown.

"That's great," I said. "I love to travel! So why do you want to be a pilot?"

By this time we were all smiling, even Margaret, Beryl's mother, whose attention came and went. There was some discussion. Beryl was quiet and Farmer John prodded her. She laughed.

"Being a pilot you get to fly many places and see the world. Also, it is well paid."

"What's the farthest you've ever been from home?"

"Kisumu," she said.

Kisumu was a 45-minute drive away.

A thousand dollars can go a long way in Kenya. As Farmer John shared all the ways he had spent the money, he pointed to them – the metal door, the red plaster on the side of his home, the solar lighting, his ailing and recovering family members, and a daughter who dreamed of flying a plane far away from it all.

———

Unlike Beryl, Collins Otieno didn't have family to support him. His parents died when he was four.

We met up with him at a roadside diner blasting Celine Dion's "That's the Way It Is."

"When you want it the most," Celine sang, "there's no easy way out."

"They pass a long time ago," Collins said. "I was so young I didn't even ask why. Later I was told it was malaria."

His grandparents raised Collins and his brothers. But they were both dead by the time he was 20. Suddenly he was the father and mother for his two younger brothers and three younger cousins.

They lived on the land left by their grandparents. He remembered those days fondly.

"You could say it was good because we went into a *shamba* [field] to dig, many of us there at once used to do a wonderful job. Three of us could work in our own *shamba* and three could work for someone else. Small jobs for coin. We could find a way to sustain our life. And also without forgetting there were some relatives who would send us some coins to help us. At the moment it isn't easy. I need to go to school. And for the last three years one of my brothers has been going to school. The lack of school fees ... the lack of food at the table ... it has been very tough."

"It's an uphill climb," Celine sang, "and I'm feeling sorry ... "

When you live in extreme poverty like Collins and his brothers and you have trouble seeing beyond today's or tomorrow's meal, GiveDirectly's lump-sum payment always seems to come just in time. He had received his first payment of 440,000 shillings ($440) a year ago.

"When the money came, we sat down as a family and we discussed how we can use that money. I took [$100] to my brother's school, and then [$200] I took to my school fees, and then the remainder we just used in the house for our well-being. We bought clothes, food."

"Don't surrender," Celine sang, "'cause you can win."

His final installment was for $660. He spent $400 to pay his school and gave the rest to his brothers. The funds allowed him to go to school for another year and not drop out, which he'd had to do after his first year.

"I used to commute by bicycle my first year. But it was somehow hectic, very tiresome riding a bicycle a very long distance."

"How long would it take you?" I asked.

"It took me almost two hours."

"Holy smokes. So you were riding four hours per day?"

"I used to go just very slowly, slowly. It was very tiresome. I could not concentrate in class so I found a friend and we combined the little resources we had and found a house near [the school].

"When I dropped, some of my friends would say, 'Collins, where are you now? The semester has started and you are not around.' I like to socialize with people. I felt very bad. In fact, I saw it as the end of my life. I believe in education so much. Survival at times becomes very hard."

"Do you go hungry?" I asked.

"At school? Yes. A lot. Because everything is money. You have to photocopy a handout? You have to forgo breakfast, even forgo two meals – breakfast and lunch."

A friend who was sponsored through Unbound, an NGO based in Kansas City, would share his meals with him.

The GiveDirectly money was gone and he was looking for other sources of income. He went to his local government official, who offered some help, but "those who are helped are coming from good families with both parents," Collins said. "The neediest people in society, in fact, don't get the money at all."

When I met Collins he was visiting his other set of grandparents and helping prepare their fields for planting. When they are able to help him, they do, as does his aunt. But he wasn't just sitting around waiting for someone to help. He was working as a day laborer from 7:30 a.m. to 5:00 p.m. at a nearby construction site.

"They give us [$4] in one day and you have to buy food. You can eat something for [$0.70] and keep [$3.30]. It is hard work. It is not a joke. You have to be strong. You carry blocks and give them to the mason. Sometimes you mix the mortar. I'm not specialized, so I'm just the muscle."

I did the math on how many days of labor it would take him to cover the [$120] shortfall that would allow him to go to school. "So ... you'd have to work 181 days." As soon as I said the number, I wished I'd kept it to myself. Also, I'm really bad at math because actually he would have to work 36 days to afford school if he didn't pay any other expenses.

"Oh," he said, too kind to correct my math. "That's the reason I need to diversify my mind."

The waiter brought us sodas, and Collins, a dedicated Catholic and a member of his school's choir when he can afford to attend school, crossed himself.

"I just want to appreciate GiveDirectly. They've done for me a very wonderful thing. One day if I finish my education, I'll also be in that pool of helping others. I'll also try to make changes in people's lives."

I've been in financial straits before but nothing like Collins has. I've never gone without food. I've gone without vacations or dining out or cable. And most of the time when I've been in those situations, I thought about the things I would have when I turned things around. I never thought about what I'd give.

*Giving Rules: Let giving more motivate you to succeed.*

"That's what my book is about," I said. "This desire to help people, to feel this responsibility, but there is so much need and each of us has limited resources and time, so what do you do and how do you help? If GiveDirectly gave you [$100] to give to make a difference, what would you do with it?"

"I like education," he said. "I believe that education is power. I'd start with our local community and identify students with ability ... after further scrutiny and investigation, because you cannot give money to somebody who doesn't like school and push them to go to school ... from there I'll try to distribute so that it can help them. I'd give it myself. I want [to be] involved. Because I know if I'm in contact with the person I want to help, direct contact, I will know the problem they are encountering and how he or she needs [to be] helped."

> *Giving Rules: Giving locally connects you to people. Giving glob-*
> *ally connects you to causes.*

I thought that this journey and researching effective altruism would help me see beyond the individual, to do the greatest good I could do, that my heart wouldn't be stolen by the single story, but Collins was worthy. He was 27, and, if he graduated from university, it was likely his brothers would follow in his footpath. Helping him would help at least two others.

After we parted, I sent Collins $35 through the same mobile system that GiveDirectly uses for deposits. His aunt chipped in some more so he was able to enroll in school. A few months later he was struggling and he sent me a message:

> Brother, I have a kind request, but [if] it looks somehow bothering... just
> forgive me. I am humbly requesting you, if you might be in a good position,
> may you save me something to put in my stomach? Otherwise, thanks in
> advance and have a nice time.

I sent him another $15, and he sent me another note that it would allow him to eat for the rest of the month and give him time to concentrate on his studies.

I sent him another $35 a few months later so he could make his next school payment, allowing him to take his exams.

Will MacAskill calls this the 100 Times Multiplier. He writes:

> The fact that we've found ourselves at the top of the heap, globally speak-
> ing, provides us with a tremendous opportunity to make a difference.
> Because we are comparatively so rich, the amount by which we can benefit
> others is vastly greater than the amount by which we can benefit ourselves.
> We can therefore do a huge amount of good at relatively little cost.[11]

Money is less valuable the more you have of it. Let's say you make $16,000 a year, putting you in the top 10% of global earners. If your income doubles to $32,000 a year, your life will change, but nowhere

---

[11] William MacAskill, *Doing Good Better*, 46.

near as much as Collins's life would change if he went from earning $22 per month to $44 per month.

Thirty-five dollars is less than my family spends on one meal at Pizza King, our favorite local pizza joint. But $35 is enough for Collins to eat for a month or stay in school.

Maybe Sally Struthers was right. It was only a few cups of coffee to me and it was an education to Collins. But like many of the people I met in Kenya who received assistance from an NGO, he asked for more. The folks I met through GiveDirectly asked me if I could get their daughter enrolled in the program, or if I could talk to GiveDirectly about offering another lump sum or maybe a paid internship. A thousand dollars was enough to address immediate medical needs, to repair your house, to pay for a semester or year of school, but it wasn't enough.

GiveDirectly recognized this, and started doing something different and even more controversial.

# 12

# Money for Nothing
# (Kenya, 2017)

*Universal basic income / Proximity to need /*
*The poor are better givers*

---

**THE POSTER ON THE MUD WALL OF** Agrippa Onywero's one-room hut read: "Happiness is not perfected until it is shared."

The poster featured a white man and a white woman lying in a field of roses (ouch) and together intimately smelling a single rose. Beneath it, Agrippa clapped and sang a song that he had written for GiveDirectly.

He sang his song of thanks. His village was in GiveDirectly's universal basic income (UBI) program. Each month for the next 12 years he would receive $22, the poverty line in Kenya, from GiveDirectly. So would his brother and his mother and 6,000 other Kenyans living in 40 villages. GiveDirectly was also giving a short-term basic income for two years in 80 villages, and was monitoring a control group of 100 villages.

An independent contractor running randomized control trials monitors the programs. It's the largest UBI study in history. GiveDirectly admits that there is a lot of buzz and controversy around UBI, but there is not enough evidence. This is an experiment, and one impacting lives.

A year into the program, Agrippa, 39, had saved up his money to pay a dowry to his wife's family, and built this home on the far edge of his family's property for $150; next, he's thinking of saving up money for music lessons.

He sings the words for the song that he wrote on the back of a flyer for a herbalist promising to treat problems such as epilepsy, evil spirits, bewitchment, erectile dysfunction, infertility, financial problems, employment issues, and relationship challenges.

"I want to bring music into the light," Agrippa said, as rain pounded on his tin roof and fingers of water crept across the dirt floor through his front door.

It hasn't been all roses for Agrippa. His wife recently left him for a reason he doesn't offer. His father died years ago and his brother was the breadwinner of the family working in Nairobi for the Kenyan Ministry of Trade. But then his brother was injured in the 1998 bombing of the US embassy in Nairobi. Now Agrippa says his brother is "mad" – he has mental health issues. When his brother wandered over, Agrippa lovingly redirected him back to his own mud hut on the other side of the property.

Before UBI, Agrippa occasionally earned money making charcoal to sell and also working in the fields of his neighbors. Rainy days like this were good for selling charcoal, he told me; wood was wet and the rain was cold.

He had seen changes in his own life and in his village.

"Now I can eat well. I can do some singing. Before, eating was difficult, but now at least I can buy meat, rice. Before, I was just taking supper only. Now I eat more. I can plan with the money. It doesn't give me much stress. Now I'm comfortable … I can see people building houses … farming. People are starting businesses, joining [saving] groups. There is development. There was a problem farming here because there was no money."

He was laid back, maybe a little too laid back. And a lot of his answers about his plans didn't jive. He wanted to save for music lessons, but had no idea how much they cost. He seemed to think he could take two months of lessons and be really good. He wanted to be a professional musician, but wasn't sure what that meant. Would he sing at parties? Would he record music to sell? He had no real plan, and John, my translator, and I were both puzzled by his uncertainty.

The biggest criticism of giving cash directly to the poor is that they'll become idle, that with their basic needs met they won't be driven to give back to society. GiveDirectly is this mix of the libertarian notion that individuals know what's best for themselves and the liberal idea of assistance to the poor: Here are your bootstraps; we're not going to tell you how to pull yourself up by them or require that you even try, but we'll watch with interest and we'll keep sending you money.

I had the suspicion that Agrippa was drinking a portion of his money. Yet he still saved enough to build his house, and, if he was drinking some part of his transfers, he was likely spending that money locally at least.

Will people spend some of their income on alcohol and cigarettes and drugs? Of course, but less than they spent before. A small percentage of the sale of the book you are reading will go toward donuts – and it will also go toward sending my kids to college. My income has about the same amount of strings as Agrippa's. Researchers at the World Bank found that more than 80% of those receiving transfers spent less on booze and cigarettes after receiving the funds, and less than 5% spent more.[1] The report concluded: "We should stop worrying that the poor are going to spend (or 'waste') their transfer income on alcohol and tobacco. They aren't. They might buy some chocolate, though."[2]

> **Giving Rules: We should worry about wasted human potential as much as we worry about wasted donations.**

They also might become givers themselves like Benter Wandolo, a great-grandma, businesswoman, and farmer (see Figure 12.1). She doesn't spend money on herself, not even on a pair of earrings, but prefers her money to multiply.

"I love farming," she said, sitting across from me, a table of tomatoes between us. "I make sure there is always food. The last transfer I bought tomato seeds. I will sell tomatoes and use the income to pay for my [grand]children's school fees."

Hopefully, an investment in education will allow her grandkids to earn more money than a tomato, chicken, maize, or fish farmer. Benter grows and raises it all. The universal basic income was the first formal, regular income she had ever received, and it has given her the freedom to invest.

I asked if I could take a photo of her, and she told me that she was too "shaggy" and disappeared to change. I sat on one of the many couches covered in bedsheets and doilies – a classic grandma move. There were enough couches to seat 18 people, which would not be enough to accomodate the family tree that she had created: seven children,

---

[1] David K. Evans and Anna Popova, "Cash Transfers and Temptation Good: A Review of Global Evidence," Policy Research Working Paper 6886, World Bank Africa Region (May 1, 2014).

[2] Rosamaría Dasso and Fernando Fernandez, "Temptation Goods and Conditional Cash Transfers in Peru" (September 24, 2013).

*Figure 12.1     Benter surveying her greenhouse.*

13 grandchildren, and five great-grandchildren. Their pictures lined the walls – weddings and graduations. It was obvious from the pictures and by the size of her property; the numbers of buildings, greenhouses, and couches; and the presence of a tractor in her courtyard that Benter had been successful before GiveDirectly.

When she returned, I asked her what she thought of the criticisms leveled at giving cash to the poor.

"I support the view that if you get a little money, you multiply money," Benter said. "That's what I've done."

Benter contributed funds to build the local school, a short walk from her house. Those who didn't have money to contribute sent cow dung to school with their students to be mixed with dirt and water to form the mortar. She also pools funds with her neighbors to contribute to families in need.

### Giving Rules: Giving creates giving.

Giving isn't a zero-sum game. And it turns out that proximity to need inspires more giving.

The World Giving Index ranked Kenya as the third most generous nation in 2017, behind Myanmar and Indonesia.

"Research has shown that when people have money and they are surrounded by a great deal of need they become more generous," says Adam Pickering, international program director for the Charities Aid Foundation (CAF).

This holds true in the US as well. *The Chronicle of Philanthropy* discovered "a compelling, counterintuitive finding" when researchers compared where wealth resides in the US versus where people are giving the most. Counties where people have the least, such as those in the South, give the highest percentage of their income. And counties whose residents have the most, such as in New England, give the lowest percentage.[3]

The proximity to need may be why African countries have seen such an uptick in their giving rank in 2017. Africa is the only continent to see an increase in all three giving behaviors in CAF's World Giving Index in 2017. Eight African nations (Kenya, Ghana, Zambia, Sierra Leone, Liberia, Zimbabwe, South Africa, and Tunisia) are among the 13 most improved countries that year.

"The big story this year is the amazing rise in giving across Africa," said Sir John Low, CAF's chief executive. "Around the world, economic development is lifting the income of millions of people, and it is truly humbling to see that the natural reaction to increasing wealth is to give back."[4]

---

[3]Rebecca Koenig, "A Mismatch Between Need and Affluence," *The Chronicle of Philanthropy*, www.philanthropy.com/interactives/how-america-gives-opportunity-index (March 12, 2018).

[4]Charities Aid Foundation, "Giving in Africa Climbs as Western World Falters Says CAF World Giving Index," www.cafonline.org/about-us/media-office/giving-in-africa-climbs-as-western-world-falters-says-caf-world-giving-index (September 5, 2017).

Kenyan Caroline Teti, GiveDirectly's external relations director, pointed out that there is only one word on the Kenyan coat of arms: *harambee*. It's Swahili, meaning: "all pull together."

"I think the *harambee* spirit has inculcated in Kenyans a strong sense of giving," Teti told me. "People traditionally view individual pressure as a matter that should concern the whole community. In many communities in Kenya, people gave materially to other community members under distress. Post-independence, I think this took a totally new dimension as people looked to improve the education of their clansmen and the larger community."

Benter and her husband, Samson, a retired police officer who tends to his small fish farm on Lake Victoria, invest and give to their community. They earn around $9,000 per year through their various business ventures, making them one of the most well-to-do families in the village. They employ two part-time workers. Benter and her husband don't need the money to survive; they invest it. She estimated that they've doubled their GiveDirectly money.

A study of a cash program in Uganda found that recipients earned on average 40 cents more through other means for every dollar they were given.[5] Benter and Samson were growing their own business, but they were also creating opportunities for others.

They were skeptical, as well, when they first heard about the universal basic income.

"Most of the locals thought it was a project supported by President Barack Obama," Benter said. "I told my brother, 'Even if it is from Obama, it was a great thing.' People in grass thatch houses could spend their money on other things to improve their lives. I was very happy about the program. The young men and women who were involved in crime – breaking into houses and stealing chickens and utensils – that has gone down because now they have income. Also, the elderly basically had no one to help them. Now they have an income and they can buy food and get what they need. This area is prone to starvation and hunger because of the climate situation. We have a very limited planting season. But now people have money to buy food and are able to fight hunger."

During the tour of her farm Benter was always tending. When she unlocked the door to her recently constructed chicken coop, the chickens

---

[5]Christopher Blattman, Nathan Fiala, and Sebastian Martinez, "The Economic and Social Returns to Cash Transfers: Evidence from a Ugandan Aid Program" (April 2013), 21.

erupted in excitement. The room was dark, and when Benter clicked on her flashlight the beam of dust fell on a dead chicken, which she picked up to dispose. In her greenhouse that she hopes to expand, she picked at the dead leaves on her tomatoes. One day she hopes to buy a cow with her savings and name it GiveDirectly.

She was thankful for GiveDirectly, but she wondered if it could double the amount. Twenty-two dollars wasn't very much money. She could use more.

That's the sentiment I heard repeatedly: We are thankful, but could we have more?

Another great-grandma, Magdalena, echoed the same thing. She wasn't as well off as Benter, but she was thankful for the funds that allowed her to spend less time working in the fields. It was hard; she was not as young as she once was, and the climate had changed, making farming even less reliable. She sat on her single couch next to her two granddaughters and a toddler wearing a reindeer shirt.

Thunder rattled in the distance announcing a storm on Lake Victoria while a hammer on a metal roof somewhere made its own thunder. If she had more money she would cement her house, send her grandchildren to school, and maybe build a cistern to catch the rainfall.

"The money boosts parents," Magdalena said. "It encourages kids. It sends kids to school and buys decent clothes. It allows people to feel worth."

"Feel worth." It was an odd phrase, maybe just an awkward translation, but it reminded me of the line in the popular Christmas carol, "O Holy Night": " … and the soul felt its worth."

The rain started. And when it rains, it rains on everyone; the rain isn't selective. It rains on thatched roofs and metal. It rains on the flowers and the weeds. It rains on those who give and those who receive. Together they feel worth.

*Giving Rules: Economically, there are haves and have-nots. But strategically, the haves may not have the best ideas of how to help the have-nots.*

# 13

# No Justice, No Peace (Kenya, 2017)

*Election chaos / Freedom versus aid / Legacy of colonialism / Human rights / Maslow's Hierarchy of Needs*

---

**MOM THOUGHT WE WERE BEING ABDUCTED.** But it was worse than that.

Her flight had landed in Nairobi at the absolute worst time of the past 10 years. After days of contention in the presidential race, the election commission had declared incumbent Joseph Kenyatta the winner. Nairobi had essentially been closed since the election – stores were boarded up, and the streets of the city of 3 million people were empty. The few times I had ventured out, it felt like the excitement and anticipation of Christmas met the hesitation and fear of a zombie apocalypse.

For Mom's sake, I tried to pretend like I wasn't afraid and made small talk about in-flight movies and how seriously London airport security took liquids left in your luggage. I looked at the crappy car's fuel gauge buried on E as the driver pulled into another gas station.

Mom thought that the driver was looking for someone to meet up with at the gas station to pass us on into some tourist trafficking ring.

But I sensed his fear, and Mom sensed mine. All the stations were closed. There were no other cabs, no cars, no one.

Residents of the slums supported the challenger, Raila Odinga, and any news about the results led to violence spilling out onto the streets. Reports of gunshots and roadblocks were already filling up social media channels. There were protesters on the street, legitimately protesting election results that would be overturned and later reaffirmed, and there were those who took advantage of the chaos to loot and create their own justice and injustice. I hated to even think about what would happen to us if our car ran out of gas in the wrong place at the wrong time.

"Welcome to Kenya! Welcome to Africa!" I told Mom, still trying to convince her and myself that everything was cool.

The driver pulled into the fourth closed gas station before giving up and making a run for our hotel.

*What kind of an idiot doesn't start this night, of all nights, with a full tank?*

If he ran out of gas, I was going to kill him myself, but we made it.

He dropped us at our hotel behind a guarded gate and drove back into the night. It was only then that I started to feel any compassion for the driver. I hoped he made it back.

To calm our nerves, Mom and I each had a Tusker beer at the outdoor bar. That was when the gunshots began.

It was like a reverse post-traumatic stress disorder. The sound of fireworks made me happy, and then the realization that they weren't fireworks, scared me. The shots sounded close. At first they popped with the frequency of an Independence Day's grand finale, or a war zone, and then faded off into a shot here and there and then silence.

"I'll take the first watch," I told Mom, when we made it back to our room. That's something I always wanted to say, something the tough guys in the movies who can fight off terrible things in the night, say. But it's not so cool when you mean it.

At 2 a.m. a shot closer than all the rest – seemingly just outside the wall of our hotel – slammed into something. I put on my shoes and got ready for whatever. I've heard gunshots. I live in rural Indiana and my neighbors seem to have an arsenal, but the thunder of a shot has a different meaning when you know they aren't directed at a target, but at a person. And then there was silence. No sirens. No yells. Dead silence.

The police had shot someone at our gate. I was conflicted how to feel about that. I had spent the previous week with people who feared the police.

I told Mom to go back to sleep as I peeked through the curtains of our first-floor room. I sat still and focused my hearing out into the night beyond the walls, searching for threats on the edge of reality and imagination.

At 4 a.m. the front gate squeaked open. *Here they come*, I thought.

I peeked through the curtain, my heart racing.

Mom sat up. "What's wrong?"

"Nothing. I heard the gate. Wait … there are people walking this way!" I yell-whispered.

I went to a different window, not because there was a better perspective, but simply because I was full of nervous energy and had no idea what to do. *Eyes. Throat. Groin.* I was prepared to go for all the places you weren't supposed to go for in my college kung fu class. A man dressed all in black was waving his arms as he walked next to another man.

*Here they come!*

Then I recognized the guy as a fellow guest, walking next to a security guard. I was awake the rest of the night.

I've rarely felt more afraid, trapped, and exposed to the violence of the world, than I did that night sitting in that hotel behind high walls with electric fencing and a guard.

The night was just a small taste of what daily life was like for so many, including the friends that I had spent time with leading up to the election, who lived in the slums.

Their night and the days following were much different.

"We are safe, Kelsey, and forced to stay indoors during the night," texted Rozy Mbone, the leader of a group known as the Legend of Kenya that promotes peace in the slums. "So far one man was killed by angry mob who were supporting Raila. Criminals also took advantage of looting and breaking into people's shops. One of our members has been shot dead."

Others sent me pictures through WhatsApp of people beaten, shot, and killed in the slums. For some reason the photos would automatically populate my photo album, so a man with his brains literally on the street next to him were adjacent to a picture of my kids' first day of school, which I had missed for this trip.

There were also pictures of Rozy and her team helping the wounded, holding peace rallies, and giving at great risk.

Days before Mom arrived and one day before the election, peace activist Selline Korir first introduced me to Rozy outside Nairobi's downtown bus station. Selline had been doing peace work since 1993.

"The 1996 election was way worse than 2007," Selline told me, "but everyone has short memories."

The 2007 election was the one that claimed the life of Thomas and Moses's brother in Mathare. It was pretty bad, but Selline didn't have a good feeling about this election either.

It was a Sunday and Selline was dressed for church. She swallowed Rozy with a hug.

Rozy, wearing a cowboy shirt, her hair twisted into tight braids, looked down to avoid eye contact with me, as Selline told me about her.

The Rozy Selline described seemed different from the one who stood before me.

That Rozy was a former gang leader turned peace activist in the slum community of Korogocho. Korogocho (Swahili for shoulder-to-shoulder) is an informal settlement (the politically correct way to say slum) of 0.57 square miles of private and government land, housing 200,000 people. The community has been labeled a "no-go" for many nongovernmental organizations (NGOs) and the international community since the violent killing of a 2004 Zambian diplomat. He was kidnapped and shot by gang members, all while his five-year-old son watched. Then they left the son in the car tied to his father's body with seatbelts.

"Korogocho is the last stop; you can't fall any further short of being totally destitute or dead," a local aid worker told a Scottish journalist.[1]

Selline had first entered Korogocho when Rozy was still a gang member. She was told that if she wanted to expand her work into Korogocho, she would need the blessing and protection of Rozy. Selline had faced down remote tribal leaders in lawless lands who listened to her with rifles across their laps, yet she had still been nervous the first time she met Rozy, and for good reason: Someone had attended the meeting to kill. I'll get to that in a bit.

Selline and Rozy held hands like mother and daughter as we crossed the street. Not all drivers would take us to Korogocho and wait for us in case we "needed to escape." Selline called one who would.

We said good-bye to Selline and got into the car, passing by Mathare, where I had spent the night seven years ago. How different could Korogocho be? I asked Rozy to compare.

"Korogocho has a lot of crime. Mathare doesn't, but sometimes those criminals feeling the heat in Korogocho hide out in Mathare.

---

[1]David Pratt, "The Women of the World's Worst Slums," *The Herald* (December 10, 2011).

Korogocho is always dangerous. In Mathare, the danger is just during political season."

A man stared intently at me as we made our way through a roundabout on the edge of Korogocho. He looked past me to Rozy and she gave him a thumbs-up. She told me that people have been robbed at this roundabout, and that she has made a point of staying friends with gang members.

Korogocho sits on the edge of the Dandora Municipal dump where 6,000 laborers scavenge for around $2.50 in findings each day. International law dictated that the dump should have closed 27 years ago, and the Nairobi City Council declared the dump was full 16 years ago, but then reconsidered when they realized they could buy more time and layers if they pushed the trash toward the center.[2]

Rozy told me that food makes its way into the dump from all over the city, including my hotel's location. It occurred to me that I threw away my leftovers last night and someone we passed could have been eating them. I wasn't sure how to feel about that – wasteful or glad that I didn't eat everything.

Tall stacks of polypropylene sacks full of plastic that had been collected and washed lined the road. Fifteen full bags fetched about $10.

Our driver asked Rozy where he should wait; then we got out and walked toward a blue tin church where a sermon blasted from speakers.

*Great. I'm going to have to make a speech.*

We marched down the center aisle and approached the altar, passing the preacher. Rozy pulled back a curtain hanging on the back wall and led me through a door with squeaky hinges into a secret room like some sort of superhero's hidden fortress – and it sort of was, but much smaller. I couldn't stand straight up, and the depth of the room was barely two shoulder-widths. There were three stools in the room, and one of them had only three legs.

One by one Rozy's team entered.

Soon there were seven of us in the room, each connected to the others by shoulder or knee or foot that touched. A spark would've jolted us all.

They are the Legend of Kenya. That's the official name of their peace-promoting group. It seemed awkward to me at first. Shouldn't "legend" be plural? Weren't they "legends," since there were seven of them?

---

[2]Micah Albert, "Kenya Poor Cling to Dump Site," *The Sacramento Bee* (April 20, 2012).

Rozy told me a little about their work, helping people overcome trauma through sharing stories. Eighty percent of residents in Korogocho have been directly impacted by violence. The group works between the police and the community to reduce violence and call for an ambulance when necessary.

I started in with questions.

"What did you do before?" I asked Stephen to my left.

There wasn't silence because only a bedsheet and a rusty section of metal separated us from the ranting preacher, but it felt like silence. They looked at one another as if deciding if they were going to share. Rozy officially introduced me and told them what I was doing. I stopped asking questions and just listened.

Kelvin went first.

"Many of my friends have been killed," he said.

Kelvin who had worked with Rozy when she was a criminal, was involved in the postelection violence of 2007. After Rozy had left the gang and started her peace efforts, she recruited Kelvin to join her.

"When Rozy first approached me, I told her to go away. I told her that I was going to work first and then maybe [join her]."

Now Kelvin is in college.

Next, Stephen decided he would share his story.

"I'm a victim of crime and I'm a criminal. I used to do bad things. My mind was corrupt. I was totally evil."

He feared mob justice, where, once the community has had enough, they beat you, lay you across a tire, and then light you on fire.

"Now I'm proud to be an agent of peace and a good person," he said.

"The darkest and best parts of him are in this community," Rozy said. "People remember him as he was and as he is."

Now Stephen volunteers at a local hospital. "An idle mind is the devil's workshop," he said.

> *Giving Rules: "It's easier to act your way into a new way of thinking than to think your way into a new way of acting." – Millard Fuller, founder of Habitat for Humanity*

Tyson, sitting on the three-legged stool, was an acrobat. He was born into a family of four and dropped out after primary school to earn money through crime.

"Life was hard. When you grow up you are supposed to take care of your family. I started with petty crimes like phone snatching. I'd go outside of the neighborhood to steal. I made other friends while participating in criminal activities."

He started to break into people's homes while they were sleeping to steal electronics.

"Some of my friends were caught and beaten to death. It was bad luck for them, I thought, but I couldn't quit. How would we survive?"

He was arrested. Beaten. Escaped from prison. But he met other criminals there who led him to bigger crimes, a whole other level. He couldn't stop. His father wasn't around and he had two siblings and his mom to provide for.

"The reason I stopped – a carjacking. My friend was shot dead. I was afraid."

The singing from the church escalated.

Rozy chimed in to tell me, and perhaps remind Tyson, who he was now: an acrobat who combined his talent with theater performances. Tyson scrolled through his phone as she talked and then held out a picture of a charred body in the middle of a dusty street.

"We keep pictures so we don't forget," he said.

"Then Rozy … ," he added, telling how he had joined the Legend of Kenya. He also joined a troop of acrobats and now does yoga and karate and trains children for free "to give them a skill." He leads peace facilitations.

Neileh's hair was dyed red, she has a dolphin nose ring, and her eyebrows were painted on perfectly. She has two kids, a 12-year-old daughter and a 6-year-old son.

"My mom left when I was 3. At 11 I turned to prostitution. One guy all night for [50 cents]. I started to carry a gun … stealing was better than working as a prostitute."

She was a prostitute for four years and then went to school to learn to do hair.

"She just did my hair," Tyson chimed in. He paid her 30 cents.

"We try to support each other like that," Rozy said.

"We don't have a lot of money," Stephen added, "but it's a peaceful life."

"Are you able to get jobs?" I asked, interrupting the string of soliloquies.

"If eating is a problem," Rozy said, "how can you buy a job?"

Jobs required appropriate papers and bribes. None of them had the resources for either.

Then it was Samson's turn. He was raised by a single mom and comes from a family of 11. "I'm the tenth," he said. Growing up, he got one meal per day … maybe. "Some days nothing." He started collecting materials around the dump at 11 or 12. Life was tough on less than $1 per day. He started to traffic guns.

"We lost Stephen's brother. They threw him in the river with the crocs and his hands chained," he speculated. "You can't ask the government about it. He just disappeared."

Then he lost his friend who was nicknamed Highway because he'd rob people on the highway. Highway was caught and a mob drove nails into him until he died while Samson watched.

"That's when I met Rozy … "

I expected his story to turn positive like everyone else's at this point, but he grew more somber.

"After my reform in August of 2015, they came looking for me." Criminals pay illegal taxes to the police, and it had been two years since he had paid. "I was reformed, but not in their eyes. In theirs I still owed them."

"I have a twin … seven bullets and I lost him. They shot him in front of his family. Even if you are reformed, you still live in fear. The team helped me bury him in the village."

Samson shifted gears to talk about the value he saw in himself.

"I'm a good organizer," he said. "When you listen good, you talk good. I've stood in front of a thousand people and talked."

"When you are doing something you are passionate about," Rozy added, "you feel happy."

**Giving Rules: Help others see the good in themselves.**

The seventh legend entered. George had a grin on his face and it takes only a half second to like him. He introduced himself as "George Bush" and passed out handshakes and hugs before showing us a video of him standing at the head of the Raila Odinga rally that had just taken place.

"Politicians have money. They use us," George said. "They pay you [$50] to beat someone."

"This election is dealing with issues of fairness," Rozy said.

Democracy is a story we tell each other, and it functions only if we believe the story. After the election of 2007, more and more Kenyans started to view their democracy as a fiction. The structures that led to the disbelief date back further.

Under British rule, officials created divisions among ethnic groups to prevent them from uniting against the government. These divisions have been exploited by politicians. Daniel arap Moi, who was the president from 1972 to 2002, fanned the ethnic divisions, hiring groups of armed men to protect his party's interests.[3]

---

[3]Stephanie Hanson, "Understanding Kenya's Politics," *The Washington Post* (January 28, 2008).

I talked with several people throughout Kenya who had received payments for their votes through the years. Some voters can earn $25 on election day "voting" for various candidates.

A 2014 report found that 50% of Kenya's wealth was in the hands of political families, including the Kenyatta and the Odinga families.[4] Incumbent president Uhuru Kenyatta, the son of Kenya's first president, was listed by *Forbes* as the 26th wealthiest person in Africa. He has "at least" 500,000 acres of land across the country, and owns the nation's largest dairy, a commercial bank, and part of a popular TV station.[5]

So there's all that, plus the fact that a few weeks before the election, an election official was killed. There were rumors that the ruling party did it so they could tamper with the election results. Others thought the opposing party killed him so they could claim the election had been rigged.

So, in this void of trust and truth and opportunity, where the unheard speak through violence, the Legend of Kenya meet in the back of a church each day. They organize debates between local candidates on all sides.

We left the secret hideout, escaped the music, and walked down the street (see Figure 13.1).

"Welcome to our chocolate city," George said. Korogocho sloped toward the base of the dump where the rusted roofs were the color of milk chocolate and the mud homes were the color of dark. Laundry dried on the roofs next to large stones that sat atop scraps of rubber, plastic, and any other material that would keep the water out.

Next we visited Rozy's home. She lived with Neileh and Neileh's mother, grandmother, and two kids. At night they had to move the furniture to make room for them all to sleep on the floor. They pay $30 per month for the home, which is more than some homes cost because they had a door that locks.

We walked down the street from Rozy's home and turned toward a stream that was actually the Nairobi River.

"On some maps the Kenyan government has the dump and the community listed as a park," Rozy said.

We walked next to the river, in which two kids played not far from two bloated, floating dead dogs.

"You often can find dead and aborted babies in the river," Rozy said.

---

[4]Patrick Nzioka and Bernard Namunane, "Political Families Own Half of Private Wealth," *Daily Nation* (February 20, 2014).
[5]www.forbes.com/lists/2011/89/africa-billionaires-11_Uhuru-Kenyatta_FO2Q
.html (2011).

*Figure 13.1    The Legend of Kenya (From left to right): Samson, Neileh, Tyson, Rozy, Kelvin, and George.*

Two men washed plastic bags in the river. The Dandora dump was on the other side of the river. Excavators crept like dinosaurs and prehistoric storks circled those who picked through the trash. The mountain rose, plateaued, and stretched as far as I could see as if it were the end of the world.

The flat layer of trash on our left was actually a pond so filled with trash that the water couldn't be seen.

"There is an anaconda in there," Samson told me.

When I asked how big it was, I was expecting a length defined by arms. Instead, Samson made the biggest possible circle he could with his arms to show its girth.

Spontaneous flames sprouted next to our path and we had to step around them and push through a wall of smoke. I felt the flame. I breathed in the noxious fumes.

A 2007 study by the UN Environmental Program found that soil samples here contained "dangerously high levels of lead," and that nearly half of children tested suffered from respiratory issues and had lead levels in their blood much higher than what was internationally acceptable.[6]

"We are going to the temple," Tyson said, as we left the valley of trash.

I'm not sure what he meant by "temple." Maybe it was another house of worship.

On the way uphill there was an exposed pipe at the bottom of an intersection in the middle of the road.

"That's clean water," Rozy said.

"You mean dirty?" I asked.

"No, we drink that. Any water that is moving is okay. This is dirty." She pointed to a mud puddle. "We could use that, too, but it takes a lot of work."

"Korogocho ends here," Rozy said at a small bridge. Then she pointed out how nice this other community was. This was the ghetto, they said, which was a step up from the slum. In the ghetto, the homes have locking doors and better construction – bricks. It's not the government land and is more permanent and legal.

In the slum, the government could take away their homes overnight. There were rumors that the government was thinking of moving the dump, and the people protested. It was the only opportunity in town. When a politician needs the votes of Korogocho residents, he claims his opponent wants to close the dump and rob the scavengers of their livelihood.

The 1948 United Nations General Assembly drafted The Universal Declaration of Human Rights, including 30 articles, which I'll quickly summarize:

We are all born free and equal; these rights apply to everyone; everyone has the right to life, liberty, and security of person; no slavery; no torture; rights apply to everyone everywhere; we're all equal in the eyes of the law; human rights are protected by law; no unfair imprisonment;

---

[6]Micah Albert, "Kenya Poor Cling to Dump Site."

the right to a trial; we're all innocent until proven guilty; right to privacy; freedom to move; the right to seek a safe place to live; everyone has the right to a nationality; right to marry; right to own property; freedom of opinion and expression; right to assemble; equal right to participate in government and elections and receive government services; right to affordable housing, medicine, education, and child care, and enough income to live on; the equal right to work; equal right to leisure and periodic holidays with pay; right to a standard of living adequate for well-being; right to education; copyright protection; a fair and free world in which rights are realized; the responsibility to help others and protect their rights and freedoms; no one can take away your human rights.

One jumps out at me as different, so I'll quote it directly from the original preamble: "Article 29: Everyone has duties to the community in which alone the free and full development of his personality is possible."[7]

### *Giving Rules: Those who have received have a duty to give.*

While the rest seem like declarations of rights, some straight out of the US Bill of Rights, Article 29 is more of a commandment: "You have a duty to help others." The Legend of Kenya members are living this each day even though, by my count, more than half of the other human rights aren't present in their lives.

This is what economist William Easterly points out is wrong with the outside-expert or "technocratic" approach to aid that supports the real cause of poverty: "the unchecked power of the state against poor people without rights."[8]

The international aid community supported Moi as he divided Kenya. Money poured in to give the poor access to food, water, and medicine, while ignoring how the government was squashing or ignoring the citizens' human rights. We've supported worse autocrats, and when asked about promoting democracy, the response is often that aid organizations don't get involved in politics. When Easterly asked the World Bank, an international financial organization, why the word *democracy* is not mentioned in its governance report, he was told the organization is not legally allowed, according to its own charter, to mention the word.

In Maslow's Hierarchy of Needs, "security" is the second step up just above biological needs – food and water. Security is more important

---

[7]United Nations, "The Universal Declaration of Human Rights," www.un.org/en/udhrbook/pdf/udhr_booklet_en_web.pdf (2015).
[8]William Easterly, *The Tyranny of Experts* (New York: Basic Books, 2013), 5–7.

than love and belonging and it is a need that, along with freedom, the aid community often overlooks.

Easterly argues that feeding a dictator's people is aiding and abetting the dictator, actually helping to keep him in power. And aid dictated by outsiders in a model that was developed between 1919 and 1949 is steeped in colonialism and racism. He concluded that "[d]evelopment ideas took shape before there was even the most minimal respect in the West for the rights of individuals in the Rest."[9]

Martin Luther King Jr., speaking out against the war in Vietnam, stated: "There can be no justice without peace and there can be no peace without justice." Rozy and her friends were living proof of that.

> *Giving Rules: If helping people makes them less free, we aren't helping them at all.*

We walked down a steep hill toward a grassy area with a few discarded tires. This was the temple. It wasn't a building at all, just a place where there was space away from people – a temple of solitude. Three rocks marked the entrance. Tyson bowed before entering.

Tyson did some crazy gymnastic things – balancing on two rocks with his arms and putting his legs out in front of him before rotating them back behind him and up into a handstand.

He did some pushups and then wanted me try. I put my arms on the rocks while he held my legs. They asked me to do 10. I did. It was a small testimonial to, an expense my monthly CrossFit membership that could send two of them to college for a year. They cheered.

Tyson did some flips and George tried, getting close. This is the location where Tyson gives gymnastic lessons to kids. Where he finds his worth and purpose. Some who have trained in the temple are performing in Saudi Arabia, and the team performing in China just had their contract renewed for two years. Tyson and Rozy told me this without a hint of jealousy. They were proud that the temple, their refuge, was a way out for some of their friends, and could be for more.

Rozy walked with me over to a tire in the shade of a tree while the others continued flipping and twisting.

Rozy was ready to share her story.

"You have to make sure that your courage covers other people's fears," she said, and I nearly fell off the tire trying to scribble the quote in my notebook.

It's a lesson she learned from Selline Korir.

---

[9]Ibid., 44.

# 14

## Giving Is Immeasurable: Change One, Change 100 (Kenya, 2017)

*Waging peace on warriors / Stepping-stones in the river of life / Education as a path out of poverty*

---

**SELLINE FELT AS IF HER BLOOD** were freezing.

The local pastors pleaded with her not to go. They warned that the warriors would kill her. They had killed women and children waiting for inoculations at a medical clinic. Why wouldn't they kill her?

She ignored the warnings.

She walked through the column of Pokot warriors. They were well organized and well armed, accessing weapons from nearby Uganda that even the Kenyan government couldn't get.

The government didn't want her there, either. Often the government instigated violence with the group, so they felt Selline and her talk of peace and reconciliation were an affront to their authority.

The leaders of the warriors sat in chairs, their manhood covered only by thin cords and AK-47s.

The National Council of Churches in Kenya had posted her to the region experiencing ethnic clashes in the early 1990s. When she first arrived, she felt as though they had brought her there to die. "You could feel the hostility," she said.

But her faith gave her courage.

"I'm serving a God of justice, a God who wants us to love. Looking at people who seem unlovable by society, I see them as clients. I want to reach out to them with love and service. My faith encourages me to give [rather] than to receive ... You look at people and they are looking for hope ... My faith gives me the opportunity to embrace the spirituality in peace building. Human beings are just not to be judged."

Selline had convinced two pastors to go with her. She gave them courage, even though she was terrified herself.

The tall pastor was the first to address the warriors. The first time he met with Selline – then a young, petite woman, from outside his community – he demeaned her by asking, "What is this *thing* looking for?" But her fearlessness, faith, and persistence had won him over.

The pastor introduced Selline and translated her words. The other pastor looked on as Selline addressed the leaders of a male-dominated culture. He would become Selline's husband.

As she talked with them, Selline thought, "My goodness, these people are actually human beings with feelings fighting because of grievances they don't understand. Fighting because they feel neglected, because they have a government that is so brutal. They have a government that doesn't care about them."

The Pokot warriors talked about issues regarding their boundaries and how no one listened to them. Selline listened and documented everything. It was the beginning of an 18-month peace process that would end with the Pokot warriors turning over their machine guns.

Selline has dedicated her career and life to the poor, downtrodden, and unloved. She could relate to them. As a girl, she would wake up at 3 a.m. to fetch water in a five-gallon jerrican – a four-hour round trip. When she returned, she would grab her books and run to school. Her father had several wives, and Selline's mother was the outcast.

"We never got things like shoes, clothes. I borrowed people's shoes and clothes ... My father and the other wives were enjoying a lot of good. We had to weed people's farms to get a little coin to buy pencils [and] to put food on the table. My mother worked hard. She never went to school. But she used to tell us education is the only solution."

In many ways Selline's mother was a human rights activist. She fought for what was right and just. She fought for the community. She hosted *wazungu* on her farm to teach a clinic on growing cotton. When they were done, they asked how they could repay her. She asked them to dig a well for her community to use so women and children didn't have to spend so much of their time and energy getting water. They agreed. When a rich man in the community tried to fence off the well and claim it as his own, she fought him. Twenty years later, on her deathbed, she was still fighting and told Selline never to let the man fence it off.

Selline's brother had won a scholarship to Cambridge, but turned it down. What was the point of getting an education and talking fancy if you came home and your mother and siblings were dead? Selline's mom sold two cows to pay for him to go to Nairobi to get a job. He worked at East African Airways and put Selline through school.

*Giving Rules: Working a 9-to-5 job to support your family may be the greatest gift you ever give.*

Selline went to a high school for the blind where she was one of six sighted students. The school gave her an education and an opportunity to serve people. She would read to her classmates and was amazed at how they could quote passages. She became a champion for the school and for her classmates.

Selline studied abroad in India and completed her master's in economics in 1993. While in India she was appalled by the caste system and spent a lot of her free time in the slums meeting people and listening to them.

It was in her role as director of Kenya Tuna Uwezo (Kishwahili for "Kenya, we have the power to change"), a program of Global Communities and supported by the US Agency for International Development (USAID), that she first met Rozy.

———

Rozy was born and raised in Korogocho, the fourth of six children. Her father's mother, a prominent political figure in the community, never approved of Rozy's mother, who sold bread and worked nights in a club. Rozy's mother contracted AIDS and the grandmother forced her to live somewhere else. Rozy was four years old when her parents separated.

Rozy's eldest brother got into crime. He went to prison for trying to rob the president's motorcade. She dreamed of going to university, but it was safer to join a gang.

In 2007, Rozy started to live a life of crime. She could read, write, and speak English, so she rose to a leadership position.

Rozy has lived a life with too many remembered dates. On November 6, 2008, her boyfriend was gunned down by the police. Rozy was devastated and shortly after learned she was two weeks pregnant with his child. His parents blamed Rozy for his death.

"I felt so bad," Rozy said. "I couldn't stop selling drugs and weed."

On July 9, 2009, despite the advice of friends who said she should kill the baby so she could find a new boyfriend, she had a baby boy.

When Selline came to Korogocho for a pilot project, someone referred her to Rozy a known and respected gang member, who could vouch for her. Before their first meeting, Rozy got high.

"People came," Rozy remembered. "Waves of bad people."

Samson, The Legend of Kenya member who had the twin who was mistakenly killed, came. He had heard that the director of Kenya Tuna Uwezo was coming to a meeting and that directors of NGOs usually have a lot of jewelry and carry laptops and other valuables that you can steal. He came to kill and rob Selline.

But Selline knew how to dress. She wore a traditional dress and shoes like blocks. She had short hair, and no wig that could be sold. She didn't wear jewelry. To Samson, she wasn't worth killing. Even so, he agonized over the decision, wondering if he had done the right thing by not killing her or if he had lost an opportunity. Later, he would confess all of this to Selline and tell her that if he had killed her, he would have lost a mother.

> *Giving Rules: The way you dress may not connect you to the people you are helping, but it certainly can remove you from them.*

When Selline first met Rozy, Rozy wouldn't look her in the eye. "These young people don't look at people ... because [of] the nature of the work they have been doing ... They never even had IDs. They didn't want to tell their real names ... Rozy's light was completely out. She had a gun. People were raiding banks ... killing people."

Selline understood them. They had developed mistrust of aid organizations coming into Korogocho and offering false hopes and promises.

"That's why Rozy was so hostile to me the first time," Selline said. She told Rozy that "the change we can make together in our lives can be a greater benefit than the thousand shillings you could earn today."

Selline saw the way people looked at her. They made her nervous and afraid.

When Selline meets with a group, she looks for the troublemakers. She asks herself: "Who can destroy all that I do?" And then she finds a way to engage them. Rozy was the troublemaker.

Maybe it was the timing of their meeting that made Rozy give Selline her blessing.

On August 6, 2012, Rozy's brother had been released from jail. Soon afterward he was shot and killed – "bullets all over."

"Before I went for the burial, I met with Selline," Rozy said. "My child has a father and an uncle who had been killed."

> *Giving Rules: Timing matters. Not everyone is receptive to help when it is offered.*

Rozy agreed to go with Selline to a trauma training, where she heard other stories of violence and survival and loss and thought that her problems weren't so big. Selline led Rozy through a storytelling exercise, drawing what Selline calls "the river of life."

"I tell them, imagine you are a river," Selline said. "Draw right from the time you were born, how your life has been. How the river winds a bit … So with that image of the river, people really dream their life … They drew good rivers… But Rozy drew the river and drew the crocodiles, drew the depths of the river, but in her river of life she explained one thing: 'I realized that even in the depth of the rivers there have been stepping-stones. The first stepping-stone was you.'"

> *Giving Rules: Be someone else's stepping-stone.*

"And now that is the mind-set we want. The rivers have been deep; they have been infested with crocodiles, but let us look for the stepping-stones."

Selline has been that stepping-stone for many like Rozy. She estimated that she has 50 Rozys throughout the slums of Nairobi.

"Sometimes I get annoyed when people are suffering next to you," Selline told me. "If you cannot help someone, why should you continue to live if you are just living for yourself? And people look at me like a radical. Sometimes I am a radical thinker. I bring ideas that people think are too much. People say, 'I can't do that.' It's okay if you can't. You have to create a society where people feel equal and accepted … and we have to go that extra mile. It has to start with you. We just can't be talking and preaching and not showing the way."

> *Giving Rules: Giving isn't talking; it is acting.*

Peacemaking and justice seeking aren't only what Selline does as a career. They have become her life.

"God has given us a family that is like-minded, Selline said. We use personal income and family income to support them. God made us philanthropists. Sometimes I say, for the years and organizations I've worked with, if I were to save, maybe I could've bought a chopper by now.

"We have developed a principle in this family. We say surely God cannot be so unfair that he gives us 100%, even if it is little, and denies others completely. So we always believe that out of what we get – from a salary, income from a friend, or a raise – we say maybe God in his grace has given us that 100%, and 50% is ours and 50% is put into our hands to be custodians for others. That is the spirituality part of it. We have impressed that so much. God wouldn't have taken me to see all of these troubles to do nothing. Maybe part of it is to give to these people."

Selline isn't a billionaire who has signed on to The Giving Pledge to donate half of her income, but she does it anyhow. Through her work Selline meets individuals, like Rozy, whom she has decided to support beyond the scope of her official work. Like her mother, Selline believes that education is the way out of poverty, and she has paid personally for the educations of many.

Before she decides to support individuals financially, she takes the time to get to know them and where they want their river of life to flow. She gives time before she gives money. She makes sure they have a clear vision of where they are going, and then she thinks about how she might help.

> *Giving Rules: Give time (volunteer and evaluate) before you give money.*

"I always ask this question: How can I make a difference in this? It helps me as a human being and in my relationships with other people. I take myself as the person who must change."

When I told Selline about my search for the Good Person Equation, she laughed.

We are moved to act by single stories. Effective altruism would say we are distracted by single stories and we need to balance our emotion with reason to act in a way that is beneficial to the greater good. That may be the case when you are a donor seeking to address global health issues that are more easily measured and quantified, but when you are working in your own community, projects are people and people are projects.

"These are human beings," Selline said. "They may help someone someday. And if two or eight transform completely, then they will have cut off a whole generation from being destructive – like Rozy, today. Her child will never be in crime. The whole of that generation has been saved. I don't look at just one today. I look at this one and they are going to marry and have children, the children will get married and have children, and their children [will have] children. If you change this, you can imagine that chain of change. And that makes me very happy – to see all those people. There are hundreds. Tens of hundreds."

"Nobody had ever hugged them," Selline said about her work in Rozy's community. "The sense and feeling that they were accepted was overwhelming. Just a hug. A hug to Rozy and to some of these young men made a big difference. [To them] it meant that 'we are human beings.'"

*Giving Rule: Some things aren't measurable, like a hug.*

———

Rozy has been a stepping-stone for others in her community. She estimated that she has 30 or so Legend of Kenya members. Some of them are professional acrobats, two are DJs, one is doing puppetry in schools, and all of them are volunteering, promoting peace.

"You don't need to change all life," Rozy said, looking over as Tyson did another flip in the temple, "just one."

Tyson brought some sugarcane he and George had cut down to give to Rozy and me as we sat on our tire in the shade of a single tree at the temple. Flies landed on us and on our sugarcane. Her gold teeth flashing, Rozy showed me how to eat it while the dump with the dinosaurs smoked in the distance.

Rozy and I got up and joined the others. We forgot to clean up the detritus of our chewed-up and spit-out sugar cane. Tyson came over and cleaned up our mess. I walked back to help him, feeling badly that I had desecrated the temple.

Before we left, we stood at the edge of the temple by the three rocks, and we bowed.

———

"We have to leave," Rozy said, as the peace rally was coming to an end. "It's not safe to be here anymore."

I had returned to Korogocho the day before the election to witness the rally hosted by the Legend of Kenya.

There had been dancers and acrobats. George had joined in with some dance moves to make everyone laugh, and Tyson had performed some

*Figure 14.1    Rozy and George planning the peace event.*

flips and contortions alongside his fellow acrobats. At the event's end, they had cut the music blasting from the rented speakers and addressed the crowd with their message of peace. (See Figure 14.1.)

The event took place on a street in front of a tire shop and a pool hall next to the most violent intersection in the community, the cross. When people wanted to make a statement, they displayed their power and violence at the cross, sometimes literally crucifying people. Not everyone could host an event at the cross without payment to the local gang, but Rozy and her group could.

As soon as we arrived, Rozy had disappeared. I saw her once during the actual event. She helped a girl do her English homework – a single sheet of paper with shapes and English words on it. Rozy appeared, helped her with a few words, and disappeared again. After that I didn't see her until she reappeared with her warning that we needed to leave immediately.

"Okay. Let's go," I said.

We drove past the police station and stopped for Rozy to pay her respects and report that there had been a stabbing. Rozy had it under control. She had talked with both parties to ease tensions and called an ambulance. The police didn't need to get involved, but Rozy wanted them to know about it.

"You can't bring peace with criminals alone," Rozy said. "Police are human beings, too, with families. Peace work involves everyone."

Rozy traveled with me by taxi to escort me out of Korogocho and shared how she wants a safe space outside of the community because it's hard to leave a life of crime when you are surrounded by it and your family depends on it to sustain them. It's not an easy transition out. People have to find their skills and something to do to earn a living to put food on the table, because you can't eat peace.

She wanted the safe space to be a place where people could share their stories, because there is power in stories to change people.

"I have lived in poverty for so long," Rozy said. "There are people who like people living in poverty because they benefit from it, especially politicians. How do we transform this community into a different kind of spot, because we are told we are a hot spot? I've been threatened. I've been shot at. I tell you one thing … If you care so much about your life, you'll be so afraid to make change. Your mind is condensed. My own mom used to live at this same place, and she moved out. She said she can't watch me die because I [had a colleague] who did the same and he was killed on February 21st, 2012. We were two of us. Many people say I'm next."

She plans on living in Korogocho until she finds a way to make the safe space happen.

"I don't want to get out of the community alone. I prefer they all go and I go last … This community has come from far. I love it. People must accept change. Bullet judgment isn't a solution to crime. What happens to the next generation? To the woman who is pregnant with child? What happens to that kid? You can't kill us all."

Rozy got a call, and the tone of her voice changed from hope and triumph to sadness.

"The news … ," Rozy said, "my friend just died."

He was killed. The taxi pulled over to let Rozy out.

I gave her a hug.

━━━━━━

Earlier I had asked Rozy about the name of the group: Legend of Kenya.

"Legends live forever. Heroes die," Rozy told me. "We've lost so many friends."

On a word level I really wanted "Legend" to be pluralized to "Legends" since there were more than one of them. English isn't their first language, so maybe it was simply an oversight. But the more I thought about it, the more I thought it was correct, although still awkward to my ear.

Legends would imply that individually they were each a legend unto themselves. But they weren't each a legend. There is no Selline without the sacrifices made by her brother and mother, there is no Rozy without Selline, there is no Samson or George or Neileh without Rozy.

We often feel we aren't positioned to make a difference, that we don't have enough money or time or talent to make an impact. I certainly feel that way. But then I take a moment to think about Rozy, Selline, and the Legend of Kenya, who grew up in a world without many opportunities and rights and found ways to act as agents of change even at great personal risk and sacrifice. If they can make a difference, we can.

Their work lives on through the lives of those they touch. Only collectively are they a legend.

> *Giving Rules: There are lone gunmen, but no one ever heard of a lone do-gooder.*

# Part III

## START LOCAL

# 15

# Growing Up Gandhi
# (India, 2017)

*Mandated giving / The Mother Teresa
controversy / Gandhi on giving*

---

**NOTHING IN THE NEIGHBORHOOD WAS OF NOTE.** The buildings were faded white and uniform. It wasn't leafy. It wasn't grand. It wasn't gated. There wasn't a sign with an arrow that read: "Guru this way!"

"Oh, I see it. I'm here," I said into my phone. I had arrived but hadn't realized it.

"Ask at the shop and they'll tell you where my apartment is."

I hung up.

"I'm looking for Gandhi."

A guy from the store walked me to a staircase outside the building.

I was sweaty. The cab ride from my room at the Royal Bombay Yacht Club had taken more than 90 minutes. Mahatma Gandhi, seen as the father of the nation, led the country to independence from the British in 1947. Yet in 1958 the Yacht Club still did not welcome Indian members. The irony of my accommodation and my destination was not lost on me.

At the top of the steps there was a wooden "Gandhi" sign. The door was open and the room was crowded.

*Figure 15.1    Tushar Gandhi and the author.*

"Kelsey!" Tushar Gandhi, Mahatma Gandhi's great-grandson, stood and shook my hand (see Figure 15.1). Picture Mahatma Gandhi and now picture the opposite. That is Tushar. He's a big guy. His hand made mine feel small. He introduced me to his audience – members of a free Tibet movement.

Two men sitting on a couch adjacent to Tushar's chair stood and gave me their seat. They stood next to a chocolate cake that sat on a stool at the edge of the circle of people. There was one piece left.

With my arrival, the meeting came to an end and the conversation focused on the cake.

"Please take the cake," Tushar said. "I'm not supposed to eat it. If it stays here I will be in trouble." I assumed he'd be in trouble with his wife.

He motioned to the youngest of the group, a woman, maybe 19. He talked about how it was important to enjoy such luxuries while you are young and healthy. He said that he used to enjoy cake and everyone said he shouldn't. And then he got diabetes and couldn't.

The guru's message: Eat all the sweets before you get diabetes.

Or perhaps: Different times in your life produce different opportunities; take advantage of them while you can.

That's the thing about gurus. If you are seeking wisdom, you'll find it even when it's just a man wishing he could still eat cake. If we sought wisdom in the words of everyone we met, I wonder how differently we'd interact with the world. Maybe we'd go mad.

They packed up the cake and still there was more talking about it: how to box it up, why it needed to go – a full 90 seconds more of cake talk.

Before they left, the young woman whom Tushar really wanted to eat the cake stood before him awkwardly. I wasn't sure what was about to happen.

"No," Tushar said. "Please, you don't have to."

She was going to ignore him.

"Please, there is no need," he pleaded. "Don't kiss my feet."

She really had to fight the urge.

*She must really love cake*, I thought.

Everyone else left, and it was just Gandhi and me alone.

There was a Gandhi shrine in the corner of the room consisting of multiple busts and statues of Gandhi all necklaced with woven cotton thread. This was one of those times I was a little uncomfortable and wished I had at least prepared some questions. I was really not sure how to talk about the journey I was on.

*I'm exploring giving and generosity and how to be good.* That seemed a little Pollyannaish and intangible.

"I've been to the slums of Cambodia and Kenya, where it is hell on earth with burning trash," I said. I've met a slave in West Africa. I feel like this stuff drives me to want to make a difference, but I'm not always sure how. I feel desperate to make an impact. I'm open to suggestions or wisdoms.

"I'm not much of a wise person," Tushar said. "But the basic ideology of making a difference … I may be of some help."

"Do you feel any of that angst to try to give?" I asked.

"I do experience that, not in myself because I'm fortunate to be associated with a lot of good work … We should give until it hurts."

"Give until it hurts." It's a quote from Mother Teresa in her address to the National Prayer Breakfast in Washington, D.C., February 3, 1994:

It is not enough for us to say, "I love God." But I also have to love my neighbor … How can you love God whom you do not see, if you do not love your neighbor whom you see, whom you touch, with whom you live? And so it is very important for us to realize that love, to be true, has to hurt. I must be willing to give whatever it takes not to harm other people and, in fact, to do good to them. This requires that I be willing to give until it hurts. Otherwise, there is no true love in me and I bring injustice, not peace, to those around me.

But even Mother Teresa, a saint and Nobel Prize winner, wasn't inoculated from the criticism of how she gave. Some accused her of not giving enough painkillers or medical treatment to the poor, sick, and dying in her more than 500 missions around the world, so their hurt was greater than if they had received proper care.

A paper by Serge Larivée and Genevieve Chenard of the University of Montreal's Department of Psychoeducation and Carole Sénéchal of the University of Ottawa's Faculty of Education examined most of the literature written about Mother Teresa and found several issues with her work and life, including "her rather dubious way of caring for the sick, her questionable political contacts, her suspicious management of the enormous sums of money she received, and her overly dogmatic views regarding, in particular, abortion, contraception, and divorce."[1]

Even if Mother Teresa inefficiently used the hundreds of millions of dollars gifted to her, the paper's authors point out that the myth of Mother Teresa may have made up for it: "If the extraordinary image of Mother Teresa conveyed in the collective imagination has encouraged humanitarian initiatives that are genuinely engaged with those crushed by poverty, we can only rejoice. It is likely that she has inspired many humanitarian workers whose actions have truly relieved the suffering of the destitute and addressed the causes of poverty and isolation without being extolled by the media."

"Philanthropy is not only about giving money," Tushar said. "It's about giving ability, giving time. Not all of us can give money."

I dumped on him about motivation, my desperation to make a difference, and how I was trying to figure out what I need to do to do enough. I told him about my fear of contentment. I started to treat him like a guru.

"There's part of me," I said, false starting. "I'm 38 now. I have a career. I've got two kids. Our life is fairly busy. We live where we always wanted to live and there is a part of me that wants to become complacent, but then to have the experiences I've had, that complacency scares me. I feel like I … like people want to know, 'Here's how much you should give, plus here's how much you should volunteer, equals you are a good person.' You know some kind of Good Person Equation?"

Tushar was concerned about a sort of Good Person Equation in India, a law that required corporations to give. In 2013 India became the first country in the world to enact such a law. Companies with net profits of $830,000 or more over the previous three years had to give 2% of their

---

[1]Serge Larivée, Genevieve Chenard, and Carole Sénéchal, "Mother Teresa: Anything But a Saint … ," University of Montreal (March 3, 2013).

net profits to causes promoting education, health, sustainability, gender equality, and poverty reduction.[2] Tushar said it makes companies complacent, as if their level of giving is enough. They are doing only what's required.

"So that the ideology of giving until it hurts has been completely killed by this sense of giving as much as is required, even when you have the ability to do more. This has actually harmed the cause of benevolence."

He was right. Some companies in India that once gave more than 2% reduced their giving as corporate philanthropy was seen less as a way to build a company's reputation than to meet a requirement. But overall corporate giving in India jumped more than 600%.

*Giving Rules: Required giving isn't giving; it's a tax.*

"They are sitting in five-star hotels sipping on coffee and they are talking about poverty," Tushar said. "What do they know about it? They haven't even smelled poverty."

Imagine what it's like to be Tushar. Some of his relatives have run from the name. There's too much pressure. People show up at your house and they want to kiss your feet and mine you for wisdom because of who your great-grandfather was. One of my great-grandfathers was a drunk. I'm not even sure about the others. I can't imagine what it would be like to be defined by their deeds. And if those deeds were as legendary as Gandhi's? I'd probably hide from my name, too. Tushar doesn't. He grew up Gandhi.

Tushar carries the legacy with grace while acknowledging the pressure.

"It's a privilege and it's a responsibility, equally weighing ... I don't pretend to be something I am not. I enjoy my legacy ... My mother worked with many of the NGOs that worked in the city. My father associated with NGOs working in the rural areas, so our vacations would be to these centers. I experienced the communities as well as the projects and the difference they made. I would see children pick up a wrapper of chocolate I had discarded and lick out the fragment of chocolate sticking to it, trying to scrape off the last bits ... That made me understand the life of poverty."

Tushar and his father, Arun, lead the Gandhi tours. Arun lives in Rochester, New York, where he is the director of the Gandhi Worldwide Education Institute, a nonprofit that seeks to "eradicate the scourge of

---

[2]Oliver Balch, "Indian Law Requires Companies to Give 2% of Profits to Charity. Is It Working?" *The Guardian* (April 5, 2016).

poverty and human degradation."[3] Arun lived with and learned from his grandfather for two years when he was a boy.

"There are two ways to give to charity," Arun had told me when I talked to him before coming to India. "One is motivated by pity and the other is compassion. When motivated by pity you go and do and then say, 'Get out of my face.' When you are motivated by compassion you think about the person's strength and what allows them to stand on their own feet and build confidence. With pity you have to keep on giving and there is no result."

*Giving Rules: Giving should be motivated by compassion, not pity.*

On the Gandhi tours, Arun and Tushar lead visits to grassroots organizations working with women and children who live in poverty.

"The majority response of the tours is that it's a life-changing experience because they come to understand the mechanism of poverty, the brutality of poverty," Tushar said. "The idealism of poverty is demeaning. In certain ways, poverty is glamorized. When you go in rural areas, you see the dehumanization and the cruel realities… Poverty cannot be experienced from glossy pictures or films. Poverty has a smell to it. Poverty is violent."

Still, I searched for a prescription, asking him what actions or guidance they gave to those who went on the tours.

"We don't tell them anything other than, 'You have learned something. Now find your own remedy. One should follow one's experience; one should follow one's own ability and intellect. You have been shown something. Now find what you are going to do to make a difference in that.'"

*Giving Rules: Experience the lives of those you hope to help.*

We have to seek out such experiences. Until we know the name of someone living in poverty, sit in their home, see them value something we have discarded, meet their families, and listen to them, can we actually expect to give even 0.1% of our income, heart, or thoughts to their existence?

Tushar told me that some leave the tour he leads and reenter the bubble of their own lives, now at least aware of the realities they ignore. He hopes to reach one or two per trip.

---

[3] www.gandhiforchildren.org/About-GWEI (March 12, 2018).

His great-grandfather is often quoted as having said, "Be the change you want to see in the world," as if our responsibilities go no further than our own behavior. The actual quote this was adapted from is: "If we could change ourselves, the tendencies in the world would also change. As a man changes his own nature, so does the attitude of the world change towards him."

Societal change is possible only if the change in us creates change in others. Arun, Tushar's father, reflects this when he talks about his work as a peace farmer. "I plant seeds and hope they become crops."

But Arun and Tushar, like the rest of us, don't always get to see the results of their work – the change in others. We don't all lead a nation to democracy and self-governance and inspire the world along the way.

Tushar encouraged me to do the work and be consistent, regardless of whether I can quantify my impact or see the results.

He didn't have an equation for me. In fact, he was totally against the idea.

"It's not an equation," Tushar said. "Only you have the equation, and you have to go beyond it. You must push it further. You need to progress in your giving."

*Giving Rules: Be the change regardless of whether you feel like you are making a change.*

# 16

# Start with Your Local (India, 2017)

*Crossing caste lines / Towers and slums / Untouchables*

---

**WHEN THE 50-SOMETHING-YEAR-OLD MUSTACHED** man wearing a sailor's suit saluted me, I wasn't comfortable. Nor was I when the hotel manager told me the man in the sailor's suit, his "boy," could carry my bag to my room and then called for him: "Boy!"

I wasn't comfortable ringing a bell at lunch so a waiter could meet my immediate need – Heinz ketchup.

I wasn't comfortable when the man in the sailor's suit saluted me as I left in the morning to make my way to the docks. I've earned no rank or status. I had enough money to buy a plane ticket to India. I was American. I knew a guy who knew a guy who was a member at the Royal Bombay Yacht Club and could get me into one of the three-room guestrooms accessed by a palatial staircase or a steam-punk elevator. None of which made me salute-worthy.

The man's spine straightened, and his heels nearly clicked. I awkwardly nodded to his salute and flagged down one of Mumbai's famous black-and-yellow cabs. To my relief, the driver turned on his meter. The day before a driver had refused to do so, intending to charge me more than the going rate, and I demanded he stop to let me out, but he wouldn't. I demanded to be treated equally, like a local. *Why should I pay more? Why should I be treated differently?* I had threatened to jump out, had my door open and everything. He called my bluff. I wasn't going to jump out of a moving car because of $1.

The driver dropped me at the Sassoon Docks. This wasn't a dock for yachts, but one of the oldest docks and largest fishing markets in Mumbai.

The women who lined the entrance of the dock didn't salute me; they motioned to the fresh catch before them.

Would I like to buy a recently killed stingray?

It was tempting, but I was heading to a meeting that a dead stingray would make awkward.

At the dock, men tossed faded pastel baskets filled with their catch eight feet up to other men standing on the seawall. Those men passed the catch to other men who auctioned the fish off to women. Auction winners walked away with shrimp, crab, and fish of all sorts balancing on their heads. They pushed me out of their way to get where they were going.

Ashok Rathod rolled up on his scooter. He wore Oakley eyeglasses and had disheveled, thick hair, and a look on his face that seemed to question everything.

We wove our way through the crowds at the dock.

"Sometimes the women will pour fish water on you to get you out of the way," Ashok warned in a gravelly voice.

Ashok is the founder of the OSCAR Foundation. He's a movie lover and named the nonprofit after the Oscar awards, somewhat incongruently with its mission and perhaps in violation of copyright, so he came up with a name to fit the acronym: Organization for Social Change Awareness and Responsibility. Ashok chose to meet at the dock to tell me about OSCAR's work using soccer as a means to promote education and empower underprivileged kids.

"I started working here when I was 10," Ashok said.

Ashok's father worked on the docks for 35 years before becoming a gardener. He did not want his children to follow in his footsteps, so he enrolled them in a government school where the teacher-to-student ratio was 1 to 65.

"The education is not good," Ashok said. "One day we decided during our break to go to the fishing market to see how our parents made money. There were a lot of fish on the floor. Everyone was busy running around to sell fish, buy fish … Whatever fish fell down, we were collecting and putting in a bucket. When the bucket was full, someone came to us: 'How much?'"

Back then, 17 years ago, fish were so plentiful that no one cared about the small fish; now the adults collect them. Things were cheaper then, too. Ashok could go to school in the morning, sneak off to the fish market at lunch to earn $2 or $3, and head back to school with enough money to see a movie and grab something to eat.

"One day my father found that I was here working. He warned me, 'If you come again, we will throw you out of the house.' So I stopped coming because if I got thrown out of the house, where would I stay?"

Ashok stayed in school, while his friends dropped out to work.

We walked past the boats to a long open-walled building beyond the hustle where men repaired fishing nets. During the monsoon the government doesn't allow large-scale fishing. These were small fishing boats only. During the main season, this dock would be full.

By age 15, Ashok's friends started drinking, gambling, and smoking. They broke into groups sort of like gangs and got into fights with other groups. When their parents found out what their boys were up to, they made them marry. The responsibilities of a family would calm them down. This was the cycle of life in the slum. Few went to school. Few left.

"Now they are 28 or 29 years old and have two to four children," Ashok said, watching the men fix the nets. "Now everything becomes expensive and their income is less ... They have to work 12 hours. It's a hard life for them to feed their children. I'm sharing this story because I wanted to become like them: to earn money, enjoy life and not to think about the future, to think of today's life and enjoy. I thought this was the best way. But because of my father, I continued school."

A white police SUV pulled in front of us, blocking our path to the end of the dock. The police called Ashok over to check out what we were doing. In November 2008, 10 terrorists came ashore on the Sassoon Docks and executed four days of shootings in a train station, café, hospital, movie theater, and hotel that claimed 164 lives. The fishermen had been reporting their concerns about strange and unlicensed boats around the docks for days leading up to the attack, but no one listened to them – they were just fishermen.[1]

The police are determined not to make the same mistake again and are extra sensitive to a foreigner walking around snapping photos and taking notes. Ashok and I walked in silence and once the police drove out of sight, I asked him to continue his story.

---

[1] CNN Library, "Mumbai Terror Attacks Fast Facts," www.cnn.com/2013/09/18/world/asia/mumbai-terror-attacks/index.html (December 12, 2017); Sujata Anandan, "26/11: It Was Mumbai Police's Darkest Night Ever," *National Herald* (November 11, 2017).

Ashok graduated and volunteered with Door Step School, a nonprofit that worked to educate kids with the goal of enrolling them in public schools. A few years later, he got his first job with another NGO, Magic Bus, which also focused on educating kids.

"One day I was coming home from work and I saw two boys from my neighborhood. They were smoking at the age of 13. They saw me, and they hid behind a car."

The kids were on the same path as his friends, the same path he would've taken if not for his father. Ashok had a vague idea of doing something to help kids in his own community.

"I identified 18 children who were school dropouts and I asked them, 'Do you want to play football?' I didn't tell them anything about education directly."

**Giving Rules: Start in your own community.**

The kids mostly played cricket, but they were interested in football – or as we refer to it in the US, soccer. They had never worked with a coach in any sport before and the prospect of having a coach and playing a sport more formally appealed to them.

Ashok told them to come to the field Saturday at 4 p.m. They did, all 18. Ashok didn't think any of them would show up, so he didn't go.

"They called me: 'Where are you? We are here to play football!' I said, 'Wait, wait, I am coming. I reached there in 10 minutes."

The kids saw him coming, empty-handed. He didn't even have a football. "Some football coach," the kids thought.

He led them in a few other games and promised he would return the following week with a football. He couldn't really afford a ball, but bought one anyway, for $6 – a quarter of his weekly salary.

"Initially," Ashok said, "they weren't willing to play each other because they were coming from different castes and religions. Everyone wanted to keep the football with them, and nobody wanted to share."

Ashok decided to mix the teams, and soon the kids were celebrating goals across castes and religions. He told them that if they wanted to continue, they had to enroll and stay in school.

Ashok was onto something.

"Basically," Ashok said, "it's about all cultures and religions living together. It's about unity."

More kids started to show up, which was great, but a problem because he couldn't afford more equipment. Fast-forward 10 years, and the OSCAR Foundation now reaches 3,000 kids. Prince William and

Kate Middleton have visited. Manchester United forward Juan Mata spent two days practicing with the kids and, no doubt, getting a similar tour that ended in the same improbable location: Ashok's home.

We made our way from the dock to Ashok's community. I sat on the back of his scooter as the monsoon season pelted us with rain from a gray sky. The Ambedkar Nagar slum in Cuffe Parade sits off the road behind a high wall painted with OSCAR Foundation art: a painting of kids raising their hands and a close-up of a girl's face.

"That is the raising hand," Ashok said, pointing to the paintings, "like coming up and also having an opportunity to help others come up. This is about women and girls. They have many challenges but they are strong and face them. Forty percent of the kids in our programs are girls."

Ashok led me past the wall and down a crooked alley. Nothing was straight. The walls of the houses weren't. The ground was uneven. For the most part these weren't the tin shanties and tarps that I had come to know in the slums of Kenya or Cambodia, but two-story structures carved out of a world of concrete. Local media outlets referred to them as "hutments." The first levels housed stores, and up above were dwellings accessed by steep steel ladders.

We passed kids in red OSCAR shirts. They asked me if I played football, probably hoping I was some less athletic European star they didn't recognize. Another kid asked me if I knew Juan Mata.

"Here they are mostly working in laundry," Ashok said.

A man swung a long white sheet across his shoulder and then whipped it down like a hammer at a carnival trying to ring a bell. An arc of water followed the tail of the sheet.

Ashok estimated that 15% to 20% of people in his community beat, scrubbed, and dried the laundry of the area hotels and the surrounding luxury apartments.

"From my hotel?" I asked, as if it mattered. Should I have more empathy or guilt or connection with this man if it were my sheet?

A man, wearing only a bleached white towel, stepped to the side as we left the laundry. He brushed his teeth, white foam gathering in the corners of his mouth.

The alley narrowed. I felt like a giant, my shoulders barely clearing the distance between buildings. Ashok climbed a ladder.

"This is the library," Ashok said.

Shelves on the walls held short stacks of books organized by grade level. There was *20,000 Leagues Under the Sea*, a *Hardy Boys* graphic novel, *The Story of India for Children*, and the somewhat creepy title of

*Crazy Times with Uncle Ken.* A cartoon frog and dinosaur were painted on the wall along with the phrase: "Send them to school."

Two office chairs sat at a desk where Ashok put his wallet stuffed so full of cards that it was round – the wallet of a man who won't let go or is too busy to bother. Other than that, the middle of the room was open. It might've been 10 feet across at the most. Ashok told me that most homes in his community were smaller than this room and slept six or seven people.

I asked him if he lived in a similar place, thinking that he probably didn't, thinking his education had lifted him to a higher standard of living, thinking that the founder of a nonprofit that had been visited by stars and princes – and who had earned the support of embassies and businesses – would live elsewhere.

"Yes," Ashok said. He reached into a cupboard and pulled out a small bedroll. "This is my bed. I sleep here."

His phone rang. He apologized and answered it (see Figure 16.1).

I looked around the room and out the short doorway. A shining apartment tower seemed to rise into infinity.

*Figure 16.1    Ashok in his office/bedroom on the phone with his girlfriend.*

Archana, the woman who first told me about Ashok and OSCAR, lived in that apartment tower. She was a friend of the man who got me into the Royal Bombay Yacht Club.

Ashok can lie on the floor in his bedroll and see the tower where a three-bedroom, 2,000-square-foot apartment lists for more than $2 million. When the sun rises, the shadows of the towers, the most desired real estate in Mumbai, reach toward the slum.

A month before my visit, the Forest Department, accompanied by 100 police officers, bulldozed more than 1,000 homes here. They claimed the homes were in violation of a law protecting mangrove cover. Residents claimed that the demolitions took place without notice, and they weren't allowed to save their belongings beforehand. They speculate that some-day their homes will become new high-rises.[2]

Residents of the slums work in the apartment towers as domestic help and drivers. They cook exotic meals they would never eat from countries they will never visit. They pick up toys they could never afford and support lifestyles they could never live.

It's not normal for someone in the apartment tower with ocean views to go down and visit the slums. Archana first visited five years ago when her staff invited her to their homes during Diwali, the Hindu festival of lights. Now she volunteers as an English teacher and, collects toys for OSCAR's community toy library. Sometimes she takes the kids to the movies on their birthdays. She has arranged for a Santa to go door-to-door delivering chocolates in the community. She inspired a friend of hers to donate his services for a dental clinic.

"Ashok is super inspiring," she told me. "He's giving back, not from a higher place, but from where he lives. He's stayed inside the slum even though he could leave."

The world has haves and have-nots, but the proximity – a short walk – and the disparity between the apartments and the slum are staggering. Yet, many who live in the apartments choose not to experience the slum even though they have a "slum view" every bit as much as they have an "ocean view."

People in the towers think the men are drunks, that the slums are dirty. They have strong opinions about a place they've never been. They may like their help, see giving to them as their charity, and see them as part of their family, but not extend that charity, empathy, or love to the other residents of the slum.

---

[2]Javed Iqbal, "Encroaching on Entitlement," The Hindu Business Line (June 2, 2017).

I once was invited to speak at a private college in Lima, Peru. The organizers wanted me, a middle-class American, to "raise social awareness" among the Peruvian students and present them with "the reality of factories, sweatshops ... the impact on society and the reality of how people live." I was nervous. What did I have to tell them that they couldn't learn looking out their windows on the way to school or to the supermarket? I chatted with the students before my talk. Many of them came from well-off families. Many of them had drivers and cooks. They had been to Disney World. They were in sight of poverty, yet they didn't see it.

In India those who believe in karma believe that those who live in hutments got what they deserved. I wondered if Mukesh Ambani, the richest man in India, who lives in a $2 billion 27-story private tower in Mumbai, maintained by a staff of 600, felt the same way.

Archana told me she believed in karma, but she also believed in the importance of spending time supporting OSCAR and interacting with people in the community.

"When you have access to so much, and all you need to do is be there, how do you not be there? It's so stupid not to do it. You have a choice to not give back. You are choosing to do things. You should feel good about yourself."

Ashok inspired her, and she inspired her friends to give, although not all of them are comfortable visiting. She sees herself as a bridge.

Ashok hung up the phone. It was his girlfriend. Speaking of divides and bridges, she's from another caste. She's getting a master's in women empowerment at one of the best schools in the country.

He's Banjara and she's Brahmin. His parents just found out about the relationship and don't approve. They are afraid he will leave. Her parents don't even know. They met five years ago when he was speaking at a conference she attended.

"I'm from a very low caste," Ashok said. "I don't believe in caste. According to [society] I come from the very bottom and she comes from the top."

In some states in India, the government classifies Banjara as an "other backward class" (OBC), a term referring to castes that are socially and educationally disadvantaged. Sometimes they are referred to as "untouchables."

On the other hand, the Brahmin occupy the top of the social structure. In Hinduism they are seen as the priests and protectors, the closest to the gods.

Ashok and his girlfriend come from different cultures and speak different languages.

People in the community look up to Ashok. He has received awards on TV and appeared alongside global celebrities, and more than that he has promoted education and unity. Kids are going to university; they are traveling abroad. Gangs, also known as groupism, have declined. He has inspired other sports programs in the community. People greet him as a celebrity, but not some unknowable, unrelatable celebrity. He's *their* celebrity.

"Now the community is going against me," Ashok said. "People are against the relationship. Because they think that here I am a famous face for the youth and the children, and they think if I get married to a different caste, other youths will also follow me."

Ashok intends to marry his girlfriend, but he worries what that will mean for his family and the community that he loves. Someone had already totaled his old scooter by beating it with a heavy rock. I could hear the pressure in his voice. It wasn't really a decision anymore. He knew what he would do. He just couldn't predict the impact that leaving would make.

"I will leave," Ashok said. "I love staying here, but, yes, I want to leave."

Two years into OSCAR, he struggled with the kids' parents. They weren't happy. The kids were always using practice as an excuse to run off. Eight of the kids dropped out of school.

Some of the parents also weren't sold on the idea of school. Unlike Ashok's dad, they didn't see the value of an education. For generations, there were set jobs for set castes. Their children would do laundry, or fish, or work in a home, or drive a car. This perception remained, despite the fact that social mobility in India – the percentage of the population escaping poverty – has been equal to that in the US for more than a decade.[3]

"If you want to learn football, you must go to school," Ashok told the kids. "No smoking, no gambling."

When Ashok started the program, no one gave him money. They thought he might misuse it.

"They were judging me because I live in a slum," he said. "Then one day in 2009, I shared this problem with the children."

---

[3] Max Metzger, "The Indian Dream? World Bank Says Social Mobility in India Comparable to the U.S.," *Newsweek* (January 21, 2015).

The OSCAR team had lost in the semifinals of a tournament. The kids were devastated. They cried. Ashok started to give them a pep talk and started to cry himself. His team had lost to teams that had more equipment than his kids had. He felt that he had let them down. He walked out of the room, wiped away his tears, and then returned.

"Competition isn't easy," he told them. "Anything you want...you have to work hard. Practice. Practice. Practice and work hard. This time we reached the semifinal; next time we can reach the final. It's not your mistake that we don't have equipment. If we had more equipment your game could improve faster. Because I don't have money, I can't buy more equipment."

What had started as a pep talk devolved into exposing the depressing truths that had brought tears to Ashok's eyes in the first place. No one believed in Ashok enough to give him money – no one except for the kids.

They had a solution. Every kid who participated in OSCAR would bring a single rupee (less than 2 cents) to each practice. Ashok used the money to fix the discarded balls from other teams, which cost him less than a dollar. He had more equipment for more kids.

OSCAR's first major financial backers were the children themselves.

*Giving Rules: If the people an organization helps are willing to volunteer and give back to that organization, you should, too.*

That was the tipping point. By 2014, OSCAR was working with 600 kids, and in 2017 with 3,000 kids.

OSCAR has grown to other communities and states in India.

I accompanied Ashok into a neighborhood interested in starting a program with OSCAR.

The flat, muddy, clay field looked like the blank slate of a future high-rise apartment building. Trump Tower Mumbai, still under construction, looked down upon us. I had seen a billboard advertising the $1.2 million condos that read: "Any resemblance to a 7-star hotel is purely intentional."

The property's website has a section on privileges, which included: "A private jet at your service: Chauffeur-driven cars are passé. As a resident of Trump Tower Mumbai, you have a private jet at your disposal, ready to whisk you away to a destination of your choice. This service is the ultimate way to travel. But then our residents are used to being spoiled."

Other privileges included a Trump Card that will allow you to "live without boundaries, limits or compromises" and stay in other Trump properties around the world, a pool where you can "soak up the luxury … located high above the ground, for your pleasure."

Far below, we were standing in monsoon mud puddles. A Cummings generator hummed rather quietly, powering a welder renovating the stands. Orlando, OSCAR's newly hired program manager, talked to me over the hum. He was as tall as I was; his hair was shaved on the sides and curly on top. If someone had told me that he was a famous Indian soccer player, I would have believed it. He was well educated and came from a family of means. He used to work in a call center and talked to English speakers all over the world.

A man in his forties arrived. He talked with Ashok and then made a call. Soon 12 college-aged students showed up, each of them with unique boy band hair – thick, coiffed, styled.

Introductions were made, and first they determined what language was best to use for everyone: Hindi.

Ashok mentioned the successes of the program, the kids, Juan Mata, and the awards. The students started to look from Ashok to one another, nodding their approval and sharing looks that said: "This is pretty cool. We should do this." But then their body language shifted when they realized they were too old to participate as athletes in the program.

Ashok won them back when he told them about the young leaders program. There were 150 active young leaders in OSCAR, led by eight staff coaches.

Behind them, a laborer stacked bricks in a wheelbarrow with a wheel that made a clunking noise once every revolution. Ashok talked of a world of opportunities beyond the field, beyond Trump Tower. OSCAR students were going to England; they were going to visit Manchester United.

As Ashok spoke, the group grew. People just appeared. By the time Ashok was finished speaking there were 20 potential coaches and players passing him their names and phone numbers.

At the end of the meeting when participants divided themselves into smaller circles, Ashok walked over to a group of kids playing cricket. He doesn't walk with the natural step of an athlete. His feet duck out a bit and he shifts from side to side in a strut. His glasses are thick, and he's short. If this were a movie, Orlando would be the leading man and Ashok his sidekick.

Ashok held a soccer ball in his hands. He offered the ball to the kids, but he really offered so much more.

"We say that football is our religion," Ashok told me. "Football never tells you, 'Don't pick me because you are a Christian. Don't pick me because you are a Hindu or Muslim.'"

# 17

# Start Small (India, 2017)

*Locals challenging societal norms / Creating leaders / The girl effect*

**I'M A 38-YEAR-OLD MAN,** but there was only so much pushing I'd take from a 12-year-old girl on the soccer field before I decided to push back. Sure, I outweighed her by a hundred pounds, but she had it coming. The key was to push her just enough to make a point– stop her from being a meanie – and to not send her facedown into the mud.

It was my last night in India with the OSCAR Foundation, and I decided to practice with the only team that I thought would not make me look like an idiot – the beginner girls' team. I thought wrong.

Imagine a competitive elephant playing soccer with small children. That's how I felt. The smallest girl on our tiny field kept stealing the ball from me and laughing as she did. My teammates stopped passing me the ball, and it wasn't because I was from another country, caste, or religion; it was because I was a horrible player.

There are 1,200 girls in OSCAR's programming, and the organization is starting a new program called Kick Like a Girl. Fifty-two girls participate in the residential training program learning the game of football and all are getting to better know themselves. Many girls in the community don't leave their homes, other than to go to school. The residential program gives them a chance to connect around the issues they face and to realize that they aren't alone. The girls even organized a Women's Day tournament all on their own and persuaded 200 girls to participate.

Many development experts believe that one of the best ways to lift people out of poverty is to educate and empower girls. UNICEF calls "educated girls a uniquely positive force for development." Regions that invest in educating girls have performed better economically. Educated women will have fewer children, and it's more likely that their kids will go to school.[1]

After our practice, I chatted with Zoya, 15, the MVP of our scrimmage. She has played with OSCAR for three years. I asked her what she liked best about today's practice.

"Each and every practice they teach us something new related to our life and our education. Today we learned that the most important thing is team coordination … and that we should always be helping. That we should not be judging. And we should keep on practicing every day to be a good person."

> **Giving Rules: Always help. Don't judge. Keep practicing to be a good person.**

Zoya's father played on the national team, and her brother is on the OSCAR team that will tour England for two weeks. She lives in the city center and yet, as a girl, still had no access to formal coaching or playing on a team until OSCAR.

The other girls agreed. One of the best things about OSCAR was experiencing life outside their homes.

We played in the corner of a giant open field, an oasis of space compared to the crowded streets and sidewalks of Mumbai. Orange cones marked our playing area. We weren't the only ones enjoying a break in the monsoon rains. There was a group of men playing rugby, one guy shooting hoops on a lone basketball court, an intense volleyball match, and several soccer practices and matches. There was a big difference between the OSCAR teams and the others on the field, who often had no shoes, no organization, no coaches, no age levels, and no guidance.

Whenever a girl on the opposing team stole the ball from me and scored a goal, the ball would roll off into another field of play. Most of the time we didn't have to run after it – someone would kick it back. No one complained. We returned the favor. It was simply the

---

[1] UNICEF, "The State of the World's Children 2004" (2004), Chapter 2.

social code: We helped others when they needed a little help because we knew we'd need help later.

The OSCAR team on the big field, including Zoya's brother, played a much older team and they were winning. Maruti coached his team. Maruti was one of the 18 kids who attended the first OSCAR practice, the one where Ashok forgot to bring a ball.

Maruti had moved with his family to the Ambedkar Nagar slum when he was five years old. His parents worked on the docks and struggled to provide enough food for him and his siblings. School wasn't even an option. While they worked, Maruti cared for his younger cousins. It was also his job to fetch water at the community well, where he met Ashok when he was 10. Ashok thought a bright kid like Maruti should be in school and made arrangements to talk to his parents about enrolling him. It took five visits before Ashok finally convinced them.

Now, at 20, Maruti was a coach.

A player got kicked in the shin and started limping. Maruti called him to the sideline. The boy slid a small shin guard, as thin as a slice of bologna, out of his sock and rubbed his leg. Maruti told him to shake it off and then worked him back into the game.

The ball hit a giant mud puddle in front of OSCAR's goal and immediately died. Two of the most skilled defenders in the world couldn't compete with the defense the puddle produced. Players kicked at the ball with all their might, but the ball barely moved. The kicks threw up more water than a shark attack.

The OSCAR team finally scored and they all celebrated. A few minutes later Maruti, fingers in mouth, blew the whistle. The players sat on the ground and stretched. One of them counted down and they all switched to a new stretch in unison. The players were soaking wet and covered in red mud. Maruti told me that in the rainy seasons most people stop practicing, but OSCAR needs them to keep coming to grow as leaders and to keep the kids in school.

As they ate homemade granola bars, Maruti gave a pep talk about the importance of education and gave examples of past success stories in the program and in the community (see Figure 17.1). He talked to them about life after soccer.

Afterward Maruti and his fellow coach Kumar invited me back to the community.

The narrow alleys of the slum were crowded at night. People flowed through the intersections like cars through a roundabout – yielding but never fully stopping. We followed Maruti, and then he disappeared and we arrived to Kumar's home down an alley so narrow I had to walk sideways.

*Figure 17.1    Maruti (right) talking to OSCAR players after a scrimmage.*

Kumar's father and mother sat on the floor, watching a small tube television. Kumar's sister popped her head out from a loft reminiscent of my college dorm days to say hi.

I had run out of water during the scrimmage with the girls and was so thirsty. Kumar's dad offered me something to drink – whiskey – and something to eat – spicy chicken. My mouth was on fire. It was the last thing I needed to quench my thirst, but I ate and drank anyway. When someone welcomes me into their home, I will eat and drink whatever they give me.

My motto is: "If it's good enough for them, it's good enough for me."

Still, I was worried because in a few hours I would board a plane for 30 hours of travel.

Six people lived in this room half the size of the sitting room in my room at the Royal Bombay Yacht Club. It was the closest living quarters I'd ever seen – not just in the room, but also the proximity to neighbors.

Kumar told me his parents were old school and that his mom wanted him to get married, but he doesn't have time for a girlfriend. He's too busy with OSCAR.

I asked Kumar to thank his mom for the food and tell her that it was very good.

"My mom did not cook," he said. "It was my sister. My mom doesn't do anything now. She's like a queen."

He shared the queen comparison with his family and they all laughed.

I think about the girls I played soccer with and all the girls tucked away in the concrete box apartments among the narrow streets where running is almost impossible. Girls go to school if they are lucky, and they do most of the housework.

We left to find Maruti. He greeted us and we followed him up a steel ladder to the room where his father sat with his nephew.

"This is where we shower," Maruti said. There was a drain in the front left corner. I asked him about water. They pay $8 per month to get six jugs a week.

Maruti commented on how small the place was, even smaller than Kumar's home. I was surprised by the comment. This was where he had lived since he was five. This was where Ashok visited five times to talk to his parents to convince them of the opportunity school offered.

Over the past few months, Maruti had worked to get passports and visas for his team traveling to the UK. First he had to convince parents, who had never been on a plane or imagined flying to another country, of the amazing, all-expenses-paid opportunity OSCAR was offering their children. Many of them were indifferent to the opportunity, but Maruti persisted, waited in lines, and shuffled papers back and forth.

It wasn't that the parents didn't love their kids or didn't want the best for them. I think they just didn't know what was possible and what was outside; and maybe, even, they were afraid that their kids would forever see the community differently, that their kids would walk into their homes one day and see how small they were, and that they, like Ashok, would want to leave.

Ashok told me that OSCAR wasn't about soccer or even about school, but about giving kids a platform and opportunity to be role models.

"If you change minds, that makes a long-term impact," Ashok said.

I asked Ashok if he had any advice for people who want to make a difference. He told me it didn't take much effort. He had started with a small idea.

Maruti and Kumar led me out of the community, past the OSCAR office, past the community well, and beyond the wall separating the community from the street. They hailed a cab for me.

I went back to the Royal Bombay Yacht Club to a world where a man in a sailor's suit saluted me, where my five nights cost more than a year's worth of rent in the slum, where a locker room attendant gave me fresh bleached white towels and mouthwash. It felt like I was in a tower of privilege looking out at the ocean view as if it were mine, something I earned or deserved. In India the haves and have-nots are in sight of one another if they take the time to see.

Part of me wants to enjoy the view, looking out and not down, but mostly I don't want to forget seeing the tower from the slum.

The lives of those in the towers and at the yacht club are closer to my own, and probably yours, than to Maruti's. I have lived in a yacht club most of my life, really. If I feel uncomfortable at the yacht club, I should feel uncomfortable in my own life, unless I do something about it.

In the tower a soccer ball is just a soccer ball. But in the Ambedkar Nagar slum, a soccer ball is much, much more.

*Giving Rules: Start small. Start where you live.*

# Part IV

## THE GIFT OF TRAVEL

# 18

# Should You Go on a Slum Tour? (India, 2017)

*Poverty porn? / History of "slumming it" / Impact of slum tours*

---

**I DID SOMETHING I NEVER THOUGHT** I'd do. I went on a slum tour.

I had talked to Tushar Gandhi and Ashok about the possibility of going on a tour of the Dharavi slum and to my surprise, neither discouraged me.

"They are a bit voyeuristic," Tushar admitted. "It has become more lucrative for the operators because of the popularity of *Slum Dog Millionaire*. Lots of tours are happening ... for locals, too."

I had read about guided tours of the slums for a few years and thought of them as a recent phenomenon, which isn't the case.

Tours of slums date back to nineteenth-century London when wealthy citizens visited the slums to experience the vibrant culture. The tours were organized and a term for it was coined: "slumming it." *The New York Times* in 1884 wrote about "the visiting of the slums ... by parties of ladies and gentlemen for sightseeing," to see "Hebrews," "squalid negro neighborhoods and tenements ... crowded with sweltering humanity" where 'sensitive olfactories' may be offended."

The modern-day version seems no more palatable. In South Africa in 2013 for $82 per night you could experience poverty in luxury at the only fake "shanty town ... in the world equipped with under-floor heating and wireless [Internet]." At one point tours of Rio's favelas were very safari-like. Tourists crammed into open-roofed SUVs stood and gawked at locals and snapped photos of them like they were zebras on the way to the watering hole. Researchers call this "the tourist gaze" in which tourists desire to consume images of tourism. They see the culture and intrude upon it, but they don't experience it.

Detractors say the tourist gaze is nothing less than poverty porn or "poorism." They claim it is voyeurism, plain and simple. People are seen as objects.

Kennedy Odede grew up in a slum in Kenya and later studied in England. He wrote in *The New York Times* about the first time he saw a slum tour:

> I was 16 ... I was outside my 100-square-foot house washing dishes, looking at the utensils with longing because I hadn't eaten in two days. Suddenly, a white woman was taking my picture. I felt like a tiger in a cage. Before I could say anything, she had moved on ... Slum tourism is a one-way street: They get photos; we lose a piece of our dignity.[1]

In post-Katrina New Orleans, tourists on an art tour passed decimated homes and a sign that read:

> TOURIST Shame On You Driving BY without stopping Paying to see my pain 1,600+ DIED HERE.[2]

Why do we go to these places? Is it enough to go and bear witness? Even though Tushar and Ashok didn't look down on the tours, I still felt uncomfortable as I waited at the crowded Churchgate train station in Mumbai to meet my guide with Reality Tours, the largest slum tour operator in the world.

A tapping sound cut through all of the commuting commotion, and I watched as a blind woman navigated the crowd. Another woman, a stranger from what I could tell, walked up behind her and took her arm – a small act of beauty, a gift, an unseen kindness.

---

[1] Kennedy Odede, "Slumdog Tourism," *The New York Times* (August 9, 2010).
[2] Mark Ellwood, "Inside the Very Real World of 'Slum Tourism,'" *Condé Nast Traveler* (March 15, 2016).

Nanu, my guide, found me among the crowd. We waited for another tourist to show up, but the tourist must have had second thoughts. It would be just the two of us.

On the train, Nanu talked to me; it was hard to hear. The doors were wide open, and warm air rushed in as the train headed inland. We arrived at our destination train station and walked to a walkway elevated above the road, over a wall, and down into the slum. Nanu reminded me of Reality Tours' no-picture policy.

"They get photos, and we lose a piece of our dignity," I thought.

*What would I get from my experience in the slum?*

"Welcome to Dharavi," Nanu said, telling me that it was one of the most densely populated places on earth, with a population estimated at between 300,000 and 700,000.

Our first stop on the tour was at a plastic recycling center in the industrial part of the slum. Two men in soiled clothes used a table saw to cut a plastic water jug. Most of the men who worked there also lived there. Nanu painted it as a symbiotic relationship in which the workers, 80% of whom were migrants, had a free place to stay, the owner had free security and employees who were never late for work.

As Nanu talked, he nodded to the men. His delivery was polished, and his quips were perfectly timed. I had worked as a scuba instructor in Key West for a few years, and I recognized the polish. I could have given my dive briefing while thinking about quantum physics, if I had actually known much about quantum physics, which I didn't. Anyhow, it was automatic.

In the countryside the men farmed and didn't earn much money, and during the rainy season there wasn't much farming to do. In Dharavi, they could make $6 per day.

"Doing something is better than nothing," Nanu told me.

Nanu led me into the room and told me to watch where I stepped. The shop was loud and hot. It was hardly different from a sweatshop I had visited in Bangladesh except they weren't producing clothes here. When we exited into the alley, the hot, sticky Mumbai air felt cool in comparison. A kid stood in a barrel of plastic pieces, washing them with his feet, like a winemaker in France smashing grapes.

We popped into an aluminum recycling center. Nanu was surprised it wasn't operating today. He said that it looked as though they had run out of charcoal.

Paint cans smoked in the corner, spewing noxious fumes into the air. Nanu said this was the dangerous part of the job – breathing. The life expectancy for those who live in Dharavi is 60 years, about seven years less than the average in India.

We walked into another recycling center. A guy delivered two small shot glasses of tea to the two workers inside. The older worker, a guy with disheveled hair and a bit of a belly, told us it was going to rain. One minute later, it was raining. We climbed a steep ladder three stories to the roof and looked out over the slum.

I asked Nanu if the owners of these businesses were compensated for letting us in on the tour. He said this owner believed in what they were doing and let them do it for free.

Bob Ma, a professor at the University of Pennsylvania, surveyed slum tourists and residents. He found that 44.6% of residents thought the tours were good, 27.7% were neutral, and 27.7% disliked the tours. As for the tourists, 37% sensed mixed feelings from slum residents.[3]

We looked out over the tin roofs, recycled plastic pieces strewn across them drying in gray daylight. Most of the roofs were lined with blue or black plastic tarps. The blue plastic tarps are cheaper than the black ones. With an untrained eye, you couldn't see the difference among the various levels of poverty or fathom the number-one factor in the price of real estate: proximity to a community bathroom.

"Dharavi is shaped like a heart," Nanu told me. I couldn't see it from where we stood. I couldn't even see any people or into the streets, just a floor of rusted metal roofs edged by taller buildings and towers.

In 1992, NGOs put a lot of pressure on authorities to legalize land rights of those in the slums. In 1995 a law was passed that all dwellings built before then were legal and any built after that were not. Eventually the date was moved to 2000.

People who are relocated to make way for developers are moved to an apartment in the distance. The private apartments are nice and maintained, but the public ones aren't. Those who are relocated may get moved to a larger place or to a smaller place. You could go from a 250-square-foot apartment to a 325-square-foot apartment. Like Ashok's community and so many other slum communities, Dharavi had become prime real estate, and developers have been circling for years.

In 2015, Mumbai's Urban Design Research Institute held an international competition, called Reinventing Dharavi, to solicit possible solutions. Proposals had to include issues beyond housing, such as

---

[3]Bob Ma, "A Trip into the Controversy: A Study of Slum Tourism Travel Motivations," Undergraduate Humanities Forum 2009–2010: Connections (2010), 12.

employment, health and sanitation, finance, recreation, and legal rights. Proposals included towers of bathrooms, a development program centered around the sport of cricket, and turning the community into a factory town like the ones in China.

The institute received 20 proposals from all over the world, but it was a Mumbai team that won with one question: "How would residents envision their future if they had their rights?" What if people had the right to participate in solving this issue, and the right to earn a living?

"We've had proposals on Dharavi since the 1970s," Jasmin Saluja, a member of the winning team, said, "but the problem is that they've never included the people themselves."[4]

> *Giving Rules: When you're developing solutions to help people,*
> *include the people you are seeking to help. Even better, follow*
> *their lead.*

People didn't have rights to the land; the government owned the majority of it, and developers wanted to get their hands on it. The team came up with the solution that the land would be turned over to a land trust governed by community members and former landowners.

Before his job as a guide with Reality Tours, Nanu had a job collecting documents. He called it being a "doc dog," or more officially, a "doc boy." One of the places in his region was Dharavi. His mom told him to call in sick on the days he was assigned that route.

When he heard about the Reality Tours job, he wasn't sure where it was. He went to the interview and learned that the job would be in the slum.

"Why would people go into the slum?" he asked.

Bob Ma asked the same question in his research on slum tourists and found that cultural curiosity was the primary motivation for tourists going on the tours. But curiosity isn't always a good thing. It leads us to rubberneck as we drive past an accident on the highway; it leads us to seek out gossip about a coworker. The most telling part of Ma's report was that "[t]ourists expressed little desire to interact with slum residents, which would have allowed them to gain a deeper understanding of slum culture, and hence a more authentic experience of slum life."[5]

---

[4]Carlin Carr, "The Best Idea to Redevelop Dharavi Slum? Scrap the Plans and Start Again," *The Guardian*, www.theguardian.com/cities/2015/feb/18/best-ideas-redevelop-dharavi-slum-developers-india (February 18, 2018).
[5]Ma, "A Trip into the Controversy," 35.

We left the roof and visited a community bathroom, where I learned there were only 700 toilets in the entire community. That's about one toilet per thousand people. Some of the toilets are public toilets and some are private.

Nanu showed me Reality Tours' community center operated by its nonprofit arm, Reality Gives. A Martin Luther King Jr. quote hung on the wall: "Intelligence plus character – that is the goal of true education." Inside, girls danced to a mix of jazz and Hindi music. The center hosts English and art classes. Reality Tours also supports a government-recognized primary school and pays the salaries of the teachers.

Reality Tours has a graphic touting how 80% of its profit goes back to the community, but when you dig deeper, it requires more explanation. The tour company actually gives 80% of "post tax profit," meaning that in a year it gives "up to 30%" of its income. In 2015 and 2016 it gave around $78,000 to Reality Gives, according to its own report.

The company sees tourism as a force for good because the tours change the opinions of foreign and domestic travelers, and as a way to fund educational opportunities in the Dharavi community. The company employs locals. It has provided education in English and given computers to 400 students between the ages of 16 and 30, has trained 15 teachers who teach 400 students, and has engaged 130 children through a variety of sports programs. Reality Tours is doing something, but is it enough?

Fabian Frenzel, author *of Slumming It: The Tourist Valorization of Urban Poverty*, sees the potential value in slum tourism. He takes a historical look at the phenomenon and finds it appears at times of greater inequality where there is growing conflict and awareness between rich and poor. Slum tourism crosses the divide between rich and poor and allows societies to address challenges that have created the divide in the first place. Solutions such as social housing and welfare have helped check inequality. Typically, this has taken place on a national level, but now slum tourism takes place in a world more connected than before. Still, Frenzel sees some positive impacts in recent history:

> Tourist interest in slums has influenced policymakers. In South Africa policy has attempted to use the tourism income streams for the cherished "broad based black economic empowerment," attempting to make the tourism industry more beneficial for the country's black and often relatively poor majority. In Rio de Janeiro, favela tourism has been embraced and supported by policy in attempt to "pacify" and normalize favelas and

to create employment and income opportunities. In Medellin, Colombia, the city government improved the transport infrastructure of Medellin's barrios by constructing cable cars that provide access to the city.[6]

Frenzel also sees how slum tourism can negatively impact communities by increasing land values, making it more likely that developers would move in and displace those who live there.

People who go on slum tours are curious about the lives of the poor. That's not necessarily a bad thing. As we learned from Paul Bloom's work, the problem with empathy is that it is a spotlight limited to those near us or like us. Those who live in the slum will never enter our spotlight of concern if we don't meet them, see where they live, and try to understand their concerns.

For instance, I go places, meet people, and write about them. Before I travel somewhere, I do some initial research about a place and the issues the people there may face. But I do struggle diving into books, articles, and journals about, say, the Bangladeshi garment industry until I've been there. After the fact, I can read these books and attach names, faces, and families to the topic.

In 2013, the Rana Plaza garment factory collapsed, killing 1,134 people. In 2007, I had spent quite a bit of time interacting with workers in this area. I played cricket with kids, I ate dinner in homes, and I even took 19 kids and one old farmer to an amusement park. When I heard about the Rana Plaza disaster in 2013, I wanted to throw up. I thought of the people I had met. *Were they in the factory? Did they lose a loved one?*

Since then, other events have led to an even greater loss of life: the 6,000-plus Rohingya who have been killed in Myanmar, and the refugee crisis of northern Africa. Intellectually, I knew these were each travesties, but I didn't feel them.

But when the earthquake hit Nepal, or a hurricane hit Key West, when some tragedy or disaster hits a place I've been to, impacting people I've met, I care more. It's a flaw and feature of humanity.

I exited the Reality Tours gift shop and thanked Nanu. I had learned a lot about Dharavi, and it was presented in a positive light.

A slum, or any community, really, isn't a place you can just show up and experience on your own. What if some foreign tourist showed up where you lived and started taking photos and asking questions? That would be weird, right?

---

[6]Fabian Frenzel, *Slumming It: The Tourist Valorization of Urban Poverty* (London: Zed Books, 2016), 2.

You need connections; you need to know someone from the community to visit. If you don't have connections or a purpose that a journalist or aid worker might have, and even those can be dubious sometimes, why would you ever visit the slum? And that's where I think my mind changed on slum tours. It's a horrible name, and I see why people are put off by it, but I feel like many who go on a tour aren't there for the wrong reasons. Their curiosity comes from a good place. They want to understand the lives of those who live in the slum, and a tour may be their best opportunity to do that. They probably won't get the chance to eat chicken curry and drink whiskey with someone's dad or play cricket with the kids. But they'll know more about life there than they did before.

However, in Dharavi, I didn't have one interaction with a resident other than stepping out of his or her way. Nanu showed me the slum much like Jacob Marley and the other ghosts showed Ebenezer Scrooge the world of his past, present, and future.

I didn't come to know the name of a single man, woman, or child. I passed real people living out their real lives. I saw them, but I didn't really know what their lives were like. I smelled the saw blade burn through plastic in the recycling center, learned the difference between blue and black plastic sheeting, and imagined a real estate market determined by proximity to the restroom. I saw their external reality, a stark contrast to my life back home and the lives of many of the other tourists who go on a tour. I saw the inequity in our world. And I won't forget.

Travel can increase caring. It's an opportunity to lift the spotlight and expand the boundaries of empathy. But not all travel is equal.

*Giving Rules: Experiences expand our empathy.*

# 19

# Joy in a Hopeless Place (Kenya, 2017)

*Safari Doctors / Following the locals' lead /*
*Go make a difference / Investing in people*

---

**THE RAIN FELL IN MY DREAMS.** And then it fell harder until I was awake and wet.

I sat up and looked at Mom, both of us shaking off the dementia of sleep.

*Where are we?* Our looks communicated the question.

Tarps flapped in a salty breeze and barefoot sailors stepped over us with purpose and grace. When I closed my eyes to try to drift back into sleep, it was as if they disappeared. Rain or not, I was tired. I could only imagine how Mom felt. The night before, we had tried to sleep in Nairobi, but gunshots directed at protesters of Kenya's presidential election had kept us nervous and awake.

We boarded the boat at 3 a.m. under the light of our cell phones and the moon and found a spot on a thin mattress on the top deck. There was a mast, but it was unlike any sailboat I had seen. I was too tired to care, so I slept.

When the sun finally pushed through the clouds, we awoke to a rainbow rising from Kenya's Lamu Archipelago and the anchor dropping into the Indian Ocean.

There's something magical about traveling at night; you know there is a world out there to be seen and discovered, and that there are people who live in that world, but you can't see it or imagine it. And suddenly it's dawn and the sail is taut, the land is wooded, the headscarves of the women on the boat are bright, and the rain clouds are gray. It's like arriving all at once – maybe the closest feeling I'll ever get to teleportation.

*How'd I get here? How'd Mom get here?*

The islands of Lamu, Kenya, are a long way from Darke County, Ohio, where we were both born and raised, and where Mom still lives. The two of us being in Lamu on the boat felt as likely as a resident from Lamu showing up in our driveway.

The crew lowered the lateen-rigged sail. The arm crossed the mast at the top like a T, and there was no boom. Such rigging dates back to the Age of Discovery. This Arabic boat is known as a dhow.

Captain Ali emerged on the bow and started tucking things away. The years added by Ali's white beard were subtracted by his smooth face. He was a weathered sailor who wasn't weathered. We sailed with him for four days. He didn't use a depth gauge or GPS; he sailed by guts and experience. Coming from a long line of woodworkers, he saved for years and built this boat himself. The Smithsonian even commissioned him to build a dhow for its museum. When he built the boat we were on, he had no idea that it would become a mobile medical clinic.

Breakfast was Swahili tea – black tea with ginger and sugar – along with fruit and bread. The crew and the staff and volunteers of an NGO, Safari Doctors, joined us.

"Lamu is the only county in Kenya that has less than one kilometer of paved roads," Umra Omar said, discussing the work of Safari Doctors. "The same thing that makes it beautiful, isolated, and pristine is the same thing that presents the challenges for access to health care. From the southernmost tip, which is in Lamu, all the way to the northernmost tip, that's a two-hour speedboat ride, about $300. For the average person from Lamu, that's not something you just cough up to run to the district hospital."

Safari Doctors brings the hospital to patients. Once a month, Safari Doctors sails with Captain Ali to provide access to medical care for 20,000 residents in remote areas of Lamu County.

My friend, Kelly Campbell, who owns and operates The Village Experience, a socially responsible travel company, told me I should sail with

Safari Doctors to learn more about their work. I asked if I could bring my mom. This was before I knew that Mom would have to poop into the ocean through a hole at the stern of the boat – not that she did – and that our one-night cruise would become four poopless nights. But our living conditions became the last thing on our minds.

A small skiff dropped us off at the first village. The villagers were waiting for us at an empty building with a tile floor. The boxes we carried from the shore were turned into a makeshift medical clinic in less than 15 minutes. The first door became a pharmacy, the second an exam room, and the third an optometry office.

The porch and surrounding area quickly became a waiting room spilling over with moms with sick kids, ill adults who wanted to be anywhere else, and grandmas who had more grandkids than teeth. Mom and I attempted to get a reaction from the kids with little success. I'm not sure what we expected. A party?

Wairimu, the program manager, opened up a giant ledger and started recording names and maladies.

I shadowed Harrison Kalu, the head nurse, as he welcomed his first patients – four soldiers who all entered at the same time and requested HIV tests. Kalu pricked their fingers, put a drop of blood on each thin strip and told them to wait. They joked and danced nervously. One of them farted. Outside, everyone else waited while the soldiers stared at their tests.

The soldiers live in a school on the edge of the village. The state-sponsored teachers had left long ago, fearing further attacks by al-Shabaab militants who operate in the area. The jihadist fundamentalist group was responsible for attacks such as the one at the Westgate shopping mall in Nairobi where gunmen killed 67 and injured 175 people. The group had spread from Somalia and recruited young Kenyans living in poverty. Al-Shabaab cut off the villagers from their fields and almost any source of income and sustenance. The soldiers were there to protect the villagers. The soldiers were also bored young men in an isolated village. They protected the villagers from al-Shabaab, but who protected the villagers from the soldiers?

The soldiers left the room, all HIV-free, and then returned for one-on-one consultations about other health concerns. Kalu, clad in a red winter coat despite the heat, welcomed the first, shut the door, and the young soldier dropped his pants and took out his penis.

"We're all men here," Kalu said and motioned for me to take a look.

He pointed with his pen to a bump on the end of the soldier's penis. The soldier was worried that it was a sexually transmitted disease.

Kalu took his time pointing and considering and explaining. Then he drew on a pad what syphilis would look like, and said something about blood and pustules, all while the soldier held his manhood and I did my best not to puke. It wasn't the sight that concerned me, but an uncomfortable question: At such an isolated outpost, who were the soldiers having sex with?

The women and children waited on the porch for the soldiers to finish their rounds.

One thought he had malaria, but didn't. Another had sprained his ankle so badly that we took him back with us to catch a boat to a hospital.

And finally, when all the concerns, aches, and pains of the men – at the peak of their physical lives – were met, a mother entered carrying her chubby baby boy. Yusuf wore a blue beanie and a wide-eyed look of trust and confusion. His mom sat him up and he reached for the table Kalu used as a desk.

I've held my kids as they've received vaccinations. All snuggled in what they knew as the world's most secure place, and then experienced the surprise and injustice of concentrated pain. I wondered if they trusted me less afterward. I wondered if it was the first time they learned a cruel reality of our world: Sometimes things that are good for us hurt.

Kalu gave Yusuf the shot and his mom comforted him just like my wife and I comforted our kids, as if hugs could relieve the pain. They can, actually. Scientists can measure cortisol, the stress hormone, in a baby's saliva. A baby who is held by a trusted adult will have its cortisol level spike, but the level will decline more quickly than for a baby who is not being held.[1] This is as true in Kenya as it is in Indiana.

Kalu, 65, has been vaccinating kids in Lamu since 1987, first for the Ministry of Health and then for a string of organizations, including USAID and an organization that did similar work to that of Safari Doctors, the Sailing Doctors.

Sailing Doctors operated from 2009 until 2012 until a series of attacks forced the organization out of the area. That didn't stop Kalu, though. He continued to travel by motorbike into the Boni forest, an al-Shabaab hideout.

"I was there for six years," Kalu said, "right in the Boni forest. It was a very good experience. I used to hear that al-Shabaab was hitting here and hitting there, but they had not come to my station until one day. It was good luck I wasn't there. I had gone to Lamu. But they burnt the

---

[1]Nicholas Kristof and Sheryl WuDunn, *A Path Appears* (New York: Vintage, 2015), 54.

motorbikes and robbed some medicine and a few records. They asked for me by name."

The al-Shabaab fighter who asked for Kalu said that Kalu had circumcised him when he was a boy.

"They wanted to get me to take me to the forest to treat casualties. But the problem could be that after treating the casualties, I could not go back. Maybe they could do away with me. Give me a bullet shot. But they did not get me. So ... that's why we want to open another station for Safari Doctors. It should be me who is there full-time."

I asked Kalu if he feared al-Shabaab.

"It was dangerous, but if I'm serving my people," Kalu said, "I was not worried. I just infuse into their shoes and become part and parcel of the community."

### *Giving Rules: Put yourself in the shoes of those you serve.*

Kalu took it upon himself to continue serving the people he could reach on the mainland by his motorbike. Umra, the founder of Safari Doctors, said that there was even a six-month stretch where her organization couldn't afford to pay Kalu, but he still made the trips.

Kalu is the only medical staff of Safari Doctors. Each month he works alongside volunteer doctors and specialists.

I watched Kalu diagnose, prescribe, and treat, and then I rejoined Mom on the porch, which was now even more crowded with patients. I struck up a conversation with one of the village elders. He walked us to his home, a dirt-floored, mud hut with a thatched roof. He was the father of seven children, some of whom were climbing on the bamboo frame inside the home. His wife welcomed us. She seemed proud of her husband or that we had come to visit. I couldn't help but think that she was putting false hope in what our presence could mean for her life.

"I tried to start a business," he said, "but it is hard because of the limitation on travel."

He tried to sell sugar, flour, rice, and cooking oil, but the roads were shut down by al-Shabaab and now accessible only by motorbike.

Some of the men fished, but only to feed their families. There was no way to make an income since they were cut off from the fields and the world.

"I'm a community health worker," he said proudly. "I was trained by the Red Cross in 2009."

He filled the gaps when no medical assistance was available. When someone was sick or injured and had a problem beyond his training and supplies, he would march up a nearby hill where he could get cell phone reception and call for a doctor.

The village relied heavily on charity. Some of the elders expressed frustration about this.

"It is really disheartening that whenever we need something we have to ask for it," he said. "We can't farm."

We walked back to the clinic and the man followed us. Before we parted he asked me if I could help him.

"Leave!" I wanted to say. "Why do you stay here? Go start a life somewhere else."

I think it's natural to have these thoughts, to see a problem and want to come up with a solution, regardless of whether we know what the hell we are talking about. *What about solar panels? What about catching the rain off the roof? Goats? Saving groups?* The intentions come from a good place, no matter how misguided. I think there is a bit of me that puts myself in their shoes and wonders what I would do – as if I could come up with some solution if I had been dealt the same hand.

Economist William Easterly writes, "There is a fear of inaction and indifference on the tragic problems of global poverty… But wrong actions are equally a danger, and they may create more indifference and disillusionment when they fail."[2]

> *Giving Rules: Sometimes the best thing to do is nothing.*

As much as I hate to admit it, if I were in their situation, I'd probably be in the same place as this man, following an American and asking if he could help. Actually, I would probably fare worse.

Stephen Jay Gould challenges us to think about how far our natural gifts will get us when our lives are oppressed by poverty or injustice.

"I am somehow less interested in the weight and convolutions of Einstein's brains than in the near certainty that people of equal talent have lived and died in cotton fields and sweatshops."[3]

I repeated to the man why I was there, apologized that I couldn't help, and wished the man the best.

Umra led us over to the school turned military barracks. We passed a crumbling latrine, long ago dedicated by an aid organization but not maintained: another broken promise.

A drunk soldier approached me.

---

[2] William Easterly, *The Tyranny of Experts* (New York: Basic Books, 2013), 15.
[3] Stephen Jay Gould, *The Panda's Thumb* (New York: W.W. Norton & Co., 1980), 151.

"I'm very happy you have come here," he said. "You have left your homes, but you are doing something good. We appreciate very much. It is not easy for a guy like you. You should be in London watching football, not in this place."

Bottles of alcohol littered the schoolyard and the edges of trenches. Hammocks were strung up between trees. Every soldier seemed to be drunk. Fifty soldiers lived here and didn't seem to be attacked by anything other than boredom and alcoholism.

Umra had arrived by a speedboat with my friend Kelly Campbell from The Village Experience and representatives of the M. Night Shyamalan Foundation, including Dr. Bhavna Shyamalan and her two daughters. Bhavna's husband is M. Night Shyamalan, the producer, writer, and director of films such as *The Sixth Sense*, *The Village*, and *Signs*.

"We travel around and look for leaders like Umra who are making an impact and a change, and then we have a leader that we support," explained Dr. Shyamalan, a psychologist.

### Giving Rules: Invest in people.

She told me that they aren't a large foundation so they look for smaller organizations where their dollars can make a real impact.

"We're looking for people who are dedicated to their community who will make it work, no matter what. They have that tenacity, drive, and passion. We look for younger organizations that we can build relationships with. There really is something special here. On the boat ride you realize how hard it is to get medication."

Their boat ride was through rough seas, rain, and seasickness. Her daughters handled it like champs.

The women of the village welcomed us into a circle, and Umra chatted one-on-one for all to hear with a woman who was a village elder wearing fabrics printed with every color of the rainbow.

In a pause in their conversation, Umra told us what they were discussing.

"We're trying to figure out what would be an income-generating activity and why there isn't anything happening right now," she said. "The mentality right now is to do business within – opening a little store or shop, selling some cigarettes or clothes … I'm asking what they could do outside. And the biggest craft they sell is the weaving."

Umra patted the large flat mats we sat on.

"The market is outside. So what I am interested in is if there is one particular thing that we can get everyone to hone in on, and then we are the ones who have to take it out. It could be as simple as doing it at our shop as a product that goes directly to the community."

Safari Doctors' office is located in the village of Shela, a tourist community where donkeys and tourists mix on narrow carless streets.

Umra and the woman began brainstorming, and the other women joined in.

"So what we'll do between now and the next clinic is we'll definitely put in an order to get the momentum started, and then they are going to brainstorm what can be done and we'll research other things they can make."

"We need to do something creative," Umra said. "Because there is nothing happening here."

------

Umra Omar was not like other girls growing up on the Swahili Coast, where most people were Muslim.

"I came from a community … where if you were young someone was making decisions for you," she told me.

Many people along the coast think girls and women shouldn't swim, their robes and hijabs making it hard to do so. Even in Shela there are very few girls jumping and playing on the long beach. But Umra loved swimming. The first time she ever got into trouble was when she made up a story that she needed to stay after school and then went swimming. Her parents were different, too. They weren't angry that she went swimming, but they were angry because she lied to them.

Recently, a man on a boat told Umra that she needed to sit more carefully or the boat might tip over and he wouldn't be able to rescue all of the women. She thanked him for his concern, but really what she wanted to do was tell him that she was a lifeguard and a scuba diver and then punch him in the face.

When she was in high school in Nairobi, she organized a poetry competition. She marched into newspaper offices and walked out with free ads. She somehow managed to convince the largest mall in the city to host the competition for free.

Children of a family friend had attended a school in Wales, and they thought it would be a good fit for Umra if she could get accepted with a scholarship.

"We think Umra would be a good candidate because she is already a loudmouth and likes climbing trees," Umra recounted them saying.

The United World School was founded during the height of the Cold War based on the idea to "bring together young people from different nations to act as champions of peace through an education based on shared learning, collaboration and understanding." Students are recruited from 155 nations, and 70% of them receive full or partial tuition assistance.

"It was four students in a room and everyone had to be from a different continent," Umra said. "That's the first place I learned about the Israeli-Palestinian relations. It was like a global classroom in the middle of sheep land in Wales. You have to take up community service. I did lifeguarding. So here was this girl from Lamu out in the Bristol Channel in a kayak freezing."

For the first time in her life she could make decisions, like eating as many white chocolate chip cookies as she wanted. She realized she was now responsible not only for herself, but also for those around her.

"Imagine your brain just being put on a table and being stretched as far as it can go," Umra said about her experiences at the school.

Jill Longson, a 1981 graduate of the school, created GoMakeADifference (Go M.A.D.), which funds 30 $1,000 student projects each year. In 2002, at the height of the AIDS concern in Africa, Umra proposed a youth awareness event in Nairobi. She was awarded the grant. Even though she still didn't know what she wanted to be or what to major in, Umra looks back on that and thinks, "Oh my God, it's pretty much exactly what I'm doing ... two decades later."

Oberlin College, a small school in northern Ohio, recruited Umra and gave her a full-ride scholarship. (So maybe it's not so unlikely that someone from Lamu would just show up in the Midwest.)

During Umra's first year, a friend at Oberlin wrote a paper asking classmates, "What do you aspire to be?"

"I imagined being a bridge," Umra said. "I imagined where I'm from and where I've been: a bridge between my roots and the experiences that have come."

She still sees herself as a bridge. She lives in Shela, where tourists can stay at luxurious accommodations and spend an afternoon poolside at a resort worthy of a glossy travel magazine spread while people bring them drinks. Yet her thoughts and efforts are directed at supporting those who live in remote areas.

"The beauty of being in such a bipolar place ... we can help those worlds merge, be the bridge between the glossy and the matte. And see how we can create those links. We're matchmakers on the island. I live in a paradise and it's because of living in a paradise that every day I can wake up and feel that I need to give and get this going."

She studied neuroscience and psychology at Oberlin. She had grown up in a culture that tried to suppress certain human instincts. She was interested in understanding how these things worked on a biological level. What happens inside of your body when you like someone, when you kiss someone?

She received her master's in social justice, and she started to make connections among behavior, fear, identity, and gender.

When the opportunity to start Safari Doctors came up, she wasn't sure at first about transitioning from job security and comfort to the unknown.

"Sometimes you might be doing something," she said, "even if it is the right thing, you have this little voice, 'Do you really think this is going to make a difference?' or 'How arrogant can you be?' It's the biggest devil I wrestle with still."

> *Giving Rules: Even people who are giving the most feel like they aren't giving enough.*

Umra started Safari Doctors in 2015 when it was just Kalu on his motorbike. They would celebrate a $50 donation because it was enough money for fuel to reach the communities. But by January 2016, they were running out of funds.

"Kalu," she recalled breaking the news, "come January I don't have a salary for you. But I have a gut feeling from June we'll be fine."

Her gut feeling was based on nothing more than optimism. There was no way she could've known what was about to happen.

Kalu told her he would be fine. He had a farm so he wouldn't go hungry, and he had a roof over his head.

Safari Doctors wasn't even an official organization, just something they did. Starting out, they needed support, but support needed history.

And then in June, CNN showed up. They later named her a CNN Hero, which came with some money but even more attention, garnering the interests of individuals and groups like the M. Night Shyamalan Foundation.

And then in July, a group of Americans looking for an organization in Lamu to support gave them enough funds to sail for a year.

To this day, she hates the question "What do you do?" In Kenya it seemed the only appropriate answers were that you were a lawyer, doctor, or accountant.

She has four jobs: Safari Doctors, property manager, regional director for a conservation organization, and the founder of a new school in Shela. But that's not what she does.

"I find joy taking care of my community and my family," Umra said. "That's what I do."

During a virtual visit, a high school class somewhere in the US recently asked her how they could make a difference.

"There is this idea in giving that it has to be something somewhere else. You have to do books for a library [in another country]. It's been sensationalized to the point where that's the only form of giving. What's in your backyard? Maybe it's doing a bake sale for the local clinic or getting a kid glasses – something really small that you can focus on.

"How can you use your education as an agent of change for your community?" Umra challenged the students. "Giving is the most basic thing you can do."

I asked her if she is ever overwhelmed by the need, and her answer, based on a quote by the poet Rumi, is still something I think about.

"You are not a drop in an ocean; you are an ocean in a drop."

---

The elder woman sitting across from Umra in the village drew with her finger through the dirt on which she sat. They were still looking for solutions.

The group discussed fixing the old latrine, but decided that it would benefit only those who lived near it. They should focus on a community center. They wanted to do something that could benefit the whole community. If they had a center they wouldn't have to have meetings sitting in the sun on dirt. They would have a place to weave, a place where women could come together to have seminars on health education.

Umra listened (see Figure 19.1). Safari Doctors visits every month. They could turn the villagers' plans into a reality.

"More than anything, I am endorsing that plan," Umra said, pointing to the elder's design in the dirt. "This is the architectural design."

In less than a year, the drawing in the dirt would become the community center the women imagined.

The women got excited and the elder talked faster. Umra recently had a baby, and the women had a party for her, but they haven't seen the baby yet. They want Umra to bring her so they could spit on her baby, chasing away any curses.

The women stood.

"We are going to have a party," Umra said to me. "Do you like to dance?"

"Mom does," I answered.

The women sang and clapped while the oldest of the elders stood in the middle; and they shook their booties, the wrinkles in their faces pulled by wide smiles.

*Figure 19.1    Umra talking and listening to women in an isolated village in Lamu.*

Umra joined them and smiled, the braces on her teeth shining in the sun. This was obviously not her first time. She mimicked the women and then added a few of her own moves that they would in turn mimic.

Two women pulled Mom in. They had her bend slightly forward and hold out her hands and shuffle back and forth as if she were guarding an imaginary basketball player. Mom mirrored a woman in a red-and-white-striped shirt and blue dress. If it weren't for her orange headscarf, she'd have looked like a dancing American flag.

A village that seemed desperate for joy and hope rang with it. It wasn't something that we brought; it was something that had always been there.

# 20

# See Yourself in the Lives of Others (Kenya, 2017)

*It's a wonderful life? / Our struggles connect us / Wisdom of traditional societies*

———

**LITTLE GIRLS LAUGHED AND CLAPPED,** and babies strapped to mothers' backs slept, while Mom danced.

A few years ago Mom told me that when she was in high school she wanted to be a travel writer. She graduated and went to a business college for a year before becoming pregnant. Mom and Dad got married in a ceremony I haven't heard much about. They moved into a mobile home, but her life was anything but mobile. Dad worked at construction and on his parents' farm. Mom worked as a secretary for an auto manufacturer that has long since closed.

She lost the baby. His name was Michael. I've always felt some connection with him. *If he had lived, would they have decided to have a third child after my older brother, Kyle, was born? Would I be here?*

Mom and Dad lived in the trailer for only a few months. I wonder, what was 20-year-old Lynne thinking in the mornings? At work? When you are 20 and want to be a travel writer, you want to move and

197

never stop. Explore, but never stay too long in one place. I remember the ache of wanderlust and the fear of being stuck.

I felt every word George Bailey had to say in *It's a Wonderful Life* when he told Mary that he wanted to shake the "dust of this crummy little town" off his feet, "see the world," "go to college to see what they know," and build skyscrapers and bridges.

But George didn't get to travel or build things. He built a life with kids and a struggling family business. His life wasn't what he imagined it would be, but he gave to his family and his community, and they all became something they wouldn't have if not for him. And Clarence the angel told him: "Strange, isn't it? Each man's life touches so many other lives. When he isn't around he leaves an awful hole, doesn't he?"

I learned to scuba dive when I was 13 in Ohio with Mom. The first time I left the country was on a trip to the Bahamas with Mom to take the plunge on our first open-water dives. We did a shark dive, too. My nose bled into my mask, and Mom didn't freak out that much. She accidentally snuck me into a topless show at a casino. She was the first to expose me to a world beyond the rural Midwest. And more than show me the world, she was the first to teach me how to see it through the books we read, the news we watched in the morning, and the conversations we had. She believed in fairness, justice, and diversity.

By DNA, upbringing, or both, Mom passed her wanderlust on to me.

After losing their business in the financial crisis, Mom and Dad bounced back. Mom started a successful yoga practice, and Dad got a new business up and running. Mom hadn't taken a two-week vacation in years, maybe never.

But this was no vacation, and I was worried about how she was doing. Besides the absence of creature comforts on the boat, her lack of sleep, and the gunshots in Nairobi, she was witnessing abject poverty for the first time.

It was a lot to process.

The dancing at the village made me feel better. It was good to see Mom smiling. But behind the smile, she felt useless. Everyone had their roles. Kalu treated, and the other staff organized. Kelly escorted the Shyamalans. I felt useless, given the realities the villagers, but I had a job: to write. But Mom?

"There wasn't a damn thing I could do," she told me.

It was low tide when we sailed up to the second village. The dinghy bottomed out a distance from the shore and we had to get out and walk. Our feet sank into the mud until they met sharp rocks, sending shocks of pain that traveled all the way to our teeth. It was slow going.

*Figure 20.1    The kids helping the author's mom to shore.*

The village sits on a hill overlooking the shore, and kids ran down to greet us. When they saw Mom struggling, three of them came to her side and grabbed her by the hands (see Figure 20.1). They appeared genuinely concerned for her well-being, like small therapists helping an adult learn to walk again.

### Giving Rules: Sometimes you are the one who needs help.

The gray sky sucked the color out of the mud and the sea. Mom's red rain jacket along with the yellow dress of the oldest girl at her side, were the only splashes of color on a drab pallette.

Mom laughs too hard at sitcoms and can outplay most of her grandkids. She doesn't act the part, but she is a grandma, 63 years young.

When the crew on the boat prepared meals, everyone could chip in to help but Mom. I think the sailors would have preferred to stab her before they would have let her cut a cucumber. The same went for when we carried things to and from the boat.

"Honor the elders, even if they are not yours," so says a Swahili proverb.

Sometimes in Western society, we think that we are at the pinnacle of modern life and that those cultures that aren't swiping smart phones want to become like us, and that we can show them the way. However, I often find that we have every bit as much to learn from other cultures as to teach. How the locals treated the elderly here stood out to both Mom and me. Our culture fears aging and values youth and beauty as if, in the words of Carrie Fisher, they were "accomplishments" and not "temporary by-products of time and/or DNA." And, in turn, traditional cultures are more likely to value the lasting by-products of time – experience and wisdom.

*Giving Rules: We have more to learn than to teach.*

Mom is my elder (although if I put it like that she would probably slap me), but I wasn't really in a position to help her. I was struggling to walk as well. And as much as Mom was being honored by the kids, I knew that if I fell face first into the mud, the kids would make fun of me. So I slogged along, cussing to myself, grimacing at each painful step.

Mom smiled at Miriam, the girl in the yellow dress, who smiled back. She was the girl that Mom would remember more than the rest.

"She doesn't know it, but I will never forget her," Mom would tell me later, as she showed me a picture collage of Miriam on her phone.

On the shore in the empty medical clinic, we helped Kalu and Robert, the volunteer optometrist, set up to receive patients, and then once again we didn't have much to do. I grabbed "the key to the world," my Aerobie SuperDisc – a Frisbee that everyone can throw – and led the kids into a grassy open area next to the playground paid for by a previous group of visitors arranged by Kelly of The Village Experience.

I remember as a kid watching Mom throw a faded red Frisbee. It defied physics as it hung in the air and curved to its target. It was one of those things that required adult coordination – like buttering corn on the cob or tying knots – which seemed unattainable.

I watched as Mom showed Miriam how to throw the disc. She was a quick learner. She also spoke English and helped Mom direct the other kids to form a circle and learn how to throw the Aerobie.

At first the kids always threw the disc back to Mom. After a few rounds, she tried to focus on the timid kids, aiming right in front of their feet.

The circle collapsed as the kids stepped forward at each throw to be the first to grab the disc.

"Big circle," Mom said, throwing her arms into the air. "Big circle."

"Big circle! Big circle!" the kids chanted, imitating Mom's voice and arms.

Kids caught the disc in their hands and, to the amusement of everyone, in their faces. When a few of the boys turned it into a game of tackle Frisbee, Mom and Miriam talked sternly to them.

This village looked much different than the first. The UK-based Al-Khair foundation constructed 28 new, two-bedroom furnished homes. The villagers had been in them for only a month. Al-Khair also built the health clinic, a mosque, and an early childhood education center. Power lines connected homes, and cisterns collected water. The kids here also acted differently. They were more playful and ornery and bright-eyed.

While Mom played with the kids, a mother of six children waiting in line at the clinic told me, "Life has changed completely. I can stand the rain and the cold because I'm living in a nice place."

The Safari Doctors did their work, and then Kalu went off by boat to visit a patient who was too sick to make the journey to the village. Mom and Miriam entertained the kids.

"When they came out to walk me in," Mom said, "she was the one who reached out right away. She was right at my side the whole time. She just reached out and touched my heart."

Mom felt useful entertaining the kids, keeping them from standing around gawking as the Safari Doctors treated people.

"Experiencing a little bit of their world was one of the highlights of the trip," Mom said.

> *Giving Rules: Sometimes you have to show up and figure out how to be useful on the fly.*

---

A Land Cruiser met us at the dock, and took us to the third village. We all piled in hip-to-hip next to the supplies.

There was no one at the medical clinic when we arrived. A boat had capsized, and the villagers, along with others from all over the region, had gone to visit the families of those who had drowned.

Kids showed up first and began sweeping out the clinic. One of the first adults to arrive was a man carrying his 18-month-old son.

"Where's your desk?" he asked, thinking I was a doctor.

What else would I be? This isn't the first time that this has happened to me. In Bangladesh and in Honduras, I had been taken to the bedsides of elderly men who were dying from malaria. Once again, I felt helpless and useless.

Ahmed lowered his son, Ali, to the ground and his legs didn't even try to stand. They folded beneath him. When he moved his head his eyes didn't follow. There was something not right. I could see it in Ali's legs and in Ahmed's look of concern (see Figure 20.2).

"Around two months old," Ahmed said, "we noticed something was going on. I took him to Lamu and they said to take him to Mombasa and that it was urgent."

He handed me a months-old note from a doctor referring him to have an "urgent" CT scan in Mombasa. He couldn't afford the $90 CT scan, the cost of the trip or accommodations, nor the time away from working as a fisherman. Besides, his wife was about to have another child and needed him at home. He was stuck worrying and waiting.

Kalu held Ali in the makeshift examination room, and attempted to have him stand. He moved his head from side to side. Kalu thought it was cerebral palsy, but there was really nothing he could do. Even if the CT scan led to a diagnosis, the list of doctors and therapists that Ali could benefit from was long and inaccessible.

Wairimu said that when she got back to the office, she'd track down how to get them to Mombasa. Safari Doctors could pay for his transport and the CT scan, but doesn't pay for accommodation because most people have family who live in Mombasa. Ahmed seemed to be the rare exception. He said his only relative in Mombasa didn't have the space to host him.

I hurt for Ahmed. When my son, Griffin, was 18 months old, our pediatrician, after ticking through the developmental checklist questions, asked us, "What do you know about autism?"

He advised us to make an appointment at a children's hospital in Indianapolis. We worried and waited for three months until the day his appointment came. We knew that Griffin needed some help or therapy that was beyond anything our love could provide or insurance could afford without a diagnosis, and we felt utterly helpless, like we were on an island alone looking for help in any direction but seeing only water and no boats.

I told Ahmed about Griffin and how great his big sister Harper has been with him.

*Figure 20.2    Ahmed standing with his children. One of them holds Ali.*

"My other children play with him and love him," Ahmed said. "But I want him to be able to interact with them more fully."

Sometimes our struggles isolate us from one another. Griffin is certainly more isolated than most kids without autism – not that he cares. Autism is also isolating for us as a family. There are the practical matters of worrying about Griffin running off at social or public gatherings or knowing that if people invite us over, Griffin will explore every room of their house. But there are also feelings that I'm ashamed to have and share: envy from watching other kids play basketball or have conversations longer than a sentence or two with their parents; self-pity, sorrow, and grief. At some point I've felt all these things and then felt guilty for feeling them because Griffin is an amazing, quirky, affectionate little dude who amazes me each day. Sometimes I look at neurotypical boys and think, "Thank God we have a Griffin."

A few years ago those stones with inspirational words such as *hope, dream, love, laugh* were popular. I kind of imagine autism written on one of those stones – let's call it a life stone – and I carry it around and never put it down. I hold the autism stone in my hand, so sometimes I don't have enough hands or the capacity to do certain things. There are some public places where it's difficult to walk around carrying a stone. I've spent days staring at the autism stone in my hands and all that it meant for Griffin and our family, wallowing in it and never looking up.

We all carry life stones around. Some are heavier. Some require both hands and a lifetime of focus. Yours probably says something different from mine. But if we get to a place where we can look up from our burdens, we will likely bump into someone carrying one similar to ours.

That was how I felt when I met Ahmed and Ali. I saw myself and my son in them.

Ahmed said good-bye and carried Ali home.

> **Giving Rules: Allow your burdens to connect you to people, not isolate you.**

I imagined what our lives would be like if we lived on Ahmed's island. It happened at other stops on our sail as well. One family entered a clinic with a son who looked anywhere but in the eyes of others. Someone always had a hand on him so he didn't dart away.

"What do you know about autism?" I asked the father, and then I told him about Griffin and what has worked for us.

Mom pointed out that the better the living conditions of the village, the more likely we were to see kids and adults with developmental delays and disabilities. Did they not survive or, even worse, were some burdens too heavy to bear? It was unthinkable, but if you had six kids already and thought your baby was going to suffer ... ?

Some of Rozy's friends in Korogocho thought she should have left her baby in the dump because it would be easier to find a new husband. It's an appalling thought, but infanticide or "benign neglect," where a mother stops feeding a child, are realities, more common in places that have limited resources such as food and health care.

"In many traditional societies, however, infanticide is acceptable under certain circumstances," Jared Diamond writes in *The World Until Yesterday: What Can We Learn from Traditional Societies?*. "While this practice horrifies us, it is difficult to see what else the societies could do under some of the conditions with infanticide … when it becomes difficult for the small number of productive adults to provide food for the larger number of non-producing children and old people. An additional consuming but non-productive mouth is then a burden that the society can ill afford."[1]

Ahmed returned alone and called us over to the shade of a tree, where he emptied a pile of coconuts onto the ground. The clinic was wrapping up, and some of the other volunteers and staff joined us. In a few expertly placed cuts Ahmed opened each coconut and fashioned a spoon to scoop out the flesh.

He gave us each a coconut and smiled as we drank them.

"I appreciate you sharing your story with me," Ahmed said. "And I hope that Safari Doctors can help my kids get the best treatment they can."

---

[1] Jared Diamond, *The World Until Yesterday: What Can We Learn from Traditional Societies?* (New York: Penguin Books, 2013), 178.

# 21

# Travel If You Can – It's Fatal to Prejudice (Kenya, 2017)

*How travel makes you a better human / Travel creates philanthropists / Responsible tourism / Reverse culture shock*

**TRAVEL CHANGES YOUR BRAIN.** We know this deep down, and science backs it up.

In *Innocents Abroad* Mark Twain wrote: "Travel is fatal to prejudice, bigotry, and narrow-mindedness, and many of our people need it sorely on these accounts. Broad, wholesome, charitable views of men and things cannot be acquired by vegetating in one little corner of the earth all one's lifetime."

When Twain wrote that he probably didn't think that years later neuroscientists and psychologists would document the mind-broadening impacts of travel. Travel exposes us to new sights, smells, languages, tastes, awkwardnesses, and cultures that ignite different synapses and alter our neural pathways.

"Foreign experiences increase both cognitive flexibility and depth and integrativeness of thought, the ability to make deep connections between disparate forms," said Adam Galinsky, a professor at Columbia University.[1]

For decades now in the travel-writing world, which I come from, there has been this debate between being a "traveler" and being a "tourist." Travelers are savvy cultural explorers in tune with the ebbs and flows of local life, moving through foreign environments while having authentic experiences, whereas tourists are gawking, culturally insensitive rubber-neckers wearing fanny packs, going on organized tours, and leaving a wake of disbelief and anger in their path.

I'm tired of the argument and have been a proponent of a third category for years: the "touron." A touron is a mix of the two.

It's impossible to check our cultural baggage at the border of a foreign land or experience. Travel is humbling, a lesson in humility learned slowly through each finger pointed, glance shot, and laugh guffawed in our direction. A touron is curious and seeks out interactions with locals, but is also a bit of a moron because it's impossible not to be when you are trying to move through a world different from your daily life.

But not all travel is equal. A slum tour may expand your spotlight of empathy, but it won't change your brain.

"The key, critical process is multicultural engagement, immersion, and adaptation," said Galinsky. "Someone who lives abroad and doesn't engage with the local culture will likely get less of a creative boost than someone who travels abroad and really engages in the local environment."

Mind-changing travel doesn't necessarily have to involve a passport or arriving at some distant port; it's more about interacting with a culture that is different from your own. I've had plenty of cross-cultural experiences in Indiana. If you go into these experiences with an open mind, willing to engage and reserve judgment, the travel magic is there.

Galinsky found that "when people had experiences traveling to other countries it increased what's called generalized trust, or their general faith in humanity ... When we engage in other cultures, we start to have experience with different people and recognize that most people treat you in similar ways. That produces an increase in trust."

According to Mary Helen Immordino-Yang, a professor of education and psychology at the University of Southern California, "to engage with people from different backgrounds than yourself, and the ability to get out of your own social comfort zone, is helping you to build a strong and acculturated sense of your own self. Our ability to differentiate our own

---

[1]Brent Crane, "For a More Creative Brain, Travel," *The Atlantic* (March 31, 2015).

beliefs and values … is tied up in the richness of the cultural experiences that we have had."

*Giving Rules: Traveling and experiencing new ways of life increase your faith in humanity.*

Seeking out, and embracing, diverse ways of life and thought changes us and helps us understand ourselves and our local and global communities better. Interacting with people who have had different lived experiences than we have had is critical to living a life of giving. Before travel shatters our preconceived notions and prejudices, it reveals them, challenging us to see the world in a new way and from the point of view of other people.

Anthropology and my college education gave me a lens to see the world that I only fully understood and appreciated with travel. I feel like my mind is, as Umra of Safari Doctors said, put on a table and stretched as far as it can go with each trip, still.

If you add up all my trips, I've spent years abroad, but that's nothing compared to my friend Kelly Campbell of The Village Experience, who introduced me to Safari Doctors.

My wanderlust is treatable with a trip here and there; Kelly suffers from chronic wanderlust. She has made a career of showing people the world, creating philanthropists, and using travel as a force for positive community change.

———

Kelly grew up in Indiana, went to school at Indiana University, and now calls Lamu Island off the coast of Kenya home for months out of the year.

After our time with Safari Doctors, Mom and I relaxed on the island, a paradise where we ate fresh fish and napped in our room that overlooked the ocean. We went on a sunset cruise on one of the boats operated by Kelly's local business partner, Captain Yusuf Ahmed Ali. We toasted lazy days with good wine. We crossed the channel to Manda Island to swim at a fancy resort straight out of a glossy magazine where we were nearly the only ones there. Often paradise is crowded. Not Lamu.

A string of attacks, attributed to al-Shabaab in Lamu County, starting in 2011 had scared off tourists. A French woman who lived next door to the resort where we swam had been snatched from her home in the middle of the night. A British couple was taken from another resort we visited with Safari Doctors far from Lamu Island. The beach was pristine and disappeared into the ocean and horizon and there was no one on it. A security expert I consulted with before heading to Kenya during the election was more concerned about my time in Lamu than in Nairobi. He joked that maybe I should take Mom on a trip to Mogadishu, Somalia's capital and arguably one of the most lawless cities in the world.

But Kelly assured me that Lamu Island was peaceful. Many of the security concerns were hours away in the far reaches of Lamu County, but when the media reported attacks or kidnappings they simply wrote Lamu. A recent headline read: "Terrorism is bleeding Lamu tourism to death."

Kelly saw this as a challenge and an opportunity to make a difference.

"When I came in 2011, we were the only tourists," Kelly said. "There was nobody here. That doesn't make me scared; it makes me want to bring tourism back. Because when I was here, all I saw were people not working, boats not going out, and fishermen with nowhere to sell their fish. It's such a fantastic place. We get a blanket State Department warning. It's irresponsible."

"In 2007 tourism was very good," Captain Yusuf said. "It wasn't easy to get rooms here. You had to book in advance."

But after the kidnapping in 2011 and the Westgate shopping mall attack in Nairobi, tourism dropped.

"Many people in the hotels lost their jobs," Yusuf said. "Fishermen as well, tour guides, shops … Sometimes it was tough even to have a meal. It was survival."

Yusuf said that 80% of jobs on the coast were lost.

"You read the news and you don't know," Kelly said. "Is it blowing up or is it not blowing up? That's one thing about getting people to come here. They can look at the headlines and then at my photos. It doesn't look like there are pirates."

One morning our boat was boarded by four-foot pirates – children from a local school. A boy climbed into Mom's lap, and stole her glasses and put them on. Singing and clapping broke out. Tambourines came from somewhere. A small girl in a hijab danced in the middle of the boat, her elbow out to her side doing some kind of slow-mo chicken wing dance. Kelly had arranged for six tourists to join the 30 kids to visit the nearby village of Matadoni. Previous tourists with The Village Experience had funded the construction of the school and latrine. The six of us funded this field trip.

We were aboard Yusuf's boat, named *Hippo Dhow* because it was the first dhow made after the rare sighting of a hippopotamus on the island.

Yusuf constructed it himself. Most dhows use the $50 paint, but he takes pride in using the $250 paint. We sat on fair trade cushions made by artisans that The Village Experience works with in India, Nepal, Indonesia, India, and Morocco.

Kelly and her sister Anne started The Village Experience in 2008. Kelly had worked in New York City and Miami in the fashion industry for companies like Tommy Hilfiger and Anthropologie. Then she got her degree in international relations from the University of Indianapolis and the University of Stellenbosch in South Africa. She volunteered in South Africa and Kenya and worked for a nonprofit in Indianapolis with a global focus. She learned a lot, including that she didn't want to run a nonprofit.

Kelly led trips getting Americans out into the world and teaching them about fair trade and how to travel responsibly. Anne focused on working with artisans on designs and finding stores to sell their goods.

The Village Experience is a for-profit business, but after a year of leading trips, Kelly was approached by some of her customers who wanted to give to support the women in India who were former sex workers, the kids in inland Kenya who were HIV positive, and a remote village in Guatemala. These tourists wanted to make a difference.

"We show these destinations and people feel our impact," Kelly said. "They feel the relationship, and they want to give."

**Giving Rules: Traveling leads to giving.**

So Kelly did something she said she would never do: She started a nonprofit to facilitate the giving of her clients.

"It is a lot of work, but it has been easy. I don't have to apply for grants and give presentations … The number-one thing we want is for people to say, 'Kelly, we bought a sewing machine; I want to see it.' I know if you are going to come to see it you are going to give more. Educated donors want to know. They want to interact."

The Village Cooperative, funded by Kelly's travelers, has given more than $2 million to communities.

"Our mission is to uplift communities in the developing world through income-generating activities," Kelly said. "But once you get in a community you end up helping with education, medical – everything comes up. The key is to make them sustainable, to help them help themselves. If I can't get a group to come to Kenya, I can't get money for Kenya. Most of the money comes from the group. They fundraise before or after.

"You can donate money once. You write one check to a church or Save the Children. There is no interaction, connection, or immersion;

you just move on to the next thing that someone asks you to donate to that you don't have an established relationship to. It's never going to last as long. If you spend your money to educate yourself, to make those lasting relationships, you become a donor and philanthropist for life. The difference is when you travel, it's a philosophy of life. You are becoming a worldwide global citizen and you are becoming a philanthropist. You aren't just a donor."

> *Giving Rules: See yourself not as a donor, but as a philanthropist investing in the good works of others.*

Kelly just wanted to travel and get others to travel, spending their tourist dollars responsibly. Now her travelers support a crew of 10 on the boats in Lamu, three walking tour guides, the education of the 30 kids who were on the boat with us, three Safari Doctor sails each year, a safari guide and a booking assistant in Nairobi, 75 to 80 kids and their teachers at a school in Kenya that Kelly sheepishly told me while rolling her eyes is named "The Kelly Academy" (not by her choice), and 40 women in a women's project. And there are the other projects in Guatemala and India and the artisans.

"Follow your heart, wherever that may lead," Kelly said. "Do not be scared to put everything else on hold and see where you end up."

The boy who stole Mom's glasses made his way to Kelly's lap. The singing continued and we all smiled so much I'm surprised no one was sidelined with face cramps. And the party didn't stop when we arrived at the dock. The villagers were waiting for us with drums and dancing.

Men showed us how they carved boats. Women showed us how they wove baskets. We were in awe of their skill and tradition.

The villagers served us lunch on large dented metal trays. The kids sat in a circle around each one and dipped into the piles of rice with their right hands. A girl sitting on Mom's lap got up and took a coconut from another kid when he wasn't looking, and then she proceeded to share it with her friends. A boy poured water from his water bottle into another little boy's mouth.

The act of eating in our culture is an individual act. You share with only the most intimate of friends.

Sharing is commonplace in the lives of these kids.

*Someone else needs to eat? Make room around the metal dish.*

*Someone is thirsty? Have some of mine.*

What if we all saw the world like this? Like there was no mine to have, only mine to give.

### *Giving Rules: Give more than you consume.*

Watching the kids share reminded me that I don't deserve more just because of where I was born. I believe that. But the world has provided me with so much more. I think it's our duty to accept our opportunities and privileges as responsibilities, to scoot over and make sure there is enough for everyone.

We were all here because of Omar, the local Rasta man who started the Twashukuru Eco School. Without him there was no school.

Omar was born and raised on Lamu Island. As a boy he got into trouble at his local school, but knew the importance of education, so he ran an hour to a different school each day.

At 21, he left Lamu and traveled to Colorado, to better support his family. He found that life in the US was much more aggressive than the *hakuna matata*, no problem, barefoot, trafficless life he lived in Lamu. He worked as a drummer and through the years also lived in San Francisco, Hawaii, and New Mexico. He still visits the US when he finds a tour that fits his school schedule.

The school happened by accident. He was sick of seeing all the plastic bottles and bags on the beaches of his beautiful home and started a recycling initiative that made plastic bags to sell to tourists.

"The women who work with us," Omar said, "their conditions were very low and they have a lot of babies. There were all these babies around, so we decided to open a small school … We pick the ones who are struggling to survive, who have no chance."

Now that tourism had died off, the school was his main priority.

"Omar is one of those people that life puts in front of you to learn from," the school's website described Omar. "Learn the values of sacrifice, effort, solidarity, respect, dignity. Learn to fall and get up again. Omar gives off an energy that without knowing reaches you. An energy with a force and a light that accompanies a very particular lifestyle, with an overwhelming personality."

Omar hadn't cut his hair in 20 years, ever since he went to the US for the first time. He tucked his long dreadlocks into his crocheted Rasta cap, and when he talked he seemed to find joy in every sentence, punctuating them with laughter.

"The kids give me more than I give them," he laughed. "It makes me happy man! Makes me happy!"

*Giving Rules: Make where you've been and where you are better.*

As we walked around, the boy who had gone from Mom to Kelly on the boat climbed me like a tree and dangled from my neck. One of my fellow tourists took our picture standing next to another tourist with a kid around her neck.

*I hope they don't put that online*, I thought.

Without context it looked like a photo that would appear in an article about great white saviors. The little boy in my arms didn't think I was saving him. I didn't think I was saving him. But I couldn't help but think I was contributing to the stereotype.

I would think twice before posing with someone else's kid in the US and posting it online. Sometimes I even ask my own kids for consent before posting a picture of them on social media. When I post photos or even write about the folks I meet, I do my best to portray them as having agency over their own lives, not as passive witnesses.

The Norwegian Students' and Academics' International Assistance Fund put together a few principles to maintain the dignity of the people we photograph on our travels to respect their privacy.

1. **Promote dignity** – Don't make sweeping generalizations that strengthen stereotypes.
2. **Gain informed consent** – Especially with kids.
3. **Question your intentions** – Are you having an exotic experience to look cooler? Are you raising awareness or funds? If so, are you respecting the other principles?
4. **Bring down stereotypes** – Don't perpetuate pity.[2]

Each photo Kelly shares online challenges the perception of what life is like in Lamu and promotes travel, which is a major employer of the community. Travel comes with the responsibility and opportunity to share your experiences in a way that honors the dignity of those you meet and to educate your family and friends.

---

[2]"How to Communicate the World," www.rustyradiator.com/social-media-guide/#checklist (March 12, 2018).

I also think we need to allow room for travelers to screw up. The first time a traveler visits a developing country, there are so many thoughts and feelings to process. I've seen people break down and cry. I've seen people worry more about the stray dogs than the people. If we criticize people wrestling with the inequality and injustice in our world for the first time, we may miss an opportunity to help them learn from their experiences and more fully understand the complexities of the circumstances they have witnessed.

We need to be quick to be inspired and slow to be offended. There was plenty to inspire us on the school field trip.

---

On our last day in Lamu, Mom and I swam on a beach all to ourselves. We floated in the longshore current like it was a lazy river.

"Thanks for inviting me," she said.

"Thanks for coming."

It took some effort on my part to convince her to come. She said no at first. I wore her down with a video of Dax Shepherd and Kristen Bell spoofing Toto's song "Africa," which I feel is a slightly awkward song since it is about an entire continent (no one sings songs about Asia or South America), but neuroscientists found that it was the best, most dopamine-releasing song of all time.[3] I sealed the deal with a quote from Mark Twain: "In twenty years, you'll regret the things you didn't do rather than the things you did do. So throw off the bowlines, sail away from safe harbor. Catch the trade winds in your sails. Explore. Dream. Discover."

We talked about our experience with the Safari Doctors – Miriam, Ahmed, and the other villagers (see Figure 21.1). We talked about Kelly's work to get Americans out in the world, and Omar's school.

"After being here," Mom said, "not doing anything doesn't feel right."

"I think it's important that we allow travel to change us," I said, trying to convince Mom and reminding myself. "It's easy to go back and get in the rut of life and forget what we've seen. As travelers we should be like a protagonist in a good book; we should change from the beginning to the end."

Months later, Mom and I sat in her kitchen.

When people asked about her trip, she didn't know where to begin. When she first tried to talk to Dad about it, she just started crying.

---

[3] Rae Paoletta, "What's the Best Song, According to Science?" gizmodo.com/whats-the-best-song-according-to-science-1796927071 (July 7, 2017).

*Figure 21.1    The author and his mom with staff from Safari Doctors.*

"I think about it daily," she said. "Most of what I think about is the unfairness and sadness."

"What do you do with that?" I asked.

"I haven't done anything yet," Mom said.

The day after she returned she went to the county fair. Rides, games, fair food – everything seemed unnecessary and excessive. She looked at the kids at the fair and compared them to the kids on the trip.

"I felt so detached… I see through a new perspective now," Mom said.

For Christmas, she made a point of giving the grandkids only one toy each and then more practical items. She thinks her house is too big and they don't need all the space.

Mom experienced a classic case of what is known as reverse culture shock. In less than two weeks she had changed, but the people in her life, her environment, and her culture back home hadn't.

She saw the abundance of things and the materialism and waste of our culture. She questioned what she valued before versus what she valued now.

One of her friends noticed that Kenya had changed her.

"I was moving through my life different, not better, than everyone else around."

She said she felt more distant from people and guiltier.

*Giving Rules: Never feel comfortable with inequality.*

At 63, travel changed Mom. She told me that she still felt useless and didn't know what to do, but the more she talked, the more it became apparent that she was doing things.

She kept in touch with a yoga instructor in Lamu and had written him a letter of recommendation. She was trying to find some local groups to which she could donate her own yoga classes. She was thinking of volunteering at a school or mentoring. She had given more money to causes and individuals than ever before, including $750 to Safari Doctors.

"It was a huge eye-opener for me," she said. "And I would do it again in a heartbeat."

Mom has begun the search for her own Good Person Equation.

# Part V

## IS HELPING HELPING?

# 22

# The Kiva Controversy (Cambodia, 2017)

*The problem with microlending / Meeting
Kiva borrowers / Giving fads*

———

**THE HELMET WAS TOO SMALL FOR** my swollen American melon, my butt
too big for the scooter's narrow seat. I thought back to my six hours of
meditation in Burma and tried to notice the pain away, but all I could
notice was my fear that we were going to crash.

Bunthoeurn, the owner and operator of the scooter, accelerated ran-
domly and so fast that I had to hang on or risk falling off the back. We
were the fastest-moving vehicle in all of Phnom Penh, Cambodia. I was
sure of it. We were on a mission.

I had given a loan to a group of pig farmers south of the city through
Kiva.org, an international nonprofit that connects people through lending to alleviate poverty. Kiva envisions a world "where all people hold
the power to create opportunity for themselves and others." The organization does that by offering microcredit to individuals and groups in
poor communities, who would typically not have access to credit.

Muhammad Yunus, a Bangladesh economist, is often credited
with the idea of microcredit. In 1976 he lent $27 of his own money

to 42 women in a village to make bamboo furniture. Banks weren't interested in lending to the poor, so the only loans they could get before were offered at high interest from loan sharks. Eventually he scaled this practice, formed the Grameen Bank, won the Nobel Peace Prize in 2006, and even made an appearance on *The Simpsons*.

While visiting the Grameen Bank in 2007, I met a woman who had been a beggar before she received a loan. She spent her first loan on a bag of candies to sell. I met another who had received several loans, each larger than the previous one. She bought a cow with her first loan, and by the time I met her she owned several apartment buildings. I was impressed.

Kiva.org offers folks like you and me the ability to extend as little as $25 of credit to entrepreneurs, allowing us each to be our own mini Grameen Banks, joining with other mini-banks. Through the years, I've funded five people around the world who've operated food stalls, clothing stores, and farms in places like Costa Rica, Ecuador, and Cambodia. I introduced my friend James to Kiva, and he's trying to lend to someone in every country to which Kiva lends.

I made my first Kiva loan back in 2009 to a woman named Mao, a mother of seven. The story that accompanied her pictures said two of her children worked in a garment factory. She was famous for her porridge and wanted $1,000 to build a small shop for her business.

I chose Mao in 2009 because I had recently traveled to Cambodia for the first time to write about the people who made my blue jeans in *Where Am I Wearing?* and Mao's daughters were garment workers. Besides, she sounded responsible, like someone who would pay me back.

Bunthoeurn and I were on our way to meet my latest borrower, Phos's group.

I chose Phos's group because they were located close to Phnom Penh, I like to support rural agriculture and female entrepreneurs, and she wanted to buy piglets. I secretly hoped there would be piglets because that would be cute.

I learned this from the story of Phos's group shared on Kiva's site:

A villager living in Kandal Stueng district's Kandal province, Phos is 40 years old. She has four children; one is still dependent on her. She has been growing rice for about 22 years as the main income to support her family.

This is her fifth loan cycle from VisionFund and she has repaid her past loans well. Her previous loans helped to provide better support for her family.

She is leading a group of five members to apply for this loan. As a leader, she will use her loan to buy piglets to raise. She hopes this new business can help her increase her income to support her family.

In this group: Phos, Phan, Phol, Pros, Chandy.

It had been a while since I had given to Kiva, and I was a little confused. Was the $1,800 loan, $25 of which was mine, going to Phos, was it going to her group, or both? She planned on buying piglets, but what about the others in her group? How was the money going to be spent?

I wanted to ask her these questions, but first we had to find her.

As soon as we entered Kandal Stueng, we stopped and woke three police officers napping on a picnic table in the shade at an intersection. Bunthoeurn explained our mission, and I showed them the picture I had of Phos's group. They talked among themselves and to Bunthoeurn and then they all laughed. Kandal Stueng was a district, not a village.

Bunthoeurn and I had had extensive conversations about our journey the day before, first at a coffee shop and then over Kentucky Fried Chicken. At KFC he acted like it would be quite possible to find Phos's group, but he laughed at me with the police. I realized he had been too polite to tell me that we didn't have enough information to go on. We were looking for a pig farmer in a district full of pig farmers.

I decided we were going to need the help of VisionFund, the field partner who facilitated the loan, according to Phos's group's Kiva page. Maybe they could help us.

A few more bumpy kilometers on a dirt road and we arrived at the locked gate of the district's VisionFund office. It was Sunday. The office was closed. We showed Phos's group's picture and profile to employees at two of the local feed stores, hoping they might recognize them as customers. They didn't.

I gave up. I was covered in a layer of dirt and sweat, and grit crunched between my teeth.

We made our way back to Phnom Penh, following a truck full of pigs. I felt foolish. It would be irresponsible of Kiva and VisionFund to give enough information to locate their customers. I was going to need help.

It made sense that I wouldn't be able to find them, although it wasn't the first time I'd had an overly simplistic take on Kiva. I wasn't alone.

In 2009, David Roodman, a research fellow at the Center for Global Development, wrote a blog post stating, "The person-to-person donor-to-borrower connections created by Kiva are partly fictional."[1] Lenders like me thought it worked like this: We scrolled through pictures and stories of people looking for loans. We chose and gave Kiva our money to give to someone like Phos. Phos repays the loan and we can lend it to someone else.

Roodman dug into the model and found that less than 5% of Kiva loans are disbursed after they are listed on its site, and most people had received their loans 20 days before their photos were published on the site. So Phos already had her money before I gave it to her. My connection with Phos was less direct than I imagined, but it really would be silly if she were waiting around for folks like me to determine her loan-worthiness.

"Imagine if Kiva actually worked the way people thinks it does," Roodman wrote on his blog post about a woman in Cambodia who worked with a local lender, MAXIMA. "Phong Mut approaches a MAXIMA loan officer and clears all the approval hurdles, making the case that she has a good plan for the loan, has good references, etc. The MAXIMA officer says, 'I think you deserve a loan, and MAXIMA has the capital to make it. But instead of giving you one, I'm going to take your picture, write down your story, get it translated and posted on an American web site, and then we'll see over the next month whether the Americans think you should get a loan. Check back with me from time to time.'"

The way I thought it worked, and the way most people thought it worked in 2009 – if they thought about it for longer than 10 seconds – would be inefficient and undignified. Who am I, sitting in my pajamas at my computer with bed head, to judge whether Phos was worthy of a loan?

Kiva wasn't blatantly hiding this, although some of its language and graphics were a little misleading. On the borrower profiles, Kiva listed that the funds had already been disbursed. But up until Roodman's post that was covered in *The New York Times*[2] and launched a thousand tweets, Kiva said its model "lets you lend to a specific entrepreneur, empowering them to lift themselves out of poverty," which wasn't exactly true.

---

[1]David Roodman, "Kiva Is Not Quite What It Seems," www.cgdev.org/blog/kiva-not-quite-what-it-seems (October 2, 2009).
[2]Stephanie Strom, "Confusion on Where Money Lent via Kiva Goes," *The New York Times* (November 8, 2009).

I knew all this as I sat in the VisionFund's Cambodia headquarters in Phnom Penh. The white floors of the bank were so shiny I could make out my eye color in the reflection. The tellers wore headsets allowing them to communicate with the rest of their team like Secret Service agents. Everything was orange and white and on-brand with VisionFund and its parent organization World Vision, a Christian relief organization and one of the largest nonprofits in the US, with more than $3 billion in annual revenue.

After a five-minute wait, a woman in a bleached white VisionFund blouse greeted me. I told her what I was trying to do. She laughed. She had never heard such a request, but she liked the idea.

"I really want to accompany you on this visit," she said. "I want to share how our clients live in the province, and how they struggle to make a living, and especially the way they use funds from our lenders."

Her enthusiasm spoke volumes about the project, but unfortunately she had end-of-month reports to finish so she couldn't accompany me. Instead, she arranged for me to meet with the branch manager of the Kandal Stueng office.

This time I took a *tuk-tuk*, a shaded chariot pulled behind a motorbike usually reserved for commuting around the city, and not for interdistrict travel. Not having to hang on for my life, I could enjoy the gorgeous blue sky, Buddhist pagodas next to lakes, and lush vegetation everywhere. When farmers looked up to see the out-of-place sight, I almost felt as though I should wave like some beauty queen leading a parade.

Before the day was over, Sok-La, the *tuk-tuk* driver, and I certainly could claim the Guinness World Record for longest *tuk-tuk* journey. It took forever. Along the way, the woman from VisionFund sent me an e-mail:

"I just got a recommendation from our management here. We don't want you to introduce yourself that you've come here through KIVA. But [you are] just here as an investor… [O]ur client might not understand well what KIVA is, and it [could] make our client feel uncomfortable to answer all your questions."

The reason Kiva shares borrowers' stories is for us to feel connected to them, but it is truly a one-way connection. I feel somewhat connected to Phos and her group, but they have no idea who the hell I am or, apparently, even what Kiva is. Again, I knew this in theory, but, I have to admit, it took some of the romance out of it. It's not really a connection at all.

"At least I'll get to see some piglets," I thought.

We followed the district loan officer on his motorbike as he turned toward a house. This was it.

I'm not the first person to follow my Kiva loan back to the borrower. Writer and comedian Bob Harris has funded more than 10,000 loans and traveled to meet borrowers in Cambodia, Bosnia, Tanzania, and beyond.

Bob was on a writing assignment that took him to some of the fanciest hotels in the world. One day he was staying at a $3 billion hotel in Dubai, drinking a $75 cup of coffee made from beans that had been pooped by a civet, and started to feel like he should do something with $20,000 of his assignment pay. Right next to the luxury he was experiencing were the people constructing and serving it.

Bob discovered Kiva and turned that $20,000 into 5,000 loans.

"It's different from ordinary charities because you are helping people start businesses," Bob told an audience at an event for his book documenting his travels, *The International Bank of Bob: Connecting Our Worlds One $25 Kiva Loan at a Time*.

"When I was a boy, we called this the American Dream. Apparently they have something similar in other countries, too," Bob said, laughing.

The thing about the American Dream, though, is that sometimes it's fueled by debt and goes up in flames. And that's precisely the concern that many have with microfinance. Think about someone you know struggling to make ends meet, or someone living in poverty. Now hand that person a credit card. Does that person's life get better?

Credit comes with opportunity, but it also comes with risk.

"My name is Kelsey," I said, bowing to Phos. "I'm an investor with VisionFund and I'm also a writer writing about some of the borrowers."

Phos looked at me and welcomed me into the shade of her home. Like many homes in Cambodia, hers sat up on stilts and had a living area beneath it that acted as the kitchen and living room. The space was strung with hammocks and partly taken up by a small SUV and a motorbike. The stilts were concrete and her house metal. A TV blared a movie. In terms of material possessions, her family seemed to be doing well.

She introduced me to the granddaughter in her arms, who immediately started to cry. Phos placed her in a hammock and rocked it gently. More grandkids appeared, staring at me.

I looked around for the piglets, but didn't see, hear, or smell any.

"Did you buy pigs?"

"Not yet. My son was in a motorbike accident," she said.

She still intended to buy pigs, but she had medical bills and a son to take care of first. Phos has four children. Three of them are married, and her unmarried son lives at home. Two work in the garment industry.

She is the head of the borrower group since she is at home the most. The others work. They spent their loan money on chickens and cows and life's necessities.

Phos walked me behind her house to a pond where they catch fish to eat and sell. There was also a fence made from small trees where she hoped to put the 35 to 40 pigs she planned to buy.

### Giving Rules: Lending isn't giving.

The Abdul Latif Jameel Poverty Action Lab (J-PAL), a global research center working to reduce poverty by ensuring that policy is informed by scientific evidence, examined seven randomized evaluations of microcredit. J-PAL found that it's not quite the silver bullet to fighting poverty that some make it out to be. In fact, the researchers found that microcredit has no impact on a borrower's income, or on women's empowerment, or on the resources families put toward school.[3]

The studies showed that access to microcredit increased families' freedom in how they earned, consumed, and invested their money. And that most of the loans went to consumption, for paying for life's things, and for medical care, as in the case of Phos's son.

Kiva loans money to its local partners, such as VisionFund, at no interest, but the partners do charge interest. Many microcredit lenders offer rates that would make a credit card interest rate look reasonable. One analysis of microcredit rates reported in *The New York Times* put the global average at 37% interest.[4]

When you think about it, extending credit really is an American way to fight poverty. Instead of the rich giving money to the poor, as is the case with GiveDirectly, we can simply loan them money, and in some cases (not with Kiva, though) even make money off the interest. Heck, we might as well saddle up the Wall Street bull, hop on his back, and hum "America the Beautiful" while throwing out sacks of money, which of course would need to be returned ... with interest.

---

[3]J-PAL, "Where Credit Is Due," www.povertyactionlab.org/sites/default/files/publications/where-credit-is-due.pdf (February 2015).
[4]Neil MacFarquhar, "Banks Making Big Profits from Tiny Loans," *The New York Times* (April 13, 2010).

As of October 2017, Kiva has lent more than $1 billion. All of its impact numbers focus on how much it has given out in loans to how many people: 81% female borrowers working in 86 countries, 219,435 borrowers in conflict zones, 526,197 borrowers who are farmers. Kiva has inspired more than 1.6 million borrowers like Bob, James, and me. These are impressive numbers, but they aren't really impacts. Some of the loans probably changed someone's life, and others were probably the worst thing to happen to a family, saddling them with more debt. A positive impact would be that borrowers created so many jobs per dollar they borrowed, that education levels increased, that families lived healthier lives, and that their incomes increased. These positive impacts can be found in individual stories or select communities, but overall, according to the most well-respected studies, microcredit isn't the poverty killer that some thought it was. It's kind of like a Shake Weight: It'll help some, maybe, but on its own you won't see many results. Perhaps the biggest criticism of it is that it distracts us from the root social and political causes of poverty.

*Giving Rules: There are giving fads, just like there are exercise fads.*

But this is the way J-PAL and effective altruism look at microcredit. Phos has a different take. She is thankful for the credit. This is her fifth loan, and if it weren't for the loan, how would she have helped her injured son?

Phos's situation reminded me of Ratana, the girl I met at the dump 10 years ago and again at the Cambodian Children's Fund office. Ratana's life was changed by a motorbike accident that injured her mother. In order to pay her mother's medical bills, Ratana's family sold their farm, like so many farmers have, and moved to the city. Maybe she wouldn't have had to work in the dump when she was 11 if her family had a Kiva-supported loan through a partner like VisionFund.

Phos posed with her grandkids for a photo (see Figure 22.1). What would their future be? It was time for me to go. She had grandkids to attend to. She was welcoming enough, but busy. I said good-bye and left. I sat in my *tuk-tuk* chariot scrolling through the pictures of Phos and her grandkids. I flipped through my notebook reading the tidbits of her life I had scribbled. All I had were a few photos and a brief story. It's not even a giving story really, but a lending one. Phos's group will repay the loan, and I'll give it back to Kiva to send to another lender.

Was I connected to her more than before?

*Figure 22.1    Phos and her grandkids.*

Bob's journey as recalled in *The International Bank of Bob* was more than just an ode to Kiva and microfinance; it was about connecting to the world. One man in Lebanon whose house had been bombed left Bob with his biggest lesson: "You love more, you win."

To see anything clearly, Bob wrote, "is simply to see where you are, look the people around you in the eye, and realize that you risk being changed by the result."[5]

We see a story and get a glimpse of someone's life. We long to connect. This is why we lend through Kiva. And this is what fuels one of the most popular ways for Americans to give billions each year internationally: child sponsorship.

---

[5]Megan Woolhouse, "'The International Bank of Bob' by Bob Harris," *The Boston Globe* (March 15, 2013).

# 23

# Sponsor a Child, Save the World? (Zambia, 2017)

*The realities of child sponsorship / Stories versus stats / Psychic numbing / Aid and dependency*

---

**ROBERTA SPONSORED TIMOTHY EVEN WHEN** times were tough.

Over the past 10 years there have been plenty of challenging times for Roberta, who is a friend of a friend and lives in my hometown. She got divorced, and, as a single mother money was tight. Her son left home to join the military. There have been moves, broken relationships, job changes, financial difficulties, and starting over in a new town.

But through all of life's inconsistencies, there was one constant: every month over the past 10 years Roberta sent $35 to World Vision to sponsor Timothy in Mbala, Zambia.

"This is my tithe," Roberta said, putting her hands on the framed picture of Timothy that typically sits on her desk. "My connection to God."

We sat in the corner waiting area of the computer repair office where she worked.

Roberta sponsored Timothy for her son Evan, who was 10 at the time. She thought the letters back and forth with Timothy would teach Evan gratitude and expand his world a bit beyond our small town in Indiana. But long after Evan lost interest and the learning opportunity was exhausted, she continued to send Timothy money. She did it for Timothy. She did it for herself.

> *Giving Rules: You can't teach gratitude. You can only demonstrate it.*

Roberta doesn't do many things for herself. She volunteers at a summer camp for adults with developmental disabilities. She loves how they "keep it real."

"Last night when I left camp, my heart was so full, and I was so thankful that I was like, 'Am I doing this because it makes me feel good?' Is it okay if I'm doing this because it makes me feel better? Other people are rejecting me. Am I doing this because of the acceptance I get from [the campers]?"

> *Giving Rules: It's okay if giving makes you feel good.*

Two years ago she did do something that was only for her. She bought a Harley.

"That's the first thing I ever did for myself. And people are like, 'Do you know how many people you could feed for the cost of your motorcycle?' Maybe I should have given it to [Timothy] or put in a well – people need water. I spent my whole life doing things for other people ... what do I want to do?"

She called it selfish; she felt she deserved it, yet she still struggled with it.

"[Sponsoring Timothy] is something I love to do and a way I relate to people and the world. But I was like, 'Oh, you're right. I spend a lot more on this motorcycle than I send to this little boy.' So am I any kind of special person because I sent him $35 per month? No. Now I'm probably going to cry. Those are the kinds of things you wrestle with."

Roberta has stopped sending letters to Timothy as much as she once did. When she writes she is very conscious about what she would say in the letter or show in a picture. Once she even cropped the background out of a picture of her cat she sent him, so he wouldn't see her house. She told me that many Americans don't want to face the inequality in the world and the privilege of our own lives.

"There's no rhyme or reason of why he's there and Evan was here."

"So what would you want to say to Timothy if he were here?" I asked.

"Gosh. I don't know what I would say to him. The first thing I would do is probably hug him and embarrass him. I would want him to know that he is loved more than he knows. There are people … lots and lots of people who love him, including me. I pray for him. I think about him. He's in my heart."

"What would your hopes be for him?"

"My hope would be that he finds his place in the world, his purpose. The obvious answer is that I hope he comes out of poverty. I hope he has a happy life … I'm not 100% convinced that wealthy people are that much better off. I want him to find out who he is, why he's here, and live into that. To believe that he is loved and worthy of anything that God has in store for him."

> *Giving Rules: Often the people we help mean more to us than we do to them.*

Roberta wrote Timothy a letter and gave it to me to take to Zambia.

"I'll do my best to find him," I said. "But sometimes organizations don't want me to come."

---

We rattled down a dirt road in a white Land Cruiser with the World Vision logo on the sides. I've seen such World Vision vehicles in most of the developing countries I've visited, but I had never been inside one.

I was in the back with various plumbing tools sitting on a bench seat with more function than padding. To see out the side windows, I had to duck down and crane my neck. We passed fields of grass burning beneath white smoke. The controlled fires helped the seeds regenerate and produce more food for cattle.

Alexie, the program manager of World Vision, turned up the radio. A gospel song blared, and he sang along: "I'm a soldier in the army of the Lord."

Before he got into the Land Cruiser, he wrapped a back brace around his torso. I wasn't sure if it said more about the state of his back or the roads we'd be traveling on.

It wasn't easy to get to Mbala. I flew from Nairobi to Dar es Salaam, Tanzania, and grabbed another flight to Mbeya, which was near the border with Zambia. From there I made the journey over land, crossing the border on foot, and grabbed a minibus to Mbala. The journey took me two full days. It was quicker to travel from Indiana to Nairobi than to make my way from Nairobi to Mbala.

The minibus was a painful experience. It was hot and crowded. I had occupied myself staring out the window and taking in the details.

Bags of charcoal as tall as a 10-year-old were stacked on the side of the road.

A woman with a child strapped to her back, as is the fashion accessory for most women during their child-rearing years, walked over a barren ridge before stopping to wave.

A little boy sat on a feedbag pulled like a sled by and older boy. Dust plumes swirled in their wake.

Houses on the side of the road were made from locally sourced mud and branches and grass. In Kenya, I met a man who lived in such a house. He called it a "temporary house," but he wanted the property to be his home forever. On a speeding bus, the houses were nearly camouflaged against the dry earth-toned landscape.

A family flagged us down. A young woman wore a prom dress with her left breast out and available for the baby boy she held. They got on the minibus, even though it felt like there was no more space to give, but somehow we always had room for one more. She covered her nose because the smell of the gas from the gas tanks inside our cab was so strong. After a few hours, I couldn't smell it any longer.

I had observed all of this while I was on the 200-mile, 12-hour minibus ride to Mbala. The views were spacious. Vast. Dusty. Shrubbed. I had written these terms in my notebook. I wanted to write another: "the middle of nowhere." I fought the urge because there was the charcoal, the waving woman, the boys at play, the nursing mother and somewhere Timothy, the boy Roberta sponsored.

As I stared out the window of World Vision's SUV ringing with gospel music, I saw many of the same scenes. We pulled into the courtyard where the chief lived. I looked forward to stretching my legs and meeting someone impacted by the work of World Vision. I had been in town a few days and I hadn't met anyone but the staff so far.

The SUV parked in the shade of a tree, and I made my way to climb out the back.

"So," Alexie said, "you will remain here."

"I'll open a window for you," the child sponsorship manager said.

*They are treating me like a dog*, I thought. And then I looked out the window and saw a dog staring at me.

———

I had expected this reception. World Vision is a giant organization with more than 42,000 staff in 100 countries supported by an annual budget of $3 billion. And giant organizations have always been skeptical of my work. Starbucks hates me because I wrote about how the farmers whom it "supports" through its own version of fair trade have never actually heard of Starbucks.

If anything, World Vision has been a great supporter of my work in the past. The World Vision Report radio program that aired on some NPR stations followed my journey to meet the people who made my clothes before there was even an idea that *Where Am I Wearing?* could become a book. Through the years I recorded around 10 essays and features for the program.

After I met with Roberta, I e-mailed a contact at World Vision. It took a follow-up e-mail and a month to get the ball rolling, and by then I was only a week away from visiting Zambia. There was concern that there wouldn't be time for a proper background check, so I rescheduled my itinerary to allow for more time. Still, they didn't think it would be possible to meet Timothy because, understandably, they have really strict procedures in place to keep the children safe. Besides, my request was less of a request than it was to say, "Hey, I'm coming to write about this; any help you could provide would be appreciated."

So I showed up in Mbala knowing all this.

I also knew that Diaa Hadid, a *New York Times* reporter, had uncovered some inconsistencies on a mission similar to mine. Hadid met Brendan, an Australian police officer who had sponsored a Palestinian boy named Othman for years but had never heard anything from him. Typically sponsors and children send notes back and forth.

"If you could ask around in your travels, I'd love to know that he is O.K.," Brendan told Hadid.[1]

She visited Othman's village of 7,000 and easily located him. The boy was five years old on the World Vision card Brendan had shared with her. When she met Othman, he was 18. None of Othman's family members recalled enrolling him in the World Vision program, nor had they received any money or support. The name on the card didn't match. Othman's middle name was wrong, but his birthday was right.

Hadid writes that Othman "liked playing Call of Duty, a popular video game. He flunked math on his final school exam, but was determined

---

[1] Diaa Hadid, "A World Vision Donor Sponsored a Boy. The Outcome Was a Mystery to Both," *The New York Times* (August 2, 2016).

to retake it this summer so he could go to a university. He wanted a job involving cars. And his relatives were rattled by the idea that some stranger in Australia knew his name and said he had sent money that they insisted they had never received."

Hadid talked with Othman's family, and an aunt did recall some white foreigners showing up and lining up kids to take their photos. And come to think of it, Othman and a cousin did receive occasional cards delivered to their local grocery written in a language they couldn't understand.

World Vision told Hadid they don't promise enrolled children more support than any other child in the community. Until 2007, the organization didn't require parental permission for children to participate in the sponsorship program. Although Othman and his family never knew his image was being used, the village was well aware of the work of World Vision. One member of the village council said that "we all benefited" from World Vision "a lot."

Brendan, who sponsored Othman for years, felt misled. He said, "People make donations based on the sense of personal connection they have with the image they are provided and that they are changing that child's life ... What level of knowledge do they have of us? It's a bit surreal, to be honest. A bit sad, in a way."

Child sponsorship is at the heart of World Vision's fund-raising efforts. More than 3.5 million children are sponsored for a current minimum of $39 per month through World Vision. The organization's home page reads: "Created to shine: Together, let's lift kids out of poverty. Shine bright in the life of a child." The statement is followed by a large orange "Sponsor a Child" button that, once clicked, takes you to a page to select a child based on the child's location, gender, age, birth month, and birthday. The page also tells you how long the child has been waiting for a sponsor.

I searched for a girl born on the exact same day as my daughter, Harper. There were four. Maria in Zimbabwe had been waiting for a sponsor for three months, Latifa in Ghana six months, Tonita in Mozambique 13 days, and Zawad in Tanzania more than a year.

I'm not sure how it was in 2003 when Brendan selected Othman to sponsor, but, if you take more than 10 seconds to read the information beyond the headline " ... you'll help that child and their community to stand tall, free from poverty," you won't be misled. The site explicitly states that "your donation combines with gifts from all other sponsors" and that "children don't get direct cash benefits," but instead it goes to the community "to create a sustainable plan to keep the community out of poverty."

Still, the whole process of selecting a kid and adding the child to my shopping basket felt a bit weird. Across all organizations, there are 9 million sponsored children. Child sponsorship is a mega fund-raising method for organizations like World Vision and Compassion International. Compassion International even has an exhibit on wheels – "the compassion experience" – that seeks to show the lives of children "suffering under the crippling weight of poverty." Visitors walk through the life of a hungry child and exit after witnessing how the course of the child's life has been changed through sponsorship.

*Connection*: That's really what all this is about. How can we connect with someone on the other side of the world who lives in a place we've never been to and may speak a language of which we've never heard when they are outside the spotlight of our empathy?

Paul Slovic, a psychologist at Oregon University, has spent decades researching why we choose to care about some while ignoring the suffering of others. First off, we care more about people who look like us and live lives more similar to our own.

Take the Rohingya in Myanmar, for instance, or the refugees of Syria, two shameful atrocities where young and old, women and children have been subjected to the worst brutalities possible. I can watch a news story about the plights of hundreds of thousands of Rohingya and in that moment I can intellectually grasp the tragedy, the senseless loss of life, and the injustice, but at the commercial break, emotionally unfazed, I could flip over to catch the end of a basketball game where the most important thing is that my team comes out on top. But if an American mother is on the news mourning the loss of her child in a school shooting, I can be moved to tears.

The same goes for the refugees fleeing Syria. I hear the numbers and understand how these people left their entire world behind searching for somewhere safe with their family. But then if my wife mentions something about going out for ice cream, I turn off the TV and head out the door weighted by the decision of what flavor to get.

Yet when I saw the picture of the lifeless body of three-year-old Aylan Kurdi, a refugee from Syria, on the beach in Greece, I was paralyzed.

I saw him and he looked like my son. I see the shirt I helped Griffin put on, the shoes we bought him. I thought about Aylan's parents and imagined being forced from my own home. What about my cat, my favorite coffee mug, our family photos, and all of the other silly and serious things that make up a home? Do you go to the ATM? Fill your pockets with cash? At some point you step out your front door for the last time and you don't have any idea where you'll sleep next, if you'll be safe, and what this all means for the future of your kids. I see my family walking. I see my family on the boat. I see my Griffin dead on a beach.

I wasn't the only one impacted by the photo of Aylan. The death toll in Syria was hundreds of thousands by that point, but when the world saw him on the beach, interest spiked. Google searches about the crisis quintupled. The Swedish Red Cross had taken in 160,000 Syrian refugees and had raised only $8,000 to support them. The day after the photo, the organization received $422,000.[2]

When confronted with a harsh reality, we should see ourselves and our family members in the mothers, fathers, brothers, and sisters impacted by that reality.

> *Giving Rules: Radical empathy is the correct reaction, but not always logical.*

Empathy should be our default setting, and in some ways it is, but it has its limits. It also causes us not to act at times.

"There are 1,198,500,000 people alive now in China," author Annie Dillard writes. "To get a *feel* for what this *means*, simply take yourself – in all your singularity, importance, complexity, and love – and multiply by 1,198,500,000. See? Nothing to it."[3]

Since Dillard wrote this in 1999, the population of China has grown by almost 200 million more. Slovic refers to this as "psychic numbing." Our empathy spotlight, our hearts, souls, and minds, simply can't process the suffering of others much beyond that of one individual.

In his paper titled "If I Look at the Mass I Will Never Act," Slovic ran an experiment to demonstrate the "identifiable victim effect." As people left an experiment, Slovic and his fellow researchers gave them an opportunity to donate up to $5 to Save the Children. The opportunity to give was accompanied with one of three different scenarios.[4]

---

[2]Brian Resnick, "A Psychologist Explains the Limits of Human Compassion," www.vox.com/explainers/2017/7/19/15925506/psychic-numbing-paul-slovic-apathy (September 15, 2017).
[3]Annie Dillard, *For the Time Being* (New York: Vintage Books), 45.
[4]Paul Slovic, "'If I Look at the Mass I Will Never Act': Psychic Numbing and Genocide," *Journal for Judgment and Decision Making* (April 2007), 79–95.

The "statistical life" scenario revealed that there was a food shortage or disaster impacting millions of people.

The "identifiable life" scenario, accompanied with a photo of a girl, shared the story of Rokia:

> Rokia a 7-year-old girl from Mali, Africa, is desperately poor and faces a threat of severe hunger or even starvation. Her life will be changed for the better as a result of your financial gift. With your support, and the support of other caring sponsors, Save the Children will work with Rokia's family and other members of the community to help feed her, provide her with education, as well as basic medical care and hygiene education.

They could contribute to help one girl or they could contribute to help millions involved in a major humanitarian crisis. A single life was worth more than millions.

Rokia received twice as much in donations because it is easier for us to relate to one than many. The third scenario was a combination of the two scenarios, sharing Rokia's story and that it was representative of millions more like her who could be helped. The third scenario received slightly more than the statistical life scenario.

> *Giving Rules: Let your empathy move you to act, and let your logic guide how you will act.*

To some extent this is a survival mechanism.

Individuals with autism may be hypersensitive to sound, hearing sounds that many of us would not notice or would simply filter out. They hear the world all at once, and it can be distracting and debilitating. Now, imagine, instead of hearing all at once, you could feel the world all at once, the suffering of millions, or even just those you bump into throughout the day. It would be impossible to function.

A picture of a little girl accompanied with her story, and the knowledge that we can help her in some way, moves us to act (remember Singer's pond?). Statistics make us feel powerless and apathetic.

This is why the narratives of Kiva and child sponsorship are so successful at motivating givers. In both cases, there's this perception that we are helping an individual or a small group, but in reality we are supporting an organization that reaches many.

*Is World Vision going to allow me to meet one person it has helped?*

Sitting and sweating in the back of the Land Cruiser, I started having doubts. Alexie and the other staff returned to the SUV. We sped down the dirt road past the dog. Two kids walking down the road stepped out of our way. I watched them cover their mouths and noses as they disappeared into our cloud of dust. I wondered if they were one of the 6,800 sponsored children in Mbala.

Three men met us at a community center and led us into the office of the cool concrete building. The men volunteer three days every week. The oldest man was the chairman of the group elected by his neighbors. The other men worked with the sponsorship program helping the kids communicate with their sponsors, taking videos and photos. A key part of their job was to register all the births and make sure that all newborns had a birth certificate. They also disseminated health information to members of their community. There were many volunteers in the community organized by one World Vision staff member. World Vision bought bikes for volunteers who specialized in agriculture to help farmers.

The youngest of the men, who had a goatee, flipped open a notebook: 326 of 400 children were sponsored. An all-capitals handwritten poster with a version of World Vision's mission statement hung on the wall:

WORLD VISION IS AN INTERNATIONAL PARTNERSHIP OF CHRISTIANS WHOSE MISSION IS TO FOLLOW OUR LORD AND SAVIOUR JESUS CHRIST IN WORKING WITH THE POOR AND OPPRESSED TO PROMOTE HUMAN TRANSFORMATION, SEEK JUSTICE, AND BEAR WITNESS TO THE GOOD NEWS OF THE KINGDOM OF GOD.

British explorer and missionary David Livingstone was one of the first to bring Christianity to Zambia in the mid-nineteenth century. At present Zambia has a higher percentage of Christians (95%)[5] than the US (80%).[6] In Zambia, World Vision works closely with the local churches. The organization works in 100 countries around the world to "serve all people, regardless of religion, race, ethnicity, or gender."

However, one could call World Vision's position of inclusion, openness, and fighting injustice into question after a 2014 reversal of a

[5]*CIA World Factbook: Zambia*, www.cia.gov/library/publications/the-world-factbook/geos/za.html (March 12, 2018).

[6]Frank Newport, "Percentage of Christians in U.S. Drifting Down, but Still High," news.gallup.com/poll/187955/percentage-christians-drifting-down-high.aspx (December 24, 2015).

decision to hire employees who were in same-sex marriages. World Vision received intense pressure from evangelical leaders and lost 3,500 sponsorships in a matter of days. So, the organization's sense of fighting oppression and injustice has a pretty big blind spot, and I personally find its position appalling. Yet its position on LGBTQ+ issues is quite progressive compared to Zambia's, where "same-sex relations" can land you in jail for 15 years to life.

World Vision has operated in Mbala since 1998. I asked the chairman if he had seen changes in his community.

"There has been a big change, especially concerning water," he told me. "We were drawing water from wells. We used to have a lot of problems, especially diarrhea. Young chaps suffered from abdominal pain, and that happens less. It was difficult to access water for drinking. Even the little ones can draw water from the borehole. The diseases have reduced. Even gardening is easier."

The other two volunteers added to the list. Before, they had a grass-thatched school, but World Vision built a new school. Pregnant women now have access to health facilities and care. They used to bury their dead wrapped in linens, but World Vision trained local carpenters to make coffins and provide them for free.

"The interventions are community-driven," Alexie added.

*Holistic* is a term that gets thrown out in development. World Vision isn't focusing on one thing; it is focusing on all of the communities' needs: financial, farming, entrepreneurial, hygiene, sanitation, hunger, water, immunizations, social welfare, and much more. The need is great in Mbala. Nearly half of children have stunted growth from malnutrition. A sign on the edge of town that seemed to be part reminder and part celebration read: The Open Defecation Free Chiefdom in Mbala.

But some locals I chatted with who don't benefit from World Vision's services question whether an international NGO is the best agent of sustainable change. What happens when it leaves?

———

The next day I sat in Alexie's office in the gated World Vision compound. I thanked him for his hospitality and communicated that I really needed to meet others impacted by World Vision's work. So far I had met only staff and volunteers. I also made one more attempt to ask for his help to find Timothy. Someone came in during our chat.

"Give me a minute. I have to deal with him," Alexie told him, nodding toward me as the one who had to be dealt with.

It was "Keep Zambia Clean" day where government offices and NGO employees took to the streets to pick up trash. They wouldn't be going into the field, but maybe he could help me.

"I'm trying to find a nearby community where we operate," Alexie said. "There is a community development worker who works in that area . . . You can't go by yourself."

Alexie called Chipo, a World Vision community manager, into his office.

"Can you be with him for maybe one hour or 30 minutes or so? He wants to talk with beneficiaries we work with."

Alexie spoke with authority. There was no doubt he was in charge. Over the course of the past few days, as serious as he was, I heard him laugh a lot. We had deep conversations about what community and family life looked like in Zambia versus in the US. He bought me lunch. He was helpful and friendly in some ways, but reluctant to let me loose on the community with all of my questions This was his compromise.

He dismissed us and then called Chipo back into his office. I assumed he gave him strict instructions about how to deal with me.

Chipo acts as the link between the World Vision office and the community.

I was staying on Chila Lake in a cabin with satellite television, Wi-Fi, and cold beer. The community where Chipo worked, Chila View, was on the other side of the lake and only recently received running water.

World Vision had constructed a borehole with a pump that filled a cistern which sat on a high platform acting as the community's water tower. Water splashed out and down the sides, but not much of it went to waste because community members had placed large plastic tubs to catch most of the overflow.

We met Agnes, a single mother of three children, at her brick home a short walk from the water tower. Her hair was braided into cornrows and she wore a skirt patterned with red peanuts.

"I thank World Vision every day," she said.

A young boy sat in the dirt and pulled a car made from a pill jar and bottle caps across Agnes's porch, a hard, swept rectangle of dirt. Another boy strummed at a homemade two-stringed guitar made out of a thin board, a corncob, and a water bottle (see Figure 23.1).

Her eldest son, who is in 10th grade, was sponsored but not any longer.

"They used to give him clothes, lotion, soap, cooking oil, and blankets," Agnes said, revealing that the sponsored kids did receive some individual perks, back then at least.

*Figure 23.1    A boy with his makeshift guitar.*

Agnes recalled receiving pictures from her sponsor, but couldn't remember where they were from.

She heard about World Vision in 1998 before she had kids. She volunteered as a community health educator traveling on a bicycle the organization provided to teach people about HIV/AIDS and how to care for patients.

"I enjoyed helping people," she said. "I stopped when I got married."

She moved to Chila View to live with her brother after her husband left her.

"I'm struggling to be a single parent. My kids are in grades 5, 9, and 10. I struggle to pay the school fees."

"If there was no World Vision, how would your life be different?" I asked.

"It would be hard for many," Agnes said, and then told me that before the tower, she fetched water from Lake Chila. The lake water made them sick, but water was life, and sick was better than dead. She spent two hours per day walking to and from the lake. Now she has a spigot of water on her property.

I asked her if she had any questions for me.

"More help. Is there a way you can help me? I could be the happiest if all the children would be sponsored. Maybe another child can be sponsored to pay for school fees."

### *Giving Rules: Giving shouldn't lead to dependency.*

Chipo explained to me and then to Agnes that World Vision no longer directly covered the cost of school for each child. The organization focused on the community and on income-generating skills so people could support themselves.

At another brick home, we met Regina, a mother of eight. Her husband didn't have an official job or income, but he spent his days fishing in the lake. They also rented space for a small garden to grow their own food.

"It is enough to take children to school. But for eating and livelihood it isn't enough."

Her oldest child, a daughter, was in college studying to become a teacher.

Regina knew the importance of education. She was heading up a local effort to raise funds to build a school in their community. A politician had visited and promised them financial support and teachers if they started the fund-raising efforts. They set a goal to raise $5 per household.

World Vision hadn't sponsored any of Regina's children, but she wondered if there was any way we could help her. Her second oldest, also a daughter, worked at a restaurant in town and could use some help as she saved for college.

Chipo told Regina what he had told Agnes, and then we caught a ride back to town. In the cab I asked Chipo how he felt when people asked for more help.

"It pains me," he said. "I came from a poor family. I'm the youngest. When Mom passed I was in grade three. The relatives of my mother were reluctant to get us ... they also lived at a poverty level. After school I used to do some piecework – harvesting maize, things like that. I used to pay for myself. I felt how it was to be poor. So I really wish that someday I could sponsor someone ... I wish that I had enough resources to help out, but the need is so wide and you can't help everyone."

When World Vision enters a community, the goal is to leave, to work themselves out of a job. The organization breaks the "Life Cycle of a Sponsorship Community" into three phases:

In Phase 1 (years 1 to 3) they listen, get to know the community, assess needs, and begin the child sponsorship program – the bedrock of their funding.

In Phase 2 (years 4 to 9) they empower community members to bring change in their own lives and take ownership over projects.

In Phase 3 (years 10 to close) lives have been transformed, a sustainable, self-sufficient future is realized, and World Vision leaves.

Alexie told me that World Vision Mbala was in Phase 3 and was supposed to transition out in 2019, but recently got an extension through 2020. I asked him what the extension was based on and when World Vision would leave. He gave me a two-part answer: Their program is underfunded so of course they weren't able to meet their goals; and if they keep thinking of work that needs to be done and keep getting funding, they will keep doing it.

World Vision has been in Mbala 19 years. It's possible that kids who were sponsored in Phase 1 have kids who are sponsored, and possibly grandkids who are sponsored.

I never found Timothy, the boy Roberta sponsors. But I did give her note to the staff at World Vision and asked them to deliver it to Timothy.

"Dear Timothy ... ," Roberta writes. "How are you? Do you know I have known you for 10 years? Since you were 3 years old! It has been very special watching you grow up in your photos. I love getting your reports and photos. I have your picture on my desk at work so I can see you every day." She shared about volunteering at the camp and updates on her son Evan, and then ended with this: "Do good; seek peace, and pursue it."

I can only wonder what Timothy's life is like and how his life has changed because of World Vision and Roberta. I'm sure it has.

But I also can't help but wonder: "If I met him, would he ask for more help?"

I shared this thought with Roberta, and she told me, "If I knew he would ask for more help, would I have still sponsored him all these years? My gut reaction is that I would. If I make an error in judgment, I would rather err on the side of generosity."

*Giving Rules: Err on the side of generosity.*

# 24

## Marine Wages War on Poverty Through Locally-Led Change (Kenya, 2010)

*Fighting terrorism by fighting poverty / Starting with the end in mind*

---

**MANY NONPROFITS AND NGOs TALK** about "working themselves out of a job," but few do. There are people with those jobs who rely on regular paychecks to feed their families and pay rent. There are people who are passionate about the work and don't want it to end, so they don't let it.

When I arrived in Kuria, a remote rural district in Kenya near the Tanzanian border, in 2010, I visited an NGO that was intent on leaving even though it had just arrived.

One of the first things I noticed about the countryside in Kuria was the corn. Some of it was short, and some of it would've won a blue ribbon at a county fair in Iowa.

Josephat waited alongside the road, dwarfed by a wall of bright green corn behind him. He greeted me with a handshake and a proud smile, and together we disappeared into his field.

The path through the corn led to Josephat's home. His wife poured corn into a tin bucket, letting the breeze blow away chaff. Their five children played in an open courtyard bordered by three structures.

"I was almost ready to give up on life," Josephat told me. "I was working a lot in the field. Two acres were getting only six bags of corn. It wasn't enough. After Nuru comes, I plant one acre and harvest 30 bags."

Nuru International seeks to end "extreme poverty in rural areas by equipping local leaders with the tools and knowledge to build self-sustaining, self-scaling" programs that focus on four areas: agriculture, health, financial access, and education.

In 2008, Josephat and his family had lived in a one-room mud hut. It was their kitchen, bedroom, everything.

When it was time to plant, he threw his seeds across his acreage, as was the local practice, and hoped for the best. Nuru taught him new farming techniques, like planting in rows, and gave him access to modern seeds and inputs. With Nuru, farmers grouped together to increase their purchasing power of seeds and inputs and to take their crops to market. Before this, they would wait for a buyer to pass through town and they would either sell it for the low price the buyer demanded or risk their harvest rotting while waiting for the next buyer to come along.

Following Josephat's first Nuru harvest, he built a larger home made out of wood. After the second harvest, which was when I arrived, he was in the process of building a much larger home out of bricks. Each home was more permanent than the last. The mud hut where they once lived was filled with corn.

Josephat has become a leader through Nuru.

"Now I visit farmers and tell them about myself – where I was and where I am right now. And I'm trying to change their lives like mine was changed."

> *Giving Rules: Local examples reach more people than outside expertise.*

The change in Josephat's life began with the change in the life of Nuru's founder, Jake Harriman, in Iraq in 2003.

"I found myself in a hole on the Kuwaiti border as the sun was setting, looking north into Iraq thinking what the heck is going on," Jake said. He shared his story with me as we sat in the Nuru house down a dirt path off the main road. His next-door neighbor sold poison-tipped arrows. Jake talked about his former life as a special operations platoon commander in the Marine Corps.

"War is a horrible, horrible thing, and what humanity has created in war is just kind of our lowest form … I'm not naive enough to think military action isn't needed. But a lot of the things I began to see in combat shed some light on information that really changed my life forever."

Jake and "his guys," who hadn't eaten in two days, were asked to set up a defensive position on a road leading south out of Baghdad. As Jake related the story to me, he lifted his imaginary rifle and looked in the direction of Baghdad; he focused on things he wished he had never seen.

A white car raced toward their position. They raised their rifles and it stopped. A man got out of the car and sprinted toward Jake and his guys. The man waved his arms wildly. They thought he was crazy. They thought he was a suicide bomber. A black military truck raced up behind the white car, and six guys dressed in black jumped out, ran up to the white car, and shot it full of holes.

"And that's when I realized what was going on," Jake said.

Saddam Hussein, the president of Iraq, had sent his special forces to forcibly recruit rural farmers to fight against the Americans. The farmers were promised that their families would be taken care of after they were dead. The guy who ran from the white car was trying to escape. His family was in the car. Jake and his guys took out the Iraqi special forces.

"But it was too late," Jake said. "I looked in the car … in the passenger seat … His wife was there and she had been shot in the face and in the chest. And she was dead. And in the backseat his little infant girl had her arm blown off and she had been shot in the face. And he was cradling his little six-year-old girl who had been shot in the abdomen and she was choking on her own blood. This guy was completely beside himself, you know, and just crying. For the first time in the war, I did something you're never supposed to do: I let my weapon down at my side. And I thought, 'What would've I done if I was in that guy's shoes? This is a guy who had no choices in life … In two seconds he lost everything.' And something changed in me that day."

Jake did another tour in southern Baghdad and kept seeing the same thing, farmers who would try fighting and not even know how to take their rifles off safety. He wanted to fight terrorism in a new way.

Jake left the military and for 18 months lived next to the beach near San Francisco. He studied extreme poverty on his own. He surfed. And he even had a stint delivering frozen fish. He tried to get a job with an NGO, but didn't quite have the resume for it. The Peace Corps and the World Bank aren't exactly looking for, as Jake put it, "trained killers."

Jake applied to Stanford's MBA program because of its strong focus on social entrepreneurism. He got accepted.

Jake wanted to fight terrorism by fighting poverty. A visiting professor put Jake in touch with his brother, Philip Mohochi, who lived in Kuria and was looking for a way to give back to his community after having had a successful business career in Nairobi. Nuru, which means "light" in Swahili, was piloted in Kuria.

The first week in Kuria, Jake was sitting on a couch checking the angle of his satellite Internet when lightning struck and blew him off the couch.

There were also the rats, the cows, the earthquake, the attempted robbery, and the malaria. But Jake and his new group of guys stuck it out and put their model of sustainable development to the test.

I joined Jake and his team for their morning meeting. Nuru's field directors, along with Philip, the chairman, met to talk about the upcoming week. Jake called on them one by one and scribbled in his notebook. The staff was on the ground for six months and then replaced. It's a key component of the group's strategy. They don't want the community to rely on an individual too much. Even Jake, who doesn't have an apartment or a home in the US, tears himself away.

Once the meeting was over, Jake and I began a five-mile walk to the granary – the heart of Nuru's operation. We passed by a school that Nuru had helped build and a well in the distance that Nuru had drilled. They weren't Nuru's; they were owned by the community. It was a walk that took us over and through two green valleys with mostly tall corn, but some short, too – a reminder there was more work to be done (see Figure 24.1).

"I walk to work every day, and [the locals] think I'm crazy," Jake said, explaining why he didn't have one of those big white Land Cruisers with logos on the doors, and he walked five to 10 miles each day visiting farmers. Jake wanted to show the locals that he would live with them as they lived. He soon earned their trust and respect as they earned his.

"These are brave individuals," Jake said. "I mean these guys are braver, more intelligent, more resourceful, and more driven than I'll ever be. They survived things that I could've never survived. They are incredible people."

*Giving Rules: Walk with the people you are trying to help.*

In less than two years, the group had achieved remarkable results, changing the lives of more than 75% of the people in the area. Crop yields had quadrupled by extending microfinance to farmers in the form of seeds and fertilizer. Much to the dismay of British American Tobacco, farmers had switched from growing tobacco to growing corn.

*Figure 24.1    Jake on his morning walk in 2010.*

The success of agriculture has led to something many in the community had never had before: a surplus of money.

People were drinking clean water. Girls who previously spent much of their time carrrying water were now going to school.

After another day and another long walk home, Jake laid out the future of Nuru.

"We want to be in the extremely poor areas where no one else is able to serve the people. We want to perfect this scalable, sustainable development model to empower the poor … in failed states in the wake of a regime change … And if that had happened [in Iraq], most of the stuff I had seen take place wouldn't have taken place because those fellas who were desperate would have had choices, would have had other opportunities to feed their kids than picking up that AK-47."

I spent a few days with Jake and his team made up of Americans and one Brit as they trained and worked alongside the local leaders of Nuru. They all talked about leaving Nuru in the hands of the local leaders. And once they perfected the model, they would take it into post-conflict areas, such as Somalia, Afghanistan, and maybe even Iraq.

But the goal was always to leave.

*Giving Rules: Aid shouldn't last forever.*

---

## KENYA, 2017

I returned to Kuria in 2017 and all the Western staff of Nuru International were gone. They left in 2014. Nuru Kenya was run by Kenyans, including my friend Josephat, who now worked as a Nuru agriculture trainer.

Josephat picked me up at my hotel, and I hopped on the back of his motorcycle. He was bundled in a winter coat and gloves. I don't think he had any skin exposed. The last time I visited him, I had walked with Nuru's staff. Now Nuru has several cars and Josephat has a motorcycle.

I had spent the day traveling with Pauline, the Nuru Kenya country manager. I had met Pauline in the morning and we traveled from Nuru's headquarters, a compound that had multiple buildings, departments, cows with Nuru tags in their ears, a mini-yogurt factory with two sizes of Nuru yogurts, and the Philip Mohochi administration building. Philip was killed in a car crash in 2014.

In 2010, there were groups organized by Nuru's Western staff. Locally elected co-ops had now replaced the groups. The co-ops, supported by Nuru Kenya's staff. have taken on the responsibility of the four focus areas: agriculture, health, financial access, and education. The goal is for Nuru Kenya to continue to phase out as the co-ops run all the programs, trainings, and organizing on their own.

At the meetings, the co-op board discussed the problems facing their community, including cattle thieves and when to take their maize to market. Someone reported on the number of bags of maize and what the moisture percentage was. Some of the co-ops were more successful than others. One had 197 registered members and 113 that were actively participating, and another had 175 registered but only 78 active members. Some co-ops had failed and others were succeeding.

"[We] want to work hard," an animated older man in a sports coat said, standing to share his thoughts, "so co-op is functional and sustainable because it will benefit our future."

The attendees discussed penetrating new markets, mobile banking, financial literacy, and health issues their members faced. The men and women leading their own communities used all the terms I had heard from Jake and his team in 2010.

"Now we can speak with one voice," said a chairman of a co-op at an info session on introducing dairy cattle. "We can even train our own children."

*Figure 24.2   Josephat and his family.*

It was at this meeting that I had bumped into Josephat again and arranged to visit his home (see Figure 24.2).

He lived much farther than I remembered. In 2010, I had walked the distance on a sunny day, instead of bumping along the dirt road at dusk trying not to fall off his motorcycle. The road was rutted and I don't know how he was able maintain control with 185 pounds of American on the back.

His home was in the same place, but it looked different. The fields had been harvested and the world looked bigger when it wasn't walled in with eight-foot-tall rows of corn.

His kids played outside; he now had nine. He also had eight cows that dragged 15 feet of rope from their necks. He told me that the local variety of cows will run more than 10 miles without stopping, but the new breeds aren't quite as good at long-distance running.

His courtyard was now fully enclosed by buildings and fences. There was even a stable for his cattle to sleep. A few years ago thieves had stolen three of his cows, but his neighbor had chased them down.

The brick home that had been under construction during my first visit was now completed and another new building connected to it. He still didn't have electricity or running water and they still lived on dirt floors, but, even so, he was proud of what he had built. He once was concerned about having enough food to eat, but now his biggest concern was paying his kids' school fees. The oldest was in school to become a Catholic priest.

He had bought more land in order to feed his dairy cows. Their milk would provide a regular steam of income. He also considered buying some land and building a house to rent.

Josephat had gone from subsistence farmer to entrepreneur in less than a decade.

"Before Nuru, my children suffered from hunger," she said.

We sat on wooden chairs in the fading light of the day in his newest home. His eldest son came in and brought two Sprites and a Coke. I didn't really want one, but Pauline had told me that it was impolite to refuse a drink from someone in Africa.

> *Giving Rules: Sometimes you are the giver and other times you are the vessel through which a gift flows.*

His eight-year-old daughter brought us warm chapati. Another child walked through with a laundry basket and another with a watering can.

Josephat's English was much improved. In 2010, he had started to attend training at Jake's house, and the trainings were all in English. He was a fast learner. He had a tough childhood, but still managed to attend school until seventh grade. His father was "crazy" and his mother moved from Tanzania to raise him with his grandparents.

"I want my kids to have an easier life than me," Josephat said.

He is a paid Nuru staff member, and he expressed concern about what would happen when the organization left for good. The downsizing had already begun.

"What happened to the others who once worked for Nuru?" I asked.

"Most of them are fine," he said. This is what Nuru wants to happen – for people to be fine when they leave. Still, Josephat was uncertain about life after Nuru, and, like many in his community, he was preparing for it.

"Nuru has helped people help themselves," he said. "Before, when Kenyans saw *wazungu* they thought they'd get free things. Nuru changed that."

Josephat's seven-year-old daughter entered and handed him a flashlight that he hung from the ceiling, clicked on, and the light chased away the darkness.

> *Giving Rules: Gifts should empower and inspire, not indebt.*

# 25

# The Little Village That Was Supposed to Change the World (Kenya, 2017)

*UN's Millennium Development Goals / Can unlimited resources end poverty? / Do we need more or less aid?*

———

**"THE LIGHT SHINES IN THE DARKNESS** and the darkness has never put it out."

The Bible verse was quoted on a shirt worn by one of Nuru's managers. We had been traveling together since 4 a.m., and I only noticed it as we piled out of the vehicles that had taken us 150 miles from Kuria to Sauri, Kenya.

Despite the lack of traffic, the going was slow. The roads were pocked with giant man-made potholes, created by supporters of Raila Odinga, the presidential candidate who was recently declared the loser of the election.

Voters felt their voices and their votes didn't matter. Odinga asserted that the election was rigged, and eventually the Supreme Court agreed with him. His supporters took to the streets in western Kenya.

They threw tires into the middle of the road and lit them. I had watched the images of the fires dancing on the news. The protesters thought maybe now they would get the attention of their leaders.

Rich politicians who lived in McMansions in gated communities and ate at Kentucky Fried Chicken bribed poor voters who didn't have fences to protect their cattle from thieves. There were rumors that police had beaten a baby to death. People went missing, their bodies surfacing in Lake Kisumu days later.

Regardless of the truth, people saw corruption everywhere and they protested. No one will ever know how many died or were injured, because not all lives are accounted for or matter as much as others.

So they threw tires and lit the fires. The holes in the road made the path forward hard to navigate. But to those who had burned the tires, it was proof they existed, that their votes might not have accomplished anything, but their fires did, even if it was only to make our early-morning drive even slower.

This was a field trip for the Nuru team to learn from the co-ops left behind by the Millennium Development Project.

In 2000, all 191 United Nations members promised to "spare no effort to free our fellow men, women and children from the abject and dehumanizing conditions of extreme poverty," and committed to eight international development goals, known as the Millennium Development Goals (MDG) to:

1. Eradicate extreme poverty and hunger.
2. Achieve universal primary education.
3. Promote gender equality and empower women.
4. Reduce child mortality.
5. Improve maternal health.
6. Combat HIV/AIDS, malaria, and other diseases.
7. Ensure environmental sustainability.
8. Create global partnership for development.[1]

Economist Jeffrey Sachs founded Millennium Village Promise (MVP), which selected 10 Millennium Development Villages, including Sauri, to demonstrate how the Millennium Development Goals could be met in rural Africa.

---

[1]World Health Organization, www.who.int/topics/millennium_development_goals/about/en/ (March 12, 2018).

"What we're trying to show is that with just a few interventions and not a lot of money, lives can be transformed," explained Sachs. "It's what MTV would call Extreme Village Makeover."

In fact, Sachs visited Sauri with Angelina Jolie and an MTV camera crew in 2005.

"This is the village that's going to make history," Sachs told Jolie. "It's a village that is going to end extreme poverty."[2]

I was excited to see the impact that a concentrated effort of global resources and expertise made on the village.

When Millennium, as the co-op leaders referred to it and referred to it often, looked for a way to exit Sauri, they saw co-ops as an integral part of their strategy. The co-op members could manage agriculture education, input distribution, and market access.

Millennium supported the dairy co-op by offering members inputs at 0% interest. Membership swelled to more than 1,000 farmers.

"The motivation to form a co-op was mainly from Millennium," Felix, one of the local leaders, said. "The push came from them. They had a lot of money."

"Now we have 35 members," Willis, a co-op member dressed like a bank manager who had loosened his tie after a long day, said. "We need to collect 300 liters per day from our members to survive. We're currently collecting 150 liters."

The Nuru team scribbled in their notebooks.

Millennium left in 2015 and for a while a German sponsor (GIZ) came on board which explained why the building looked like a German flag – red, yellow, and black.

In our informal chat before the meeting, Willis was funny. Everything he had said got a laugh. Now he was somber.

"We are praying for another group like GIZ," Willis said.

When it was time for the Nuru team to ask questions, it became apparent that the Sauri dairy co-op should be visiting the Nuru co-ops. But the Nuru co-ops were still supported by Nuru and Sauri's were on their own.

One of the Nuru team calculated the number of cows supporting the dairy and their daily production. "That's really low," he said.

The agriculture agents once supported by Millennium had been absorbed by the county. Farmers used to be able to get their assistance for free, but now agents had to charge.

"How do you measure success?" another Nuru team member asked.

---

[2]"The Diary of Angelina Jolie and Dr. Jeffrey Sachs in Africa," MTV (September 14, 2005).

The question went unanswered, and Willis told us that the co-op had a deficit so would have to delay payments to the farmers to make ends meet.

But perhaps the biggest factor leading to the 97% decline in membership was because the co-op, which had to cover operational and staff costs, had to charge interest on all loans. Millennium had provided no-interest loans to farmers to buy cows.

Fatuma, the head of Nuru's co-op efforts, took a sharp breath.

"Without Millennium, are you able to stand?" she asked.

"We are willing to stand," Willis answered.

I felt badly for the Sauri co-op members. They were circling the drain. Nuru hoped to learn from its mistakes. When it left Kuria, it didn't want the co-ops to have to search for the next Nuru, but wanted them to stand on their own.

We moved from the dairy co-op to the cereal co-op, where we sat in a tall barn with a tin roof that seemed to magnify the heat of the sun. It was so hot that I kept passing out or napping, although I wasn't sure whether the difference between the two mattered. I was conscious enough to get the gist of the meeting. It was the same story here.

"We haven't gotten to the level we anticipated," one of the leaders reported. Since Millennium left, co-op membership had fallen from 1,600 to 400. The co-op on its own couldn't afford to offer interest-free loans and the other technical and educational supports that Millennium had provided.

Members used to be able to get credit with tears, according to one of the members. There was no documentation required at first. From 2011 to 2013 Millennium loaned $27 million and collected only 25% of it. From 2013 to 2017 $3.3 million was loaned and 60% of it was collected.

"We run to Millennium," one of the members said. "It was so easy to get loans. Things were free. You were given 4,000 shillings of inputs, but you only have to pay back one bag of maize, which was only worth 2,000 shillings."

The plastic chairs on which we sat, the building we were in, the wooden pallets that held the maize, and the motorbike and tractor parked outside were all stamped with MVP: Millennium Village Promise.

Its mark remained, but the promise of the future was not guaranteed.

*Giving Rules: How will your gift live on after you are gone? If you can't answer this, reevaluate.*

I parted ways with Nuru and came back to Sauri, where I met with John, who was a local political leader when MVP started in Sauri. He welcomed me into his brick home with a concrete floor and invited me to sit on the couch.

"Angelina Jolie sat there," he said.

A picture of John with Jeffrey Sachs hung on the wall.

"It was a good project. We got a lot. We wanted it to last forever."

Before MVP, farmers weren't using fertilizers. They were harvesting only five bags of maize per acre. During Millennium, they were getting 18, and now since Millennium left and farmers were getting the previously provided supports, they were getting only 10 to 12 bags per acre.

Millennium paid for school fees and provided meals. Now the schools are on their own.

The roads and schools that Millennium constructed are still there, but it is harder to pay for teachers now, and some of the roads, which are maintained by the county, are returning to the forest.

"I blame the leaders who took over," John said.

"Compare life before Millennium to life now," I suggested.

"Life has slightly improved," John said. "It didn't change the world, but it was a good experience."

"What would you say to Jeffrey Sachs if he were sitting right beside me?"

"'Thank you!' I would be so happy to see him. I'd hug him."

Jeffrey Sachs is a rock-star economist. Bono wrote the foreword to his book *The End of Poverty: Economic Possibilities for Our Time*, which made the argument that poverty could be ended if only we, the Western world, gave it the attention and resources it deserved. Poverty could be ended for only $250 billion a year, which is much cheaper than having wars, he'd say.

"Jeff really changed the way we think about the problem of health," Paul Farmer, the well-respected founder of the NGO Partners in Health, said. "What we were always saying is, 'Do this because it's the right thing to do,' but Jeff said, 'Yeah, it's the right thing to do – and it also is going to open the door to real development. Because you can't have development if everybody is sick all the time.'"

But he wasn't without his critics.

Simon Bland, who had worked in development for 30 years, said, "I know that if you spend enough money on each person in a village, you will change their lives. If you put in enough resources – enough *mzungu*, foreigners, technical assistance, and money – lives change. I know that. I've been doing it for years. I've lived and worked on and managed development projects … The problem is when you walk away, what happens?"[3]

A prominent citizen in Dertu, Kenya, another Millennium Village, filed an official 14-point complaint against the program with the Kenya Parliament, including: "1. The project was supposed to be community driven, but MVP staff [drove the] project; hence this created dependence syndrome; 2. The project is supposed to be bottom top approached but it is [vice] versa; 3. No sense of ownership of the project; 4. No transparency and accountability."

These are classic arguments against aid that have been leveled at Sachs and top-down interventions thought up by outside technical experts.

Where Sachs has been the ultimate optimist, saying that we can end poverty by 2025 if we work hard enough, his critics such as William Easterly believe that the West has wasted more than $2.3 trillion of aid in Africa that ultimately only inhibited the self-determination of Africans.

**Giving Rules: Do something, but not just anything.**

Personally, I believe that long-term aid can create dependency, but it also has saved millions of lives. It's impossible to say what would've happened in Kenya or Zambia if there hadn't been aid. It's also hard to say that all aid has been a waste. Peter Singer does the math and calculates that $2.3 trillion was spent over the course of 50 years. That's about $46 billion per year or $60 per person per year living in affluent nations over that period of time.[4] So suddenly that number doesn't look so big. Aid eradicated smallpox by 1973. Smallpox previously killed 1.5 to 3 million people per year. Its eradication has saved between 60 and 120 million lives. Immunizations have decreased deaths from preventable diseases by 3.6 million between 1960 and 2001. Malaria deaths have declined by 3.1 million per year, and deaths by diarrhea by 3 million per year.[5] Aid isn't responsible for all of these lives saved, but it played an important part.

The UN's Millennium Development Goals program ended in 2015, and have been replaced by Sustainable Development Goals, which apply to all countries, not just those considered developing countries.

---

[3]Nina Munk, *The Idealist* (New York: Anchor, 2014).
[4]Peter Singer, *The Life You Can Save* (New York: Random House, 2010), 106.
[5]William MacAskill, *Doing Good Better* (New York: Penguin Random House, 2016), 45–47.

Even critics of the Millennium Development Goals agreed that focusing and having conversations on defined goals as a global community was important. The number of people living in extreme poverty was more than halved. In 1990 47% of people in developing countries lived in extreme poverty and by 2015 that had been reduced to 14%, although the results were uneven across countries, and the gains in the growing economies of China and India met the goal on their own. Other goals such as child and mother mortality rates were missed. Dean Karlan, an economics professor at Yale, said he wasn't against global yardsticks like the Millennium Development Goals, but "you can't compare one country to another. It doesn't give us much, in terms of telling us what to do." Poverty can be focused on from a global level, but it's the successes and failures of local actions that really matter.[6]

Before I left Sauri, I met with a farmer who had attended MVP's first meeting.

"We fell apart because of lack of finance," he said, and added that he had a message for Sachs: "Remember us and try to uplift us again."

Doing good isn't always easy. Even experts with nearly unlimited resources often fall short of their own and our expectations. It's easy to be cynical. But maybe the failures of MVP will bring future efforts one step closer to success.

*Giving Rules: Don't let the failures of others and your own stop you from giving. We learn more from dreamers than from cynics.*

---

[6]Somini Sengupta, "Global Poverty Drops Sharply, with China Making Big Strides, U.N. Report Says," *The New York Times* (7 July 2015).

# Part VI

## OUR GIFTS CONNECT US TO THE WORLD

# 26

## The Strength in Your Story (US, 2011–2018)

*The art of listening / The gift of your story*

**STORIES ARE HEAVY, AND TOO MANY** of them are untold. All of us carry them, tell them, and listen to them. They constantly change us.

I hope the stories I've shared throughout this book have reached your heart and head and changed you in some small way, but there is no doubt the person who has been changed the most by them is me. These are people I've met, shared meals with, stayed in touch with (when possible), and had the responsibility to carry and share their stories.

*Giving Rules: Listen more, speak less.*

The stories of factory workers and farmers, mothers and fathers around the world have changed the way I live my life as a father, husband, giver, volunteer, and global and local citizen.

They inspired me to become engaged in my community and volunteer with TeamWORK for Quality Living, the nonprofit in Muncie that worked with individuals fighting their way out of poverty. I started to think about ways I could get others involved in the act of storytelling.

When the 2010 census was released showing that one-third of people in Muncie lived in poverty, a debate played out in the newspaper. An economist pointed out that the number included Ball State University students, who, he argued, really shouldn't be included, and that only 15% of Muncie residents actually lived in poverty.

Statistics are important to help guide policy and community efforts, but there was something that I really didn't like about the debate. It didn't include the most important poverty statistic: one.

"Do you know one single person living in poverty?" I wrote in an editorial in our local paper.

So often in our nation we judge people who live in poverty or who are immigrants or who are addicts, yet often we don't know a single person who faces that reality. And until we have a face and a name and a story to match with the statistics, are we really qualified to understand the issue and create policy or interventions?

I wanted to find a way to lift up the stories of my friends in Muncie who lived in poverty to educate the broader public. I started to bounce ideas around with the staff at TeamWORK, including Jim Flatford and Molly Flodder, but I wanted it to be more than just someone writing his or her story and others reading it. I wanted people sitting face-to-face and having one-on-one conversations like I've had in so many homes around the world. I wanted it to be a community-wide effort.

As a Big with Big Brothers Big Sisters, my Little and I had interacted with Ball State University's "Writing in the Community" class led by Professor Barbara Bogue. Barbara matched us with student Logan Moeller, who met with us several times and then wrote a fictional story about us that he read at a community performance. That program planted the seed for what would become Facing Poverty.

We recruited 17 other nonprofits to spread the word about the project to find people willing to share their stories. We recruited writers to meet with them and collaborate on the lived narrative told from the point of view of the person facing poverty. The stories were collected in a book, and actors brought them to life at a public performance.

I missed the performance. I was in Colombia talking with coffee farmers. One of the writers I recruited, J.R. Jamison, found the experience to be meaningful as he sat next to his storyteller while an actor performed her story. I thought the project was important and might be something that could be repeated in Muncie. J.R. had a bigger vision. He thought the project should be replicated in other communities to empower people to tell their own stories, choose their own issues to face, and use their narratives to create community-wide conversations and change. J.R. said we could put together a tool kit to share. I wasn't exactly sure what a tool kit was. J.R. had worked for 15 years as community-engagement specialist in higher education, so he guided the process. Eventually, we cofounded The Facing Project as a nonprofit, and its model has spread across the country, and has been adopted by more than 75 communities.

> *Giving Rules: When possible, include others in your giving. Be a part of a community of giving.*

Stories from Facing Sex Trafficking in Atlanta were used in a kiosk at the Atlanta Hartsfield-Jackson airport to educate travelers about human trafficking and how to identify it at the airport.

The Facing Autism in Muncie books are used by the Indiana State Police to educate officers about working with individuals on the autism spectrum. My wife Annie shared our own story, and four years later she still gets people who connect with it, and reach out. Annie has helped quite a few families figure out where to get a diagnosis, find a therapist, and providing comfort by listening to them. And so many who are on Team Griffin today are folks I met while organizing Facing Autism.

The Facing Project has helped people see the strengths in their own stories.

Think about the most challenging thing you've faced. Maybe it was a loss, an injustice, a death, or a disease. It's that life stone that you carry around, that burden that you can never put down. Remember when you first felt the weight of the burden? Remember how alone you felt in those first moments, as if you were the only person ever to face such a thing?

But you're not alone. Chances are there are people much closer to you than you realize who've faced the same challenge.

What helped you move forward? I bet it was the story of someone else who had been where you were, and knew what it was like and where to turn for help.

When our son Griffin was diagnosed with autism, we felt alone. We didn't know anyone who had a child on the autism spectrum, but there were people a lot closer to us than we realized. We found comfort and a path forward through their stories, and now we're those people for others.

The Facing Project has shown me that one of the greatest gifts you have to give is the gift of your story to the right person at the right time.

> *Giving Rules: That thing that makes you feel weak can actually give strength to others.*

I've volunteered thousands of hours and donated thousands of dollars to The Facing Project. I've never given more of myself, expected so little, and gained so much from anything (other than my family). It doesn't make sense. It's not logical, but it is part of me.

When I think about Scott Neeson in Cambodia, Rozy and Selline and Umra and Jake in Kenya, Tim in Myanmar, Ashok in India, and so many of the other people I've met on this journey, I often just shake my head and ask, "How do they exist? Why do they do this?"

They give so much.

It's not logical. They can't even explain it. They just started doing a thing and then they did it again without expectation, and it grew. And their life skills, experiences, passions, and gifts coalesced to create a life's work, a mission greater than the sum of its parts.

For me that's The Facing Project (see Figure 26.1). It's not all-consuming. It's all-producing.

As a writer for a Facing Autism project, I met a mother who shared the lengths she and her husband went to help their eldest son, and how, when their youngest son unexpectedly died, they came to see the emotional

*Figure 26.1    The author championing The Facing Project.*

distance the eldest kept from his younger brother as a gift. They realized that their teamwork facing autism made them stronger as a family to face even the most heartbreaking of circumstances. She told me this story in her kitchen. I felt her story all at once and I sobbed uncontrollably. She comforted me. Now when I see her, we hug. She asks about Griffin, Harper, and Annie.

As a writer for Facing Disabilities, I was charged with writing the story of Jerrold, who didn't have a lot of words to express his views. After my first conversation with him, I was worried I wouldn't be able to tell his story. I visited Jerrold at work and watched him interact with coworkers. I chatted with him while he stuffed envelopes. I talked with his supervisor and his coworkers. I went on a date with Jerrold and his girlfriend to KFC. I watched Jerrold be shy, be funny, and be ornery. I watched and I listened, and, even though Jerrold doesn't have an abundance of words, I heard Jerrold's voice. His was a voice full of life, laughter, and wisdom. His was a voice that had a lived book's worth of stories.

I've shared my story for Facing Mentoring, and my friend Michael Brockley, a poet, listened to the thoughts and feelings I had never processed as a volunteer Big Brother, and Michael gave them life.

I've seen storytellers embrace and take pride in stories they once kept secret. I've seen writers, storytellers, and actors become more engaged in their communities, through listening to those stories.

I look at The Facing Project and I see the influence of Khenpo Sange, Amilcar, Annie, Ratana, Harper, Griffin, Barbara, Molly, Jim, J.R., and my parents. I see their gifts flow into the lives of other people and other communities. And just as rivers flow and don't question their purpose, we do our work.

There are all sorts of Venn diagrams meant to help you find a life of purpose and meaning. I like to call this sweet spot the Axis of Awesome, where your skills, life experiences, and passions intersect, but the best diagram, and concept, comes from Japan. The Japanese call the Axis of Awesome *Ikigai*, which means "reason for being." It's at the axis of what you're good at, what you are paid for, what the world needs, what you love: your passion, mission, profession, and vocation.

However, staring at a Venn diagram isn't all that helpful. Meaning isn't something that can be thought; it comes from experiences gained on a journey.

So far The Facing Project has flowed through the lives of 7,500 volunteers and reached more than 200,000 others.

*Giving Rules: The best giving doesn't cost you, leaving you with less; it grows you, leaving you with more.*

J.K. Rowling has a great quote that sums up what I feel about The Facing Project:

> The power of human empathy, leading to collective action, saves lives, and frees prisoners. Ordinary people, whose personal well-being and security are assured, join together in huge numbers to save people they do not know, and will never meet ... [U]nlike any other creature on this planet, humans can learn and understand, without having experienced. They can think themselves into other people's places. We do not need magic to change the world, we carry all the power we need inside ourselves already: we have the power to imagine better.[1]

---

[1] J. K. Rowling, "The Fringe Benefits of Failure, and the Importance of Imagination," speech presented at Harvard Commencement (June 5, 2008).

# 27

# The X Factor in the Good Person Equation

**ON EVERY STEP OF THIS JOURNEY,** the amazing givers I met taught me something else about living a life of generosity and giving, and they also made it more unlikely that I would be able to solve the Good Person Equation I set out to find.

But I promised. So here goes.

## THE GOOD PERSON EQUATION

To do at least our part to make the world a better place, we should …

**Volunteer 100 hours per year.** According to the 100-hour rule, you'll be happier and more connected to your community. Even better if you could put a special skill to use. Only 25% of Americans volunteer. Do it!

**Donate 2% of your income to the most effective organizations fighting global extreme poverty.** Singer's www.thelifeyoucansave .org has a great tool to determine what percentage of your income to give. According to the tool, someone who makes $12,000 per year should give a minimum of 1%. At $60,000 per year, the average household income in the US, that jumps to 2.1% and at $100,000 to 4.6%. If you give at least this much, you'll be doing your part to end extreme poverty, and giving about 20 times more than most. Find organizations at www.givewell.org and at Singer's www.thelifeyoucansave.org.

**Donate 2% of your income to the most efficient organizations helping those in poverty in your community.** Early childhood reading programs are especially effective.

**Donate 1% of income toward arts**, a friend in need fund, or your "when some kid hits you up for a school fund-raiser" fund.

*Note:* None of these suggestions includes giving to religious institutions. That's between you and your God. And since 40% or more of Americans' giving goes to religious institutions, you may be doing this already. Just keep giving what you are giving in addition to the 5% of income allotted for global, local, and your art/friends fund.

**Annually Engage in six acts of citizenship or political engagement** (donating blood, attending a rally, calling a politician, writing an editorial, signing a petition). According to a Pew poll, highly engaged citizens, representing the top 13%, took part in five or more acts of citizenship.[1]

So here's what the equation looks like if you're math-minded:

(# of hours volunteered / 100)

+ (% of income toward fighting global extreme poverty / 2%)

+ (% of income toward fighting local poverty / 2%)

+ (% of income toward arts or friend in need fund / 1%)

+ (acts of engagement / 6) = Giving Score

0 = Uh, you need to give more. You'll be happier.
5 = Average. Thanks for doing your part.
10 = Amazing! You are setting an example for the rest of us.

Find your score and then give more.

――――――――――

―――――――――――
[1] Aaron Smith, Kay Lehman Schlozman, Sidney Verba, and Henry Brady, "The Current State of Civic Engagement in America," Pew Research Center (September 1, 2009).

The X Factor in the Good Person Equation is you. This is my first attempt at the equation. I suspect it will change and evolve over time. Yours is probably different from mine. The important thing isn't finding an answer; it is wrestling with the question: Am I doing the most good I can do?

And we should always struggle with this question, and it should always make us a little uncomfortable. Because the reality is uncomfortable.

I don't want to be comfortable when I live in a world where kids die of diarrhea, where the rights and lives of individuals are threatened by the government meant to serve them, where slavery still exists, where people are persecuted because of their religion or skin color, where poverty kills, and where kids in my own community go to school hungry.

Tushar was right. We can give more.

Rozy was right. We have to let our courage cover the fears of others.

We can start small like Ashok.

We can be an ocean in a drop like Umra and Kalu.

We can start with the one like Scott Neeson and help the many.

We can be as optimistic as Jeffrey Sachs and as pragmatic as William Easterly.

We will accept the responsibility of our privilege like Peter Singer.

We will live lives of gratitude by allowing the gifts of others to flow through us.

Initially, I thought this journey was to figure out the Good Person Equation. I wanted to prescribe for myself and for you the least we should all do. But somewhere along the line that changed. Giving isn't about the least we can do, but about the most we can give to others with the gifts we have.

There are no rules for giving; however, if we are at our best, giving rules our lives. Giving isn't a prescription, although it can treat many of our ailments and help us live happier and longer. If we look at our lives as givers, giving becomes a philosophy that helps us see the best and most generous versions of others and ourselves.

When you look for people doing good in the world, they aren't hard to find. Be one of them.

It has been a gift for me to wrestle with these thoughts through these pages. I'm thankful for the gifts of knowledge shared with me from the amazing givers I have met around the world. I'm grateful to have shared them with you. I hope you found something worth passing along.

After all, a gift is only a gift if it never stops.

# ACKNOWLEDGMENTS

We are the products of the gifts that have been given to us. So many people have shared their gifts with me to make this book possible. Besides those I wrote about in the book, there are many to whom I owe sincere thanks. In fact, there are too many to name here, so let me admit my failure up front. Each has my gratitude.

My patient, even-keeled wife, Annie, is the realest person I've ever met. She is afraid that I'll get too sappy in my acknowledgments, so I'll just say this: Home is my favorite place on earth, and it's wherever she is. I'm forever thankful for Annie.

My daughter, Harper, was upset each time I set out on a trip and didn't take her with me. She's already a great traveler, whether that's exploring the Wizarding World of Harry Potter, or our backyard while shooting the next episode of her YouTube Channel, Time to Explore with Harper, or snorkeling in Puerto Rico. Just as much as she wants to go on these trips with me, I want to stay at home and explore with her. I'm grateful to live with one of my best friends.

Every night I'm home I read to my best buddy Griffin and then snuggle with him. There isn't a person alive whom I have more spoken and unspoken inside jokes with than Griff. His curiosity about global plumbing can be surpassed only by how lucky I feel to be his dad.

I remember sleeping in a tent at Scout camp fighting homesickness, trying not to cry. I was homesick every day of the trips in this book as well, except for the days my mom Lynne was able to join me in Kenya. I enjoyed seeing the world through her eyes as we sailed around Lamu. Thanks for going, Mom, and a big thanks to my dad, Ken, for encouraging her to go and always being the rock in our family. I would be doing something else other than writing books if it weren't for my parents believing in me.

My in-laws, Jim and Gloria Saintignon, are always there whenever Annie, the kids, and I need any help with floods, broken appliances, or to provide a kid-less weekend. They each give so much. Jim will sit on a beach with a homeless man and talk about the weather. Gloria is a one-woman community center.

I see the gifts of Mom and Dad and Jim and Gloria in Harper and Griffin, and I love each of them even more.

It's a peace of mind knowing that Annie's sister Emily and her family, Jon, Jared, and Cale, are only a few miles away, and always there to give us a hand or play with the kids, as are my brother Kyle and his family, Jenn, Max, Ollie, and Ainsley. Kyle was my first adventure companion and is always one of my early readers.

In the course of living this giving journey, my path crossed with that of J.R. Jamison, who has become some strange mix of my brother and son. There are few people in this world whom I'd rather share a page or stage with or the joys and burdens of founding a nonprofit. I'm thankful that J.R. was able to pick up my slack while I traveled to keep the important work of The Facing Project moving forward. I owe him 452 coffees … at least.

Before I wrote any of my thoughts here, I bounced them off my friends Jay Moorman, Matt Carder, James Mitchell, BJ McKay, Scott Smalstig, Larry Olson, and Justin Narducci.

It's easier to leave my family when I know they are surrounded by friends like the Clawsons, the Carders, the Davises, the Nolans, the Moormans, the Hunters, the Misslers, the Truexes, the Mosiers, the GoodFunners, and Annie's CrossFit cult.

This is the third book I've worked on with John Wiley & Sons and editor Richard Narramore. I'm grateful that somehow Richard decided my stories were worth sharing. Thanks to Peter Knox for spreading my stories and to Vicki Adang for helping me tell them better.

Thanks to Justin Ahrens and his team at Rule29 for a great cover and for being such a great example of how business can be a force for good and fun.

My literary agent, JL Stermer at New Leaf Literary, helped shape the idea of this book from the very beginning in a way that didn't make me look like a vainglorious goober.

Thanks to the Eugene and Marilyn Glick Indiana Authors Award for supporting me and other Hoosier writers with encouragement and resources.

Every writer needs gifted friends like Jama Bigger, Kelly O'Dell Stanley, Gail Werner, Michael Brockley, Jeff Pearson, Holly Miller, Barb Kehoe, Cathy Shouse, Shelly Gage, Joe Roper, Sarah Schmitt, Lisa Wheeler, Terri DeVries, Irene Fridsma, Annie Sullivan, Matthew Clemens, Ashley Ford, Cathy Day, and Jane Friedman. They are all fantastic literary citizens who fill the world with important stories.

Sometimes I make plans, and sometimes my plans go astray, but most of the time I fly by the seat of my pants. During this journey the following people helped shape my path: Jay Zimmerman introduced me to Tushar Gandhi, Ro Selvey saved me from a storm, Stephanie Fisher allowed me to rant in the harbor, Libby Hogan, Robert Sterken, and Victoria Milko helped me understand Myanmar, Andrew Scheffer made me more mindful, Joseph Beckett at the Cambodian Children's Fund introduced me to students who give me so much hope, Nari and Ai in Cambodia made time to reconnect, Matt Gross shared his Frugal Traveler connections, Aditya Parikh made me feel like royalty, and Billy Williams and Brian von Kraus made sure I came back.

To the thousand people I left out, remember, a gift should be given without expectation. Thank you!

# ABOUT THE AUTHOR

Kelsey Timmerman is the author of the *New York Times* best seller *Where Am I Wearing?* and *Where Am I Eating?* He is also the cofounder of The Facing Project (www.facingproject.com), a nonprofit community storytelling initiative that helps individuals and communities see the strength and connections in their stories. His writing has appeared in the *Christian Science Monitor* and has aired on NPR. Kelsey lives in Muncie, Indiana, with his wife, Annie, and kids, Harper and Griffin.

# A

# Giving Appendix

## TEACHING GIVING

If you are a teacher or professor using this book in your class, you can find resources at www.kelseytimmerman.com/teaching-giving. Don't hesitate to email me – Kelsey@kelseytimmerman.com – if you have any questions. Maybe we could even arrange a virtual class visit.

## SPEAKING OF GIVING

I also have done hundreds of in-person talks through the years. If you are interested in inviting me to speak to your campus, community, conference, or group, visit kelseytimmmerman.com/kelsey-speaks.

## DISCUSSION QUESTIONS

A good journey often leads to more questions than answers. You've traveled around the world with me as I've wrestled with why and how to give, now it's your turn. My good friend and cofounder of The Facing Project, J.R. Jamison developed chapter-by-chapter discussion

questions, curriculum, and reflections at www.kelseytimmerman.com/
giving-discussion.

Here are a few questions to get the discussion started:

1. Which Giving Rules did you relate to the most?

2. Who has helped you get to where you are today? How are you a product of their giving?

3. When was a time you wanted to give, but didn't? When was a time you gave, but regretted it?

4. Of all the givers in the book, who did you find the most inspiring?

5. What challenges have you faced that connected you to others more?

6. Would you alter Kelsey's Good Person Equation? How?

7. Is giving a responsibility or something that we do that is above and beyond what is expected of us?

8. Thinking about The Four Pillars, the Ikigai Venn Diagram, and Kelsey's Axis of Awesome, how are you using your gifts and talent to make a difference in the lives of others?

9. Who are you investing in?

10. Of all the people and organizations highlighted in the book, whom would you most likely give to? How?

If you have questions about using the *Giving* curriculum, contact J.R. at jr@facingproject.com.

---

## GUIDE TO GIVING LOCALLY & GLOBALLY

You read the book and now you are looking at how to give more? I think that's the greatest good I hoped this book could achieve. Thanks!

I'm not so comfortable telling people what they should do, but with the Giving Rules, the Good Person Equation, and the suggestions and resources below, I think you'll find ways to give meaningfully of your time, talent, and resources.

### 1) Giving Audit

If you have a budget, you probably track how much you spend each month on dining out or on groceries. Let's take the same approach with giving globally, locally, volunteering, and acts of engagement. How much have you given of each in the past year? What's your Good Person Equation score?

Before you can take Tushar's advice and give more, you have to know how much you are giving already.

## 2) Give Intentionally

If your giving decisions are based on what shows up in your mailbox or email, or the clerk at PetSmart asking if you'd like to give money to puppies, you need to put a bit more thought into your giving. Make a list of local and global causes to which you feel connected or would like to be connected and research organizations that do the most good in those areas.

Check out givewell.org, givingwhatwecan.org, thelifeyoucansave.org, to find top charities by cause.

## 3) Evaluate

Who cares how much a CEO makes? The real question we need to ask is: What outcomes does the organization produce?

GiveWell.org has a fantastic resource organized by cause that will arm you with questions to ask an organization's staff. www.givewell.org/charity-evaluation-questions.

## 4) Career

Career advice isn't often centered on how to make a social impact. Yet, you'll spend more time working, approximately 80,000 hours, than almost anything. How you spend that time is one of the biggest decisions you'll ever make, so spend some time making it.

You can find the career guide that I wish I had when I was in school at 80,000hours.org.

You can find links to all of these resources and more at kelseytimmerman.com/giving-guide.